return to
SPIRIT LAKE

return to
SPIRIT LAKE

JOURNEY

THROUGH A

LOST LANDSCAPE

CHRISTINE COLASURDO

Photos by Celeste Colasurdo

SASQUATCH BOOKS
SEATTLE

Printed in the United States of America.
Distributed in Canada by Raincoast Books Ltd.
01 00 99 98 97   5 4 3 2 1

Cover design: Karen Schober
Cover photograph: Oregon Historical Society OrHi 42304
Inset photograph: Celeste Colasurdo
Interior photographs: p.12, top: Marita Ingalsbe, ©1970; p.12, bottom: A.J.
Colasurdo, ©1975; p.13, top: Oregon Historical Society, OrHi 70E90;
p.13, bottom: Celeste Colasurdo, 1993; pp.14–20: Celeste Colasurdo, 1995.
Maps: Rolf Goetzinger
Interior design and composition: Kate Basart

Library of Congress Cataloging in Publication Data
Colasurdo, Christine.
        Return to Spirit Lake : journey through a lost landscape /
        Christine Colasurdo : photos by Celeste Colasurdo.
                p.   cm.
        Includes bibliographical references.
        ISBN 1-57061-081-9
        1. Natural history—Washington (State)—Saint Helens, Mount,
Region. 2. Volcanoes—Environmental aspects—Washington (State)—Saint
Helens, Mount, Region. 3. Saint Helens, Mount (Wash.)—Eruption,
1980. 4. Colasurdo, Christine. I. Title.
        QH105.W2C63 1997
        508.797'84—dc21   97-16044

SASQUATCH BOOKS
615 Second Avenue
Seattle, Washington 98104
(206) 467-4300
books@sasquatchbooks.com
http://www.sasquatchbooks.com

    *Sasquatch Books publishes high-quality adult nonfiction and children's books
    related to the Northwest (Alaska to San Francisco). For more information about our
    titles, contact us at the address above, or view our site on the World Wide Web.*

For my parents, Angelo John and Marie,

who knew one kind of Spirit Lake,

and for Tom, who has come to know another

———————————

Please Note

Many of the areas mentioned in this book are not open to off-trail travel by the public. The Spirit Lake basin in particular is off-limits except for designated trails. Backpacking into the Mount Margaret backcountry is by permit only. To climb Mount St. Helens between May and September you must also obtain a permit. Please contact the Mount St. Helens National Volcanic Monument for up-to-date information on where you may legally hike and camp inside the monument and to obtain backpacking and climbing permits.

Contents

MOUNT ST. HELENS

pre-eruption

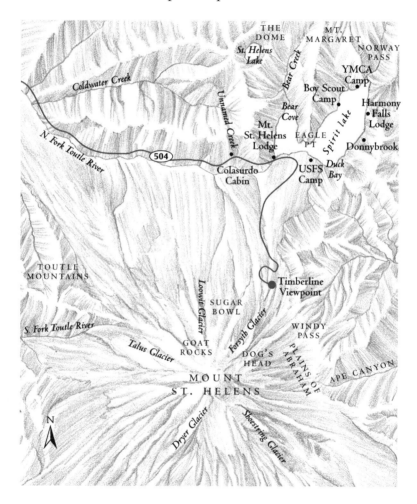

post-eruption

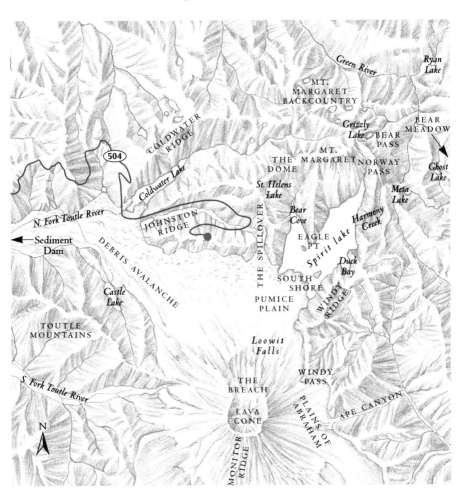

I can at best report only from my own wilderness.
The important thing is that each man possess such a wilderness
and that he consider what marvels are to be observed there.

—Loren Eiseley, *The Immense Journey*

T ake a look around. You'll notice that you can't see the mountain. It's behind us, hidden by trees. Those forested ridges across the lake—that's the backcountry. The trail starts from here at Duck Bay, but let's not go there now. Let's sit a while on this log sawn flat on top and listen to the water lapping. That is a sound you can hear anywhere at Spirit Lake—water lapping against a log, or upon the pumice shore.

On our left is a white beach where hardly anyone goes. See how the land juts out there, near those cottonwoods? My sisters and I sunbathed there once, but the flies were so thick we ran back to the campground screaming. We named that beach Fly Island, not because it is an island but because island sounds like fly—deer fly, horse fly, black fly. They all bite at Fly Island.

Across from Fly Island is Eagle Point, on the lake's north shore. From there you can see nearly everything: the outlet where the lake drains to become the Toutle River; the south shore; and the mountain, so close you can see the ice sweat on its glaciers. From here we can't even see Harmony Falls, the giant waterfall, although in winter we might hear it. One summer my sister Elizabeth and I floated in an inner tube from here to Harmony, then rolled it back three miles along the trail. Dust gathered on the wet rubber like brown sugar. We laughed as we chased after it: we had no shoes. By the time we returned our feet were as brown as the tire.

Here at Duck Bay there is no brown dust—only pumice, white as bleached bones. Pick up a stone: it's so light it's as though you held nothing. Now toss it into the lake. See how it floats? It's a trick of nature, the same way all those huge trees hide the mountain.

Your pumice landed just beyond the boat dock. At that spot the water is already twenty feet deep. That's a good place to see how clear Spirit Lake is. Let's walk there now.

It will be hours before your pumice sinks. Shall we dive in and race to it? Kneel down. Cup some water: it's so clear it's as though you held nothing. Too cold? That's what many people say. Wait here, then, and listen to the water lapping. Perhaps with each wave you will hear the seeping of lake water into pumice—a brief sizzle of a sound. That is the chant of a mountain hidden by trees. The song of nothingness coming into being.

Reflection of pre-eruption Mount St. Helens at Bear Cove

Headwaters of the Toutle River draining from pre-eruption Spirit Lake

Harmony Falls at pre-eruption Spirit Lake

Daybreak over Spirit Lake and Mount St. Helens' crater

Circles in ash sketched by windblown tips of blast-zone colonizer

Blast-blown logs amid pearly everlasting

Spirit Lake, seen from its new South Shore

Blast-blown log suspended beside trail to Coldwater Peak

Blast-directed snags and fallen branches near Coldwater Peak

Snags and blast-combed logs lining canyon of Coldwater Creek

Standing dead forests and replanted trees in scorch zone near Ryan Lake

Dead snag amid blown-down logs, new seedlings, and standing dead trees

Spirit Lake basin, seen from the Pumice Plain's upper slopes

Broken bits of mountain and pearly everlasting on the Pumice Plain

Loowit Falls, created by the May 18, 1980 eruption

Bumblebee dozing on dew-tipped pearly everlasting

Introduction

Within a few months of the May 18, 1980 eruption of Mount St. Helens I began to experience recurring dreams. In each dream a lake shimmered before me—a ghostly place of blue water and trees. Wherever I went the same image rose up in my sleep, and I recognized it as I would my own face: Spirit Lake, on the north side of the mountain.

After some time the dreams mixed with nightmares. In one nightmare I stood alone, paralyzed, on the lake's shore. Spirit Lake was radioactive—I was being contaminated with radiation even as I stood there—but I could not take a single step to leave. In another dream, I flew over the poisoned lake in a helicopter about to crash. In another I was alone and treading water in the middle of the lake, surrounded by boulders. In still other dreams—dreams that I continue to experience—I am standing in the old-growth forest between the lake and the volcano, staring up at the dark crowns of enormous trees. I have only minutes to escape. Sometimes I am with others, mostly I am alone. In all of these dreams I am near panic: I have to get out.

When I first experienced the dreams, I thought nothing of them. As a child I had experienced insomnia, nightmares, even sleepwalking, and considered the dreams another chapter in my nocturnal wanderings. But when they continued for ten years, I pondered their bizarre contents and geography. Nothing in them made sense. I kept traveling all around the Spirit Lake wilderness—to the Toutle River, the Mount Margaret backcountry, even the mountain—with no order or reason. In one dream I found myself digging into the earth at St. Helens Lake. In another, I flew over Windy Pass, my arms for wings. Wherever I went, I encountered strange objects and people I had never met in my waking life. A yellow quilt, a map, a shovel, a blind woman—what did they mean? Most recently I dreamed of a pencil sketch of Spirit Lake on faded rag paper. I caressed the image in the dream, thinking that I had drawn it. But in reality I had never executed such a drawing.

Even today, as the dreams continue, I awake from each one feeling as though I were privy to the roar of laughter rising from a distant room but not the joke itself. I suppose I could spend the rest of my days poring over the dreams' nonsensical symbols. But I would be chasing shadows. For the dreams' fantastical images and surreal geography cloud my memory of things that really existed at Spirit Lake—places and things lost forever.

Where in my dreams, for example, is Bear Creek frothing under mossy logs? Where are the lake's chipmunks, otters, and mergansers? The salmonberry bushes bent with berries? The raucous gurgle of the occasional raven perched in a distant tree?

And where in my dreams is Jim Lund, grinning and strumming his guitar as though his life depended on it? Jim Lund lived a stone's throw from my family's cabin on the Toutle River and befriended each of us from the moment my parents purchased the cabin in early 1977. Why have I not watched him, chainsaw in hand, fall a snag as nonchalantly as one might tie a shoe? But my dreams do not bring back Jim's weathered cabin, adorned by a single clump of bone-gray antlers. Nor do I dream of Pearl, his three-legged dog, howling at the moon, or Jim's front tooth, hand carved out of solid jade. Nowhere do I hear him shouting and laughing, telling us how well his dog can play the piano, and how no one could pay him enough to swim in that freezing, deadly lake called Spirit.

And Laura—how could I not dream of her? Within a week of my arrival at Harmony Falls Lodge the summer before the eruption, Laura had nicknamed me Crayteeana and taught me how to wait tables without dropping dishes. Ten years older than me, she seemed to know everything—how to drive a pick-up, cut firewood, bake bread, run a restaurant, and seduce any listener within earshot by singing the blues on a twelve-string guitar. Some people thought we were sisters; others thought we were part American Indian, with our brown hair and summer tans. But Laura and I were just suburban dropouts, preparing meals in the lodge's dilapidated kitchen, driving to Longview for gallons of milk and hampers of eggs.

Nor have I dreamed of the only item I retrieved from the lodge—a small sugar bowl Laura gave me one afternoon as we stood hunched in the lodge's cramped attic. In the semidarkness, surrounded by dusty stacks of old plates, Laura handed me the cream-colored bowl, with its tiny, hand-painted border of maroon and blue leaves. Like Mount St. Helens' Sugar Bowl, a lava dome roughly 1,100 years old, my Harmony Falls sugar bowl is round and smooth and liable to crack. But also like the mountain's bowl, it has somehow escaped destruction. A mammoth hump of gray lava, the old dome is the only landmark left on Mount St. Helens' exploded north slope. And my porcelain bowl, the sole surviving piece of china from Harmony Falls Lodge, is the only object I possess from those days at the lake. But it has never appeared in my dreams.

And I have never dreamed of the only item rescued from my family's cabin: the "mountain cabin journal," as it was called. On several occasions during the months before the May 18 eruption, different members of my family tried to reach the cabin to retrieve the canoe, disconnect the propane, and haul out snowshoes, books, and my father's handmade stained-glass butterflies. All were stopped by the Skamania County sheriff and the National Guard, who had orders from Washington Governor Ray to block all traffic leading to within several miles of the active volcano. Only four miles north of the volcano's summit, my family's cabin lay well inside the state-defined Red Zone, where no one but authorized personnel were allowed.

For several weeks Spirit Lake cabin owners protested the restrictions. Then, on May 17, law-enforcement agents escorted the owners up Highway 504 to retrieve personal property. A second caravan was scheduled for 10 A.M. the next day. My family was not made aware of either escort, however, and lost everything in the cabin, not to mention the cabin itself.

However, on April 17, one month before the owners entered legally, my mother and two other family members persuaded the roadblock guards to allow them to enter on foot. They strolled past the sawhorse gate and within minutes were offered a ride by two women who had driven in on an abandoned logging road. At milepost 44 my mother declined to continue to the timberline parking lot to see the mountain up close. Instead, she trudged through the late-spring snow by herself to the two-story A-frame, which had a view of the mountain from its back deck.

Inside, she thought of making herself tea, but was too afraid to drink from the ash-infused faucet water. So she popped open a bottle of beer from the propane-fueled refrigerator and sat down on a patio chair to sip it. Outside, in the warm spring air, she watched as the clouds lifted to reveal the volcano's north face, looming as though it were close enough to touch. The slopes were covered with snow but dusted, too, with ash. One particular area on the volcano's north side—between a dome named Goat Rocks and the summit—had not yet bulged with magma, although it would do so dramatically over the next month, growing as much as five feet a day. But on that day, the famous "bulge" had yet to swell, and Goat Rocks still looked like Goat Rocks.

"Mount St. Helens looks normal," my mother wrote in the journal. In fact, April 17 was a relatively calm day for the volcano; geologists observed only twelve plumes between 7 A.M. and 1:30 P.M. But after a few sentences, my mother watched a wisp of smoke from the summit grow into a minor eruption. It was one of two plumes that would mushroom 500 feet that day. She waited nervously for the car to return, feeling unwelcome in the silent forest. When the group finally arrived, she grabbed the only valuable thing she could carry—the journal. As the car sped down the old Spirit Lake Highway, my mother thumbed its pages distractedly. The cabin was locked and the propane shut off; everything was going to be all right.

Handmade by my sister Terese, the lavender-covered journal is now creased and worn. Its pages are littered with the ruminations of a family of nine ragtag teenagers and their friends. But after my mother's April entry come the pages following the eruption. These pages are as white and smooth as the snow that once coated Spirit Lake all winter.

A tiny sugar bowl and a dog-eared, unfinished journal. Is this all that remains—these fragments and a heap of garbled dreams?

For years I stayed away from Mount St. Helens. With my family's land condemned by the government and Harmony Falls Lodge destroyed, it was simple to do. I pretended I had never been there. I feigned forgetfulness, endured a sleepy amnesia, even traveled to live for three years in a foreign country where no one paid attention to an active Cascade volcano. In the moments when I did think of the mountain, it was with anger. Angry at a mountain? Impossible. And so I went back to sleep.

But dream-wandering without a map grows tiresome. For no dream can replace an actual landscape.

In 1993, thirteen years after the 1980 eruption, I located an old topographic map of Spirit Lake. Printed before the eruption, the national forest map shows an extensive trail system built during the Civilian Conservation Corps era of the 1930s. As a child I had my own worn copy of this map and walked many of the trails shown on it between the ages of seven and seventeen. From 1993 to 1995, with this pre-eruption map in hand as well as a post-eruption one, I traveled in search of Spirit Lake. My journeys begin with a river valley, the way I first traveled to the lake as a child. The center is the lake itself, a deep basin around which all other points collide. The journeys then progress to the Mount Margaret backcountry, a remote territory I had only just begun to discover as a teenager. And they end at a mountain I had never scaled before the eruption—but one I cursed for more than a decade from hundreds of miles away.

This is the story of what I found there.

A Common Wildflower

My return to Spirit Lake began in earnest the day I happened upon a wildflower so common some call it a weed. Our group of four had set up camp high above Spirit Lake when I noticed it at dusk one late-summer evening. Nighthawks swooped about. A coyote bark drifted up from the east arm of the lake, 2,000 feet below. We stood, ears clipped by wind, on a 5,000-foot-high ridge as the day came to a close and the sky opened. A summer storm that had drenched the area earlier was clearing off, cloud by cloud. The sharp edges of twisted snags and cracked branches softened in the twilight as the last cumulus in Mount St. Helens' crater slipped west, disclosing the volcano's dome. Spirit Lake's steep basin filled slowly with shadows, but sunlight still caught the crater rim and, in the distance, the snowy summits of Mount Hood, Mount Adams, and Mount Rainier. We were high up on the ridge's spine, eye level with four of the Cascade Range's major mountains, the only shining things in the wake of the setting sun.

That was when I first glimpsed, after years of shouldering the loss of a vast green landscape, how I might find a path out of my grief—a grief so strange it seemed more like vertigo than mourning. For one thing, the Spirit Lake wilderness bore a strange new name—"blast zone"—to define the area where the volcano's lateral explosion had swept through, blowing trees over and burning them. The words bespoke violence, as though I were returning to a bombed-out house identified as Ground Zero. Worse still, the lake and its surrounding ridges deserved their new name. For 230 square miles the land was so changed its volcanic aftermath had to be catalogued: scorch zone, blowdown zone, mudflow, pyroclastic flow, avalanche. What were those? The first few times I saw Spirit Lake after the eruption, I looked everywhere—at my feet, straight ahead, to the side—trying desperately to get my bearings. Here was once a river. There, a shaded beach. Over there, a grove of old cottonwoods. And on all of the ridges—trees. Everywhere I turned, what should have been lush and cool was desiccated and barren. Low valleys were high; dry land was now water; dark *forests were sunbaked plains. I've been here before, I murmured each time. But not only had I lost an entire landscape, I myself was lost—a stranger in what should have been familiar land.*

But that summer evening, after zigzagging up through the back-country's blast-flattened forests, I finally tripped upon a compass. There, at my feet, blooming undisturbed in the rain-patted ash, was a four-foot-wide clump of pearly everlasting, a flower that once bloomed all over Spirit Lake. Like a ghost returned from the forested past, the tall-stemmed wildflower illuminated its small patch of earth with creamy blossoms flaming with failing sunlight. The narrow, spearlike leaves glowed a soft green. Each stem terminated in a fist of flowers. Nothing grew within two feet of the clump, which appeared about three summers old. I could tell the plant's approximate age because scattered below the upright stems were dead ones—the withered skeleton of the previous summer. And below those were others, and still others, fanning out in matted rags across the dark ash.

I might as well have tripped over the doorstep of that bombed-out house. Here was something I could understand. Pearly everlasting was one of the last wildflowers I saw at Spirit Lake before the eruption. I had sketched it, picked it, dried it. I knew its shape and size, could recall the exact places where it had bloomed—and here it was again. I looked south, east, and north at the sunlit Cascade mountains I had known since childhood, four alpine islands in an ocean of temperate green foothills. Volcanoes. I stood next to the everlasting clump as it shook slightly in the wind, and waited for the last bit of light to abandon the land.

Like many wildflowers at Spirit Lake, pearly everlasting (Ana-phalis margaritacea) is a perennial herb that rises after each snow melt. Its Latin name, margaritacea, *means "pearly" and describes the small, beady flowers that are composed of white papery "involucral bracts" instead of petals. The bracts encircle the tiny yellow florets containing a hundred thread-thin seeds. If picked before they mature, the blossoms—bracts and all—remain intact indefinitely when dried, hence the plant's name. I thought of the everlasting flowers I had dried before the eruption. They had kept their shape and scent for years until I forgot about them. Where were those flowers now?*

Pink light moved up the first of the four Cascade mountains encircling me. The shortest, youngest, and most violent, for 40,000 years this volcano had pummeled the land where I stood with searing winds, ash, and pumice. Light struck the dark basalt of one of its old lava domes. It was the peak closest to me, a hundred beats of a raven's wing away. Gusts shook the lake's surface. Bats joined the nighthawks to feed. I counted the stems of the pearly everlasting beside me: nineteen.

Although it is common in North America and northeast Asia, no one has paid much attention to pearly everlasting. Nineteenth-century naturalists like Thomas Nuttall and David Douglas ignored it. Thoreau considered it the "artificial" flower of September pastures, and the Scandinavian author Neltje Blanchan asked, "Who loves it?" She denigrated the wildflower as "stiff, dry, soulless, quite in keeping with the decorations on the average farmhouse mantelpiece . . . the most uncheering of winter bouquets." Its ubiquitous presence produces no excited exclamation or praise. At the turn of the century, the wildflower reached its own humble pinnacle of usefulness as the principal flower in funeral wreaths.

But here, at my feet, the illuminated flowers were glowing cold, swaying in the wind, cupping their seeds in bracts that folded like tiny frozen roses. A plane soared over the lake basin, then disappeared west down the Toutle River. Behind me, the backcountry lakes were jammed with logs, steeped in night. Before me, the peach glow hummed: light was leaving that first mountain.

Native people in the Northwest have also, for the most part, been indifferent to pearly everlasting. Most tribes have neither a name nor use for it. On the Olympic Peninsula, the Quileutes traditionally used the plant in a steam bath for rheumatism, but the Makah forbade their children to play with it because it caused sores. Pearly everlasting can't be eaten like wapato, camas, or wild ginger. It has no berries to rival those of huckleberry, thimbleberry,

*Oregon grape, or even salal. It lacks the medicinal properties of
Pacific yew or cedar. Its blossoms wax sallow next to purple penstemon or orange columbine.*

*However, over the last century, as the Northwest's woods have
been burned, logged, and sliced by roads, pearly everlasting has
been useful in one regard: as an erosion-controlling colonizer.
Because of its "weedy" properties—vigorous growth, prodigious
seeds, and resilience to extreme conditions—pearly everlasting has
often been one of the first plants to revegetate a clearcut or burn.
Within months of fire or logging, pearly everlasting will sprout in
a sunny patch and, along with fireweed, will brighten the spaces
between the blackened snags with tall, waving stems loaded with
blossoms. By autumn, the two will compete to litter their surroundings with seeds so light they float on the faintest updraft.*

*Light left the second Cascade mountain—a narrow cone that
trembled from time to time with shallow earthquakes. Only fifty
miles west of its summit, thousands of people in the Portland
metropolitan area were finishing dinner at this moment, washing
plates, putting children to bed, thinking of anything but sulfurous
fumes rising from one of its warm vents. Pearly everlasting flourished at that mountain, too.*

*When Mount St. Helens erupted in 1980 it exploded sideways,
knocking down thousands of acres of forests. As a result, moun-
tainsides that once held cool, shaded forests were now as sunny
and exposed as any clearcut or burn. This seemingly lifeless terrain
was inhospitable for many deep-forest species, but for pearly everlasting it was a vast new land upon which the flower could scatter
its progeny. Along with fireweed, lupine, thimbleberry, and
groundsel, everlasting was sprouting in the blast zone within three
months of the May 18 eruption.*

*I remembered the pearly everlasting flowers near my family's
cabin. They lined the highway to the mountain like beach foam
lapping against the conifers. This was a plant that loved sunlight
and didn't care how it obtained it. No wonder it was prospering
here, atop a windblown ridge.*

As a "generalist," pearly everlasting was well equipped to rein-habit Mount St. Helens' harsh terrain. A tough opportunist, the adaptable wildflower wields silver-green leaves whose color deflects the blast zone's intense solar radiation. From stem to leaf tip, the plant is covered in tiny white hairs that trap heat during freezing subalpine nights. Its tenacious roots and rhizomes knit themselves so tightly into the pumice soil no gust can extract them. But per-haps most importantly the plant is able to sprout from mere root fragments, and its plentiful feather-light seeds catch the blast zone's winds to colonize vast distances. It is a wildflower that thrives on disaster.

Shadows moved up the third Cascade mountain. Like the others, that volcano had erupted frequently and violently for thousands of years. It, too, could blacken the eastern sky in moments with stinging, suffocating ash. But pearly everlasting grew there, too.

Five years after the eruption, pearly everlasting was the most common wildflower in the blast zone. The flower swept over the landscape with the same abandon as the eruption itself, clinging to eroded cliffs, loose pumiceous soils, and log-jammed hillsides. But while the horizontal eruption was dramatic, immediate, and televised round the world, everlasting's quiet, seasonal advance transpired with little acclaim. Only the scientists noticed that it was improving the harsh habitat for other living things—that it was providing mulch for the volcanic ash, shade and food for insects and rodents, and an anchor for other seeds.

The cold began to cut through layers of wool; the wind howled over rocks. My eyes teared. Below, Spirit Lake's giant log raft—all that remained of the forests surrounding the lake—was breaking up. The raft was created when the volcano erupted sideways, causing a giant wave that washed all the trees into the water. Now, pushed by wind, the massive raft was moving, log by log, to the other end of the lake. It was time to go back to camp. Only a little light remained.

As pearly everlasting reappeared in the blast zone, so too did the mountain's other flowers. As I stood on the ridgetop, I noticed

*tangles of fireweed five feet high. Beyond them rustled meadows
of pasqueflower, paintbrush, and false-hellebore. Shrubby willows
and alders drew green spheres on the brown slopes. Huckleberry
shrubs proffered tiny blue berries. Young noble and silver firs rose
up like little green islands, fifteen feet high. Coyotes who had survived after the eruption on little besides insect carcasses and ash
now had fragrant wild strawberries to feast upon. The trail we had
taken to the ridge was littered with strawberry-studded coyote scat.*

*I looked up: one star. I rubbed my nose: ice. Then I looked at
the volcanoes: nothing. The everlasting clump, too, had gone dark.
I bent down and buried my face in its flowers to inhale their bees-
wax fragrance. The drab pearls in my palm were a tunnel to the
inhumed past—when Norway Pass was dark and cool; when the
mouth of the Toutle River sang under its burden of snow; when
Spirit Lake, clear of its log raft, reflected at night clouds of stars.*

*I released the beads and the plant swung back. I was shoul-
dering an old loss like a chunk of wet firewood, but at dusk on
the ridge east of Mount Margaret I paused beside a flower some
call a weed, and rested.*

*And when coyotes howled around our camp at midnight, I
rose from the tent to look at the stars. The lake's logs had disappeared west, disclosing its east arm—a huge, flat path of sparkling
obsidian. I gazed up at the sky, then at the same image below:
there were the stars, clouds and clouds of them, tiny ice-white
flecks in the lake's black waters. The last time I had seen them,
the lake was 200 feet lower, and hundreds of trees had crowded
its shores. Now it was higher and wider and could accommodate
more of the heavens. Thousands of stars floated below, constella-
tions beyond my comprehension. The coyotes' cries drifted for miles
across the broken timber. Lost in the galaxies, I took one wide look
at the dark land around me. So this was the blast zone. I was on
my way home.*

THE RIVER

An Unnamed Creek

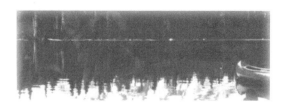

The mountain stands far,
And toward that I am traveling,
Toward that I am traveling.
On the top of it,
The clouds stand far above.
Many are the songs the mocking-bird is singing,
And following his songs the edge of the morning appears
And from there the morning comes.

—Papago Indian Song,
Girls' Puberty Dance

One of the places pearly everlasting bloomed before the eruption was a slip of a creek that, as far as I know, didn't have a name. It knocked, gurgled, and whistled as it plunged down a steep, forested ridge behind our cabin, one and one-half miles west of Spirit Lake. Spring-fed, even its backwater eddies swirled clear and cold.

As an adolescent I used to stroll a short way behind the cabin to watch the creek fall down the folds of the 1,100-foot ridge. The ridge had been swept by fire a couple of decades before; perhaps that was why the sun-loving everlasting thrived there. A worn path wandered through the young forest up to where a thick black hose, the water line to our cabin, lay anchored in the center of a round pool. There the trail ended, and I had to climb the creek's banks to follow it higher. I jumped over boulders and bent low under branches to hike as far as I could. Pumice peppered the forest's humus. A struggling understory of vine maple and bracken fern competed with the slender, dense conifers. Eventually fallen logs, cliffs, and my own fear of the unblazed wilderness discouraged my progress, and I stopped to listen: nothing but the roar of water. No jay's complaint, no mountain lion's scream, no cheeping of chipmunks: only the throaty knocking of side streams could be heard as they filled their bouldered pools.

Captivated by the incessant fall of water, I crouched beside its constant crash. I hardly thought about the creek's downstream path, although I knew it emptied into the North Fork of the Toutle River, a quarter of a mile below. From there, the North Fork gathered other tributaries for twenty miles until it met the South Fork and became, simply, the Toutle. It then rushed fifteen miles west to empty into the Cowlitz, which in turn journeyed south another twenty miles to the Columbia River, which completed its 1,200-mile journey from British Columbia by swirling another seventy miles to the frothy breakers of the Pacific Ocean. At sixteen, as I watched the creek percolate through the moss on its banks, I never considered that the water flowing behind my family's cabin would drift under fifty bridges, join one of the largest rivers in North America, and travel as far as 300 miles out to sea before it dissolved into salt water. For me, the creek was rooted in the landscape in the same way the tall white snags soared on the ridgetop: it stayed in one place. Fluid but unchanging, it was my own small wilderness—where no trail traveled, where no one else thought to spend an afternoon.

Perhaps I felt such privacy because the creek had no name. A tiny blue line on the U.S. Geological Survey topographic map, it ran nameless into trail-less territory. Its source lay at the top of the small ridge, a saddle between two larger ridges, none of which had any names. In the folds of this ridge, the creek cascaded down to a small valley where a handful of cabins sat near the river. My family's cedar-shaked, two-story A-frame stood in this pocket of cabins. Unlike the creek, it had a name: *Casa di Montagna,* or Mountain House.

When my parents purchased the cabin in early 1977, they gained water rights to the creek. My brothers bushwhacked through the young firs and burnt snags to explore its source—a noisy underground cavern high up the ridge. My brother Bernie fell and cracked a rib as his reward for reaching the spring. Each of my eight siblings drank from the creek. With so many people, potential names for the creek could have been endless, but instead we drank from it year-round and left it unnamed.

It also went unphotographed. Views of the mountain and other panoramas were worth shooting, but not the little creek. No one thought to document it, except as a water source. As the only water supply on the north bank of the Toutle besides the river itself, the unnamed creek was not unimportant. My father had heard stories of cabin owners fighting over the creek. During some of the disagreements, some owners had cut other owners' lines. There was not enough water to go around, people argued. Perhaps a name for the creek was used then; perhaps documents now destroyed contained that name, or another. But no one in my family remembers. It is a slip of water eluding the most human of impulses—to name.

We name things to hold onto them, to make them ours. A four-legged creature who hops from a leaf is already something else if it is known as a tree frog, and something else again if it is referred to as *Pseudacris regilla.* Names announce the familiar and permanent: a

bend in the road taken slowly becomes the Hairpin Turn; an outcropping becomes Inspiration Point. By naming places, things, even
ourselves, we freeze characteristics and hold them to a description—words like Grand Canyon, which is indefinitely grand, or
weeping willow, which indefinitely weeps.

It is no secret that in the Pacific Northwest European explorers—
transients who passed through the land—renamed places, plants,
land formations, and animals that were previously named by native
peoples. In some cases, the explorers copied down the native
name—as with *Spilyai* and *Wahkiakum*. But this transcribing was com-
plicated by the fact that the original namers were from an oral
tradition and had no written version. The result was often a cor-
ruption: *Killimuck* became Tillamook; *Quamash* became Camas. In
many cases, the native name was replaced altogether by an English
one, as with *Hood, Adams,* or *Baker*. Mistakes abounded. Indigenous
conifers were given Eurocentric names like *hemlock* and *cedar* when
they were neither, and the Pacific Northwest's most common tree
was triply misnamed: Douglas-fir *(Pseudotsuga menziesii)* is neither a
fir, as its English name claims, nor is it related to hemlock, as the
Latin *Pseudotsuga* implies, and David Douglas was not the first European to catalog it. In his book, *Having Everything Right*, Kim Stafford
discusses the disconnectedness of this type of naming, noting that
"The Kwakiutl people of the Northwest coast had a habit in their
naming. For them, a name was a story . . . a place-name would not
be something that is, but something that happens."

Mount St. Helens was named for a British diplomat who never
traveled through the Pacific Northwest. The volcano was given its
current name on October 20, 1792, by Captain George Vancouver
in honor of his friend Alleyne Fitzherbert, Baron St. Helens. In
1791, Fitzherbert helped Britain resolve a territorial dispute with
Spain regarding Nootka Sound on Vancouver Island and received

the title of Baron St. Helens that same year. He lived in London rather than St. Helens, the village in Lancashire, England, from which the title originated. The village of St. Helens was itself named after a Catholic church there devoted to Saint Helen (A.D. 250–A.D. 330), the mother of Constantine, the first Christian emperor of the Roman Empire. The original name, Helen, became famous with Helen of Troy, who was kidnapped more than once on account of her beauty, and whose abduction by Paris led to the Trojan War. In ancient Greece, early records refer to Helen as a moon goddess. Oddly enough, like a traveling moon the name has journeyed west over 1,500 years to rest upon an active volcano.

Among the volcano's many Northwest Indian names, the most common, *Loowit*, was also related to a woman who, like Helen of Troy, caused a great war on account of her beauty. The Klickitat legend documented by Ella Clark in *Indian Legends of the Pacific Northwest* begins long ago, when people were neither cold nor hungry. At that time, two brothers began to quarrel over the land. One night, the Great Spirit took the brothers to a new land with mountains and a "big river"—the Columbia. There, he woke them and told them to shoot their arrows in opposite directions:

"Where your arrow falls, that will be your country. There you will become a great chief. The river will separate your lands."

One brother shot his arrow south into the valley of the Willamette River. He became the father and the high chief of the Multnomah people. The older brother shot his arrow north into the Klickitat country. He became the father and high chief of the Klickitat people.

Then the Great Spirit built a bridge over the big river. To each brother he said, "I have built a bridge over the river, so that you and your people may visit those on the other side. It will be a sign of peace between you. As long as you and your people are good and are friendly with each other, this bridge of the Tahmahnawis [divine spirit] will remain."

It was a broad bridge, wide enough for many people and many ponies to walk across at one time. For many snows the people were at peace and crossed the river for friendly visits. But after a time they did wicked things. They were selfish and greedy, and they quarreled. The Great Spirit, displeased again, punished them by keeping the sun from shining. The people had no fire, and when the winter rains came, they were cold.

Then they began to be sorry for what they had done, and they begged the Great Spirit for fire. "Give us fire, or we will die from the cold," they prayed. The heart of the Great Spirit was softened by their prayer. He went to an old woman who had kept herself from the wrongdoing of her people and so still had some fire in her lodge.

"If you will share your fire, I will grant you anything you wish," the Great Spirit promised her. "What do you want most?"

"Youth and beauty," answered the old woman promptly. "I wish to be young again, and to be beautiful."

"You shall be young and beautiful tomorrow morning," promised the Great Spirit. "Take your fire to the bridge, so that the people on both sides of the river can get it easily. Keep it burning there always as a reminder of the goodness and kindness of the Great Spirit."

The old woman, whose name was Loowit, did as he said. Then the Great Spirit commanded the sun to shine again. When it rose the next morning, it was surprised to see a young and beautiful maiden sitting beside a fire on the Bridge of the Gods. The people, too, saw the fire, and soon their lodges were warm again. For many moons all was peaceful on both sides of the great river and the bridge.

The young men also saw the fire—and the beautiful young woman who attended it. They visited her often. Loowit's heart was stirred by two of them—a handsome young chief from south of the river, whose name was Wyeast, and a handsome young chief *from north of the river, whose name was Klickitat. She could not decide which of the two she liked better.*

Wyeast and Klickitat grew jealous of each other and soon began to quarrel. They became so angry that they fought. Their people also took up the quarrel, so that there was much fighting on both sides of the river. Many warriors were killed.

This time the Great Spirit was made angry by the wickedness of the people. He broke down the Bridge of the Gods, the sign of peace between the two tribes, and its rocks fell into the river. He changed the two chiefs into mountains. Some say that they continued to quarrel over Loowit even after they were mountain peaks. They caused sheets of flame to burst forth, and they hurled rocks at each other . . . Loowit was changed into a snow-capped peak, which still has the youth and beauty promised by the Great Spirit. She is now called Mount St. Helens. Wyeast is known as Mount Hood, and Klickitat as Mount Adams.

Loo-wit-lat-kla, or "Keeper of Fire," appears in other stories, most of which describe the volcano's transformation from snow-capped peak to ash-covered crater and back again. The volcano was also called *Lawelatla,* or "One from Whom Smoke Comes"; and *Tah-one-lat-clah,* or "Fire Mountain," referring to the volcano's violent past.

It is not surprising that at the same time Vancouver named the volcano, he indicated its position. "Latitude 46 degrees 9', and in longitude 238 degrees 4'," he scribbled in his log. Names are handles on the land. They not only bestow an identity, they position the observer in the landscape. Names tell us where we are, where we have been, where we are going; they carry the weight of history and the course of the future. One October day after the eruption I took a morning flight from San Francisco to Portland, and as the plane circled to land, a snowy Mount Hood, Mount Adams, and Mount Rainier popped into view. Mount St. Helens was gray and snowless in contrast. The woman sitting behind me asked, "Which mountains are those?"

"That's Mount Hood behind us," I answered, "Mount Adams on the right, Mount Rainier in the distance, and Mount St. Helens."

"*Which* is Mount St. Helens?"

"The one with no snow on it," I smiled.

"Oh right!" she laughed.

Would it have helped to say, Loowit, the old woman who keeps the fire in her belly? Or Lawelatla, Smoking Mountain? To name a volcano after a diplomat who was named after a church that was named after a saint is to clothe a cougar in a riding coat sewn from altar vestments. Neither name nor garment fit. And yet that is what we have.

On the south shore of Spirit Lake, sitting around a huge campfire year after year, people laughed in disbelief when the Forest Service ranger announced that Mount St. Helens would erupt before the end of the twentieth century. As sparks from the huge fire spiraled off into the dark ceiling of fir boughs, crowds of campers would burst into guffaws at the notion of an active volcano in their midst. Huddled in my jacket, I laughed, too. And when an earthquake rattled the kitchen cabinets inside Harmony Falls Lodge the summer before the eruption, I considered the mountain's movements a passing thrill.

Sometimes we wake to a dark wood and don't know where we are. When that happens, names are a false security, and whatever knowledge we acquire is by a different kind of knowing. After the 1980 eruption, new names were needed for a new landscape: Pumice Plain, The Breach, Willow Springs, Castle Lake. Old names were obsolete or forgotten: Bear Cove, Duck Bay. And a pair of forested ridges that had once been nameless gained new names: Johnston Ridge, Harry's Ridge. But beyond them all cascaded a wild hum of water that still splashes inside me. Four miles north of

Loowit's summit and one and a half miles west of Spirit Lake it flowed, supplying my family year-round with sweet springwater that needed no filtering. My mother used to haul gallons of it back to Portland to fortify us when we were away from the mountain. The container that held this water was usually labeled Spirit Lake, only because Spirit Lake was the name that described the entire wilderness we felt we belonged to and which we thought belonged to us. But the water we drank to remind ourselves of this wilderness was not Spirit Lake water. It was water from a creek that no longer exists, buried under 400 feet of rock and mud. A creek that had no name, and will no longer need one.

But perhaps even now pearly everlasting grows there.

The Toutle Mountains

You never know
what you are going to learn.

—Wendell Berry

My first task in returning to Spirit Lake was to return to a river—a river that once carried the water of both Spirit and the unnamed creek. For although other routes have been used to access Spirit Lake— including logging roads, half-blazed "way" trails, and helicopters— since I was seven there seemed to me but one way into the Spirit Lake wilderness: up a river called the Toutle.

Before the eruption, the Toutle River carved a V-shaped gorge through a series of forested mountains as it carried Spirit Lake's water west to the Cowlitz River. The source for the undammed, wild river was two-fold: the Toutle's South Fork began on the mountain, and its North Fork drained from the lake itself. For nearly all of its journey the river was accompanied by a two-lane road called the Spirit Lake Highway, or State Route 504. Built in 1903, the Spirit Lake Highway began at Castle Rock, then followed the river's North Fork to Spirit Lake, and finally ended near timberline on Loowit's north flank. Before the eruption, it was the only paved road into the lake. My family called the road Highway 504 and knew every twist, straightway, and bend. We had to—driving recklessly meant getting hit by one of the many logging trucks that thundered by at top speed, its red flags flapping from the sawn tip of the trailer's longest log.

When roadblocks were erected on Highway 504 in March 1980, I felt a door close with a soft, tentative click. My family's cabin was suddenly off-limits, but I felt certain I would see it again. Harmony Falls, too, was off-limits, but I had every hope of returning to work there after I graduated from high school. In fact, I counted on it. Spirit Lake was not so much a vacation place for me as an obsession: I wanted to live there, permanently, year-round.

By late April, when restrictions stiffened, I waited patiently for the door to open. A potential eruption had not figured into my plans. I would finish school just in time for Spirit Lake to return to its former anonymity, for summer to begin. But on May 18 the door slammed shut with a boom heard as far away as British Columbia and northern California. The volcano exploded upon the river's upper reaches, generating a huge mudflow that bulldozed its way down the valley for hours. By late afternoon Highway 504 was crumpled, buried, or flushed downstream. Five-ton blocks of glacial ice—along with snow, ash, trees, and heated rocks—turned the Toutle into a 90-degree-Fahrenheit flood of slow-moving mortar. The tepid, silty porridge ripped houses off their foundations, tore bridges from their supports, and stained tree trunks gray. More than 45 million cubic yards of sediment were dumped into the Columbia River, decreasing the channel's depth from forty feet to thirteen and blocking shipping traffic for two weeks.

Six months after the eruption, I traveled to the valley to see the destruction for myself. Minutes after exiting Interstate 5, I encountered a roadblock. The door seemed locked for good.

But it turned out I was wrong. Thirteen years, forty-three miles, and $165 million later, the new Spirit Lake Memorial Highway was built. When I heard that the highway would be open in May 1993 for the thirteenth anniversary of the eruption, I phoned my twin sister, Celeste, and proposed a trip upriver.

We planned to hike to the old cabin site and camp somewhere that reminded us of the valley's huge trees. We both recalled the highway as a gray sliver sliced out of a gigantic coniferous jungle. From any angle there had been trees and more trees—western hemlock, western red cedar, Douglas-fir, bigleaf maple, vine maple, cottonwood, red alder. And the highway knifed uphill through all of them to reach the blue, sunlit plain of Spirit Lake.

As I arrived at the Portland airport on the eve of our trip, every river and stream below the aircraft shot back bright cumulus clouds and blue sky. The watery land glistened in a hundred blue-white mirrors. I thought of the Toutle: would its silty waters run clear? Even in 1912 it had been described as a "stream of milk" by geologist Carl Zapffe. The Harmony Falls crowd had referred to its glacial tributaries as "milkshake rivers." Would it, too, throw back blue light? And would some remnant of its giant trees cast shadows in the deep valley?

The next morning I awoke in Celeste's downtown apartment to clouds hugging the volcano. Potential rain. We crammed her small blue car with our backpacks and bid good-bye to her husband as low clouds sailed overhead. Cruising north on Interstate 5, I hung my head out the window and let the cool air rush over my face. It had been so long since I had spent time alone with my twin sister that even the air seemed delicious.

Although Celeste and I had shared a bed for most of our childhood and an apartment during college, upon graduating we traveled oceans to live apart. For three years I studied literature and worked in France while Celeste volunteered for the Peace Corps. My letters from Paris crossed hers mid-air from Honduras; I wrote about Henri Matisse while she wrote about amoebic dysentery and some "mysterious thing that bit me while I was fording the river." I slept in a mouse-infested tenement while she stayed up nights trapping bats that had crawled through the rafters of her *casa*. Then Celeste left the Peace Corps around the same time that I was nearly deported from France for lack of working papers. She returned to Portland and I moved to San Francisco, 600 miles away.

But now the mountain had pulled us together again. We had swung wide like geese to circle back to familiar territory. Or so we thought.

In fact, we were trailed by a strange haze of confusion everywhere we went. And being twins, we failed to rid each other of the affliction. After only two days, I was convinced that my twin sister would be the last person I would want to be with if I were lost in the woods. We would devise the same wrong escape route, shudder with the same paroxysms of fear, or eat the same bad mushroom. No doubt we would perish in the best of company, but it might be better, just the same, to live.

The first hour of the trip seemed ordinary enough. Daisies and lupines lined Interstate 5 as we drove north past Woodland, Kalama, and Kelso—old logging towns from the nineteenth-century boom-and-bust days. The bust seemed to endure; on our right, a plywood-covered storefront announced CLOSED VACATION

REPAIR. But the boom endured as well, with acres of logs still lining millyards and the scent of pulp polluting the air. For most of the drive, mountainous piles of gray silt sprawled beside the freeway— volcanic mud dredged out of the Columbia River by the U.S. Army Corps of Engineers. The gray mounds rose up like trail markers telling us we had entered Loowit's territory.

We smiled in sudden nostalgia as we exited at Castle Rock, where we would begin a journey up a valley we loved as much as Spirit Lake itself. But our confusion began at Silver Lake, five miles east, as late-morning clouds shuffled over the hills. We entered the Mount St. Helens Visitor Center, a handsome stone building constructed five years after the eruption, and immediately noticed a large sign with a famous quotation by the ancient Greek philosopher, Heraclitus: "Nothing is permanent except change." It made us think about the volcano, but there lay the start of our confusion. For the first thing we saw after leaving Silver Lake and driving east was not change due to volcanism.

For a moment we thought we were at the beginning of the blast zone. We had read all the displays at the visitor center and considered ourselves prepared. We had read how the streams in the region were the most sediment laden in the world, how the Cowlitz River salmon were expected to perish after the eruption but survived by their own resourcefulness, how the lateral blast blew down more than 1.6 billion board feet of timber within national forest boundaries. The Forest Service had been faced with a difficult decision: What to do with all the dead trees? Should they be left to rot— thereby endangering nearby forests with the threat of insects or fire? Or should they be harvested? We had read that some of the wood was removed and the most dramatic areas left untouched. A compromise between conservationists and the timber industry had been reached.

We continued up Highway 504 gazing right and left. Was this already the blast zone? Couldn't be. But if it wasn't, *where were all the trees?*

Slouched in the passenger's seat, I stared over my right shoulder. The sun had broken through the clouds, and there, across the river, stood the Toutle Mountains. Known also as the Green Mountains, these gently folded, 4,000-foot ridges formed the valley's south wall and separated the river's North Fork from its South. In some places, such as Spud Mountain, their ancient, crystallized volcanic rock dated back 32 million years—an eternity compared to the volcano's 40,000 years. Like the forked river encircling their north and south slopes in a watery necklace, they disappeared west, yielding to the broad Columbia River basin. But the mountains' geology was not foremost in my mind as I stared out the window. Because before me the Toutle mountain range rose road-rutted, skid-marked, checkered in brown.

"Celeste, they cut all the trees."

"Are you sure this isn't the blast zone?"

"I don't think so. The blast zone is supposed to be ten miles away."

"Then where are we?"

My eyes returned to the road, where I read wooden signposts planted left and right—just like other signs planted along the highway before the eruption. The pre-eruption signs, sprouting from small clearcuts along the road, had announced confidently, "Your Forest 2025." Today, the new signs stated simply, "Weyerhaeuser St. Helens Tree Farm, Planted 1985" and "Commercially Thinned 1992."

We were in the middle of the largest tree farm in the state of Washington. The devastation we found so shocking was ordinary clearcutting. We sat stone-faced in the car, confused. How could it be that in the last thirteen years the valley had been completely logged? While Celeste was teaching Honduran villagers Western nutrition and I was lecturing American students about French châteaux, Mount St. Helens' trees were being felled, bucked, yarded, shipped, and milled. Against conservationists' protests, the Forest Service and Weyerhaeuser even removed the majority of the blast-blown logs. Ash-dulled chainsaws were fixed or replaced. Nothing got in the way.

We stopped at Hoffstadt Bluffs, twenty-seven miles up the highway, to take in a full view of the valley. Here, no doubt, was a place to orient ourselves. Instead we were distracted by a group of tourists photographing what they thought was volcanic devastation, their cameras angled at the sweeping clearcuts.

At the time of the eruption, roughly 55 percent of the forested area affected by the lateral blast was state and U.S. Forest Service land; the remaining 45 percent belonged to Weyerhaeuser Company, the world's largest private owner of merchantable softwood timber and the largest producer of softwood lumber. Compared to the company's holdings in Canada, which number 17 million acres, the amount of land the Weyerhaeuser Company owns in the state of Washington seems small—only one million acres. The company's holdings west of the volcano, the St. Helens Tree Farm, span 440,000 acres. However, in contrast, the Mount St. Helens National Volcanic Monument barely totals 110,000 acres—only a quarter of the size of the tree farm and a fraction of the original 230-square-mile blast zone.

We climbed higher up the valley's north wall, past the North Fork and Elk Rock viewpoints. Clearcuts and replantings lined both sides of the valley. It was impossible to tell where the industrial timber activities stopped and the volcano's blast zone began.

By the time we reached the new visitor center at Coldwater Ridge, Celeste and I knew we wouldn't be camping along the Spirit Lake Memorial Highway. We finally understood our mutual delusion. There was no old growth *at all* along the new road. We had been driving the dreamscape of our childhood. Whatever ancient forest had escaped the eruption had been clearcut after the blast. We spent the afternoon hiking down the Elk Bench Trail to Coldwater Lake. Stumps marked the treeless land like tombstones dotting a cemetery. False-dandelion weeds and grasses bloomed undaunted, not yet baked by the rampant sun.

We hiked back to the Coldwater parking lot as afternoon clouds cast enormous shadows over the bald hills. Tomorrow we would have to drive some other road to find dark, shaded woods. Before leaving, we stopped inside the new visitor center, which was closing after its first day. Inside, a ranger told us that it was impossible to hike anywhere near our family's cabin site from Coldwater Ridge. No trails had been built in that direction, and off-trail travel was prohibited. In front of a panel of gigantic windows facing the mountain, we asked another ranger where we could find a trail through ancient forest. He paused. "Well, there's the Lewis River Trail on the south side. It has some nice 500-year-old trees. You'll have to drive around to the south."

Was that all?

"And there's the Green River Trail, on the north side. That's another long drive."

So was that it? More than one million acres of trees in the Gifford Pinchot National Forest, and that was all the old growth near the volcano?

"Well, there's Cedar Flats."

A small, 680-acre preserve. No more than a fifteen-minute stroll.

"And Quartz Creek Big Trees."

Even smaller. A 60-acre preserve on the north side, barely larger than its parking lot.

"And the Dark Divide."

A large stretch of roadless land indeed, but one that stretched east toward Mount Adams.

We opted for the Lewis River, spending the night at a motel at Silver Lake, our packs stashed against a wall.

We sat down in two vinyl-backed chairs to eat our dinner of backpacker's soup at a small formica table. Shouts and laughter erupted in the distance. A group of fishermen were having a party by the lakeshore. As the kitchen light burned overhead like an interrogator's lamp, we nursed our shock with the hot corn chowder. I felt like a swallow that had just bashed into a window.

"It would be hard to understand what's missing around here if you never saw the Toutle before the eruption," Celeste said, crossing one leg over the other and blowing at a spoonful of steaming soup. "All those huge trees."

I felt the hot fluid on the back of my throat. We were the last generation to see those trees. Even if the new, replanted trees grew back, they wouldn't be the same forests. Straight lines now ran all over the hills, and pockets of alders marked old clearcuts that weren't replanted. I suddenly felt extremely old, like an octogenarian who had witnessed the disappearance of a valley of dairy farms lost to subdivisions, or a series of falls swallowed by a dam.

Celeste yawned. "And to think I just wanted to take a little stroll down Memory Lane." Amid the distant shouts and laughter, we crept into our beds and fell asleep.

The next morning we drove to the mountain's south side, stopping in Cougar for breakfast. As we spread strawberry jam on our toast, a gray-haired man in a tan shirt and jeans entered the cafe and talked with two other men at the counter. All three were truck drivers who had worked for decades hauling logs out of Mount St. Helens' forests. All three were unemployed. One was trying to sell his house and move to the Oregon Coast, but couldn't find a buyer.

"I gave everything I could, you know," he said, shaking his head our way. "Got nothin' in return."

We didn't know what to say. We were enduring our own weird return of nothingness. My response lay somewhere between wanting to shake the man, and patting his shoulder in sympathy.

We left Cougar for the Lewis River. There indeed was an old-growth forest—a fourteen-mile stretch graced by roaring rapids and water ouzels streaking upriver. But it was not the old growth of our childhood. The Lewis River was a low-elevation forest overhung with mossy bigleaf maples. We hiked five miles of the spiderwebbed path—hardly the sort of pumiceous trails that once wandered through the cold 3,200-foot-high forest encircling Spirit Lake. We stepped off the trail every so often as small flocks of mountain bikers shot past. Then, as both daylight and bikers disappeared, we camped by the river, which paralleled the highway on its other bank. We awoke at dawn to the roar of logging-truck wheels and the whine of gears.

Upon leaving the Lewis River, we found that we could not travel to Mount St. Helens without crossing a clearcut. The volcano was enveloped by monoculture tree farms—vast acres planted at the same time and of the same species of tree. Some of the clearcuts were in various stages of replanting. In one, fir trees stood fifteen feet high. In others, seedlings were just breaking shrub height. But all were as uniform as a field of beans. By the time we explored the mountain's south side, we knew that we were looking at something more tremendous than this century's largest eruption in the lower forty-eight contiguous states; we were witnessing the great age of western deforestation—endless tracts of ancient forests whittled down to vestigial pockets in less than a hundred years.

Loowit's forests began drawing loggers more than 150 years ago. During the late-nineteenth century, western Washington's immense stands of Douglas-fir lured hundreds of lumbermen from the Lake States in a mass migration that continued into the early part of the twentieth century. By the 1920s, the amount of wood cut in the Northwest exceeded the combined total of all of the nation's other forests. And the fragrant foothills surrounding Loowit had been among the most fertile of all. The first mill in Cowlitz County was built by Alexander Abernathy and James Clark in 1848, the same year gold was discovered in the Sierra Nevada. The Abernathy and Clark mill was followed by scores of others, including the Ostrander mill in 1890, which became famous for producing the longest timbers in the world. As a result, during the first decade of the twentieth century Cowlitz County's average yearly shipment of old-growth logs was 26 million board feet. By 1948, the two largest lumber mills in the world—Long-Bell and Weyerhaeuser—were employing thousands of people in Longview to cut more than one million board feet of lumber a day.

During the 1960s—the decade in which Celeste and I were born—the Forest Service began clearcutting aggressively in the national forests as old trees became scarce on private land. By 1970, the first time Celeste and I traveled the Toutle River, clearcuts had marched secretly up the valley. At that time, fifty-foot-deep buffer stands of trees left uncut along the road led us to believe the forests were all untouched. We gazed upon them with the eyes of children.

But on that unstable spring day in 1993 we were no longer children, and the fifty-foot-deep roadside stands had been abandoned. Everywhere we looked logging operations had cut straight down to the highway's shoulder.

I sighed in dismay as I realized that the blast zone itself was hemmed in by replanted tree farms. There was no way to tell where the blast winds had subsided; dense green seedlings camouflaged the old ragged line of the scorched and blown-down trees. I discovered later that within a year of the eruption, Weyerhaeuser had removed 850 million board feet of timber from its blast zone land and replaced the blown-down logs with 14.6 million seedlings. The Forest Service had removed more than 200 million board feet of blast zone timber and replanted 14,000 acres with 10 million seedlings. These efforts were called the "new forests" of Mount St. Helens. But instead of forest Celeste and I saw only rows and rows of baby trees—rows so perfectly straight they reminded us of grid paper.

Finally, we gave up looking for an old-growth experience and headed down a logging road instead. Most of the Toutle mountain range was now owned by the Washington Department of Natural Resources. Of the state's 80,000 acres, all but 1,200 had been cleared and replanted, mostly with Douglas-fir scheduled to be cut every sixty years. Like Weyerhaeuser Company, Burlington Northern, International Paper, and other timber harvesters at Mount St. Helens, the state had yet to implement an alternative to clearcutting and monoculture farms.

We parked the car and walked quietly down the old dirt road, which was slowly being carved into a creek bed by seasonal rains. Eight-foot-tall alder saplings were reclaiming the road root by branch, and we walked in their shadows amid horsetails and bracken fern. A deer skull, crushed into the ground by four-wheel-drive tread, lay on the right-side track, its shell-like fragments stained green as moss. As we rounded a curve, the alders disappeared, and the sun-washed expanse of the clearcut stretched before us. Replanted stands of thin-trunked Douglas-fir bounded the east, north, and west sides of the straight-edged, deforested square. The clearcut itself, an acre or two, was shrubby and green. Salmonberry vines trailed the ground. Tough-leaved salal and Oregon grape thrived in thick bunches. A Douglas-fir seedling here and there poked its crown above the scrub. Red-flowering currant and vanilla-leaf bloomed in the windless noon. Near the road, bullet-busted beer cans lay scattered beside a short chunk of forgotten log. Uphill, a spring-heavy creek glugged and drummed a soft, regular rhythm. Robins and dark-eyed juncos chirped and swung from shrub to earth.

We waited for something to happen—for a tree to fall, for a deer to crash through the alders, for the wind to stir. But there was only the creek's glug-glug and the birds' quick trills. We sat down on the short chunk of log, and my eyes rested on a young clump of pearly everlasting. I thought of the blast zone's everlasting, the blast zone's silence, its sun-washed slopes, its birds. Like the blast zone, this square before me had endured its recent annihilation and was recovering in a wide and gentle silence. But unlike the federally protected monument, the clearcut would not be allowed to persevere through a slow, indefinite metamorphosis. Its tiny Douglas-firs would not crash and rot after soaring skyward for 500 years. It was a nonspace, a tilled and sown field awaiting autumn. It straddled its violent past and tall-treed future as uncomfortably as any urban lot anticipating a gray-trunked skyscraper. Its patchy, disrupted present was a cipher only nature claimed, a nonpresent bounded by past commodity and future profit. Foresters and conservationists alike were waiting for the clearcut to become something other than it was. Loggers congratulated themselves for their fait accompli; conservationists mourned it as damage done. As we sat on the log, somewhere miles away both parties were waiting, like us, for something to happen. But what of the clearcut as it was? It was embraced only by indiscriminate nature, with seeds that wanted to root, wings that wanted to land, and hooves that traveled miles for sweet leafy food.

We strolled back to the car wondering how many times the patch of land before us had been clearcut. Once? Twice? Three times? At what point would the rich volcanic soil erode away or become exhausted?

As we slammed the doors shut, I thought of how in one place alone did our confusion subside: in those few areas where the blast-blown logs had been left on the ground. There, amid the gray quilt of decaying debris, it was clear to see that an untouched forest had soared before the eruption, and now another one was slowly taking its place. A thin coat of ash still dusted the logs there, as though the eruption had happened only yesterday.

"Each tree tells its own story," Celeste had observed in front of the blown-down logs. "Each tree shows you, years later, how it died and which way the blast winds came."

But the clearcut had no such story to tell.

We drove slowly away, our confusion as thick as the dust clouds rising behind the car. It was supposed to be a celebration—a return to old haunts transformed by nature. But neither of us would ever forget the group of people photographing what they thought was volcanic destruction. And I would never forget my first glimpse, after thirteen years, of those gentle hills known as the Toutle Mountains. I had counted on them to help me get back to the river's headwaters. But it would require more than one journey up the Toutle to reach its wild heart.

The Toutle River

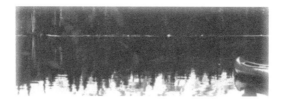

The nature of the road describes the nature of the travel.

—John Steinbeck

Six months after our journey up the Toutle in May 1993, Celeste and I returned to the river, splashing north out of Portland one autumn morning in a tumult of driving rain. The windshield wipers danced like frenetic metronomes as the car ambled past the Trojan nuclear power plant, which loomed over the swollen Columbia River near Rainier, Oregon. Celeste told me that the plant had been closed recently due to malfunctions. I recalled the little brown plastic pellet we had received on a field trip to Trojan when we were schoolkids. About the size of an elk dropping, the pellet represented how much nuclear waste was left over after the plant had heated thousands of homes. I wondered how many of those pellets were lying in the cooling ponds now. As we cruised past, the tall gray cooling tower disappeared into a milky November sky that bore down upon us, threatening snow. By the time we reached Castle Rock, the clouds disintegrated into torrents. Not quite ready to face the river in such a deluge, we wandered around the old part of town, stopping in antique stores, chatting with residents. In one store, the shopkeeper accused us of being related.

"You're twins," she said, grinning. "Fraternal or identical?"

"We don't know," I answered. "The doctors never decided."

"What do you mean?"

"The pathologist thought one thing, the obstetrician another. And since we were the seventh and eighth children my mother had, she was too busy to ask for details."

"Huh," she said, tilting her head as we exited the warm store into a wall of cold, steady rain. We skipped across reservoir-size puddles to reach the car.

"Having to go into all those details is exhausting," I complained.

"Just say we're identical," Celeste replied.

"But we don't know that."

We left Castle Rock and headed east upriver. Mist clouded the young firs replanted along the road. The river flowed like runoff from a cement mixer. Just beyond the small town of Toutle, we parked the car on a curve rising over the riverbank so that Celeste could photograph the bony red alders beside the muddy river. Splattered raindrops turned the windshield into a kaleidoscope. Clouds descended over the trees. Then, out of the fir branches near the road opened two gigantic wings that banked and circled toward the car.

"What is *that?*" Celeste asked, as trucks and campers pounded past. Whatever it was, it liked fish. The huge bird swooped down through the alders to land on a silt bar in the middle of the river. It kept an eye on our parked car as well as the tumbling current. It waited for two minutes, maybe three, then unfolded its wings again and spiraled back toward us, flashing its underwings at the windshield and departing north into the trees. We weren't the only ones looking for life along the rain-troubled Toutle in the belly of autumn.

"A golden eagle," Celeste said.

"Must have been. Or an immature bald eagle."

Young bald eagles lack the white head that makes them easy to identify as adults. We sat for a few minutes before realizing a positive identification was impossible. It didn't matter: a shadow lingered upon us despite the snow-cloud sky. Would it return? We stepped out of the car to wait and watch the river in the rain.

It wasn't the first time I had been broadsided by surprises in this valley. Since we first traveled it as children, the Spirit Lake Highway had been a long snake of surprises. The tree-walled road was where I saw for the first time in my life, visible only as moving shadows among the still shadows of firs, a small herd of Roosevelt elk feeding at dusk. Often the road itself teemed with ambulant raccoons, migrating frogs, skittery maple leaves, or black-tailed deer. And on certain stretches it offered its most powerful vision: between the canyon of trees, just at the road's vanishing point, soared a mass of rock, snow, and ice—the mountain.

Because we are not born on mountaintops, every mountain begins with the journey toward it. As every climber knows, there is no mountain without first going to the mountain. For those traveling to Loowit's north slope before 1980, climbing to timberline meant climbing through the Toutle River valley. Each traveler experienced the road's winding transition, from the flat, pulp-perfumed strip of Interstate 5 to the berry-scented lake basin shadowed by high ridges and trees. There, within fifty miles, the gradual transformation from burg to wilderness took place. Summer breezes cooled degree by degree; lawns surrendered to woodlots; the scent of alder and fir rose on the air. On our first journey, it seemed that the cool air wafting down from the forests had disappeared, perhaps because the forests themselves were gone. But on that rainy autumn day, the eagle seemed to glimpse things we could not, and perhaps heralded a returning forest that would one day bring the cool breezes back.

We waited near the bank as our boots gathered raindrops, but the bird was in no hurry to return. As we headed back to the car, Celeste glanced down.

"Look at that," she said. The highway's metal guardrail ran straight into a mound of gray mud. At first I thought it was a buried piece of the old highway, but one post was dated 1989. Even construction a few years old was vulnerable to the valley's convulsions: the last five feet of rail simply disappeared.

It was no wonder the state's engineers had run the thirty-seven miles of new road high up the valley's north wall. Steeped in contradictions like liquid earth, feather-light stones, horizontal forests, plugged drainages, and irruptions of new life, the Toutle River valley was wild. This was a valley that rolled, cracked, burned, flooded, and remade itself time and again. Best to run the new road high.

The valley's elk were another surprise. Eliminated by the eruption, the Toutle's Roosevelt elk populations rebounded in the 1980s with human-planted forage areas. More elk than ever strolled the valley that autumn day, to the delight of hunters parked along the highway in trucks and campers. But the only ungulate we glimpsed near the town of Toutle was a gutted doe lashed to the roof of a four-wheel-drive vehicle; the elk were hiding upriver.

We continued upriver ourselves, our eyes on the Toutle's silty wash. The water bore no resemblance to the fir-shaded stream of our childhood. Its mossy boulders were gone. It had no canyon. Like streamers changing course in high winds, it braided its floodplain in gray ribbons. We cruised past great thickets of red alders claiming the old mudflows that had gushed for ten hours in 1980. New trunks, roots, and branches were beginning to disguise the valley's wild past—at least for a while. Then they too would have their turn at sudden death; the volcano dictated so.

It was a 40,000-year-old dance, this relationship between river and mountain. The forests here had been pounded by pumice and buried by mudflows for centuries. As a result, the river's human past was a mystery. Trails, artifacts, or dwellings that might have once existed had long ago disappeared. The word Toutle originated with the Hullooetell, an obscure tribe, but it is unclear whether the tribe actually resided in the valley. In 1806 Lewis and Clark observed that "On the same [Cowlitz] river, above the Skilloots [a Chinook village at its mouth], resides the nation called Hullooetell, of whom we learnt nothing, except that the nation was numerous." Roy Wilson, traditional spiritual leader of the present-day Cowlitz Tribe, believes that the Hullooetell were not an individual tribe but one of four bands (Upper, Mountain, Lower, and Lewis) of the Cowlitz nation. Two of the bands—the Lewis and Lower Cowlitzes—lived near the Toutle and probably traveled through the valley in summer to forage for huckleberries and conduct their vision quests near the mountain. (Cowlitz means "the people who seek their medicine spirit.") Long familiar with the Toutle River, the Cowlitz had their own name for it, *Sickuku*, which Wilson had heard from his tribe's elders when he was young.

The nineteenth century was a turbulent time for the Cowlitz Indians. The volcano erupted frequently and violently from 1800 until 1857, making it difficult for them to hunt and gather berries near the mountain. Worse still, the influx of European diseases decimated the tribe. According to one account, more than 80 percent of the Cowlitz died during the winters of 1829 to 1831, due to a mysterious epidemic that swept along the coast and up the Columbia River.

The valley's first white visitors were a handful of nineteenth-century fur traders. Then came the loggers, who spread upriver soon after the volcano went dormant in 1857. By 1895 a railroad had been constructed to serve eight logging camps halfway up the valley floor. Less than a decade later, the Spirit Lake Highway was constructed to satisfy prospectors looking for gold. Robert Lange, a Polish immigrant from whom my family's cabin property descended, was one of the prospectors who pressured Cowlitz County Commissioner Studebaker to blaze the road. In the 1880s, Lange had hiked alone up the valley to reach Spirit Lake and knew only too well what a convenience the road would be. Hacked out of the forests in 1903, the narrow wagon road was too arduous to transport ore effectively, and Lange's as well as other mining operations folded in the early part of the century. The muddy, one-lane road became instead an access route for mountaineers, hunters, and campers. Retlaw Haynes, who first visited Spirit Lake in 1922, recalled the last portion as a "tortuous stretch," where trees rubbed both sides of his family's 1919 Willys Knight. Pumice lodged in the tire treads. But by 1938 a tongue of asphalt ran up the valley, opening Spirit Lake year-round to hundreds of tourists. By 1962 the highway continued past Spirit Lake to timberline, where it terminated in a circle just below the Sugar Bowl. What had taken Lange three days to hike in 1887 now required one hour to drive.

The 1980 eruption changed all that. The new highway Celeste and I drove in 1993 no longer ran as far as timberline. The old timberline parking lot had been crunched and buried by landslides and pumice, and the portion near my family's cabin lay under 300 to 600 feet of mud. A valley that rippled and slipped: best to run the new road short.

The very first route into Spirit Lake was probably not up the North Fork at all. Early American explorers used the Spirit Lake Way trail, or so it was called in 1897 by Charles Elliott, an army geographer. This "way"—a series of blazes rather than an established trail— began on Loowit's south side, not far from the present-day town of Cougar, veered east and north through the South Fork's valley, then terminated at Spirit Lake. The way trail was the route innkeeper Harry Truman (no relation to the future president) used when he first traveled to Spirit Lake in the 1920s. The well-known proprietor of St. Helens Lodge named one area Dead Horse Canyon because he had lost a horse there. Truman kept a jar under a rock in the canyon for several decades so that he could drink easily from a nearby stream. By the 1970s Truman hadn't visited the canyon for years, but he told Forest Service ranger Chuck Tonn about the trail. Tonn hiked the poorly marked trail amid "hundreds of mountain bluebirds" and found the jar under its rock, where it had sat untouched for more than a decade. Then the volcano destroyed most of the trail—not to mention the canyon, bluebirds, and jar.

As we sped along the highway upriver, it seemed the problem of human access into Spirit Lake had yet again been resolved by engineers. But how long would this new road last? It is well known among geologists that Loowit erupts nearly every century. This gives the highway, with its state-of-the-art bridges, a potentially brief existence.

With the rain continuing to pelt the windshield, we turned off the highway at milepost 21. In contrast to the road's easy access for automobiles, below us lay something that since 1989 had blocked access for other travelers through the valley—the Toutle's fish. The local agencies called it a Sediment Retention Structure, or SRS. I knew it as a dam. It had been erected by the U.S. Army Corps of Engineers to block silt, ash, and mud draining from the volcano. But in the same way that the dam kept the volcano's sediment from journeying downstream, it also kept the river's anadromous fish from journeying upstream to spawn.

I knew those fish well. The stretch of the Toutle River that once ran near my family's cabin contained its own pools of scaled glimmers. Fingerlings swam there beneath my bare feet like so many wiggling brown fingers. They hung back under the shadows of fallen logs, disappeared under the glare of a sunny patch of water, then re-emerged in another shaded pool. I watched them nonchalantly, along with the caddisflies in their pebbled cocoons. I never thought that one day they wouldn't be there.

Known as some of the best runs in the state of Washington, the Toutle's anadromous fish were hit hard by the eruption. Although they had survived centuries of volcanic disturbances—including one deadly ash eruption as recent as 1842 that killed thousands of fish—the river's native fish were obliterated by the 1980 mudflows. An estimated 47 billion gallons of melting glacier water combined with 1.4 billion cubic yards of ash, mud, rock, and debris flushed and scoured both forks of the Toutle. The river's native sea-run cutthroat, steelhead, coho salmon, and chinook salmon were all killed, along with several hatchery runs planted in the 1950s and 1960s. Most of the fish were either cooked by high temperatures or suffocated when their gill filaments were scratched by the sharp-edged ash particles. Early observers witnessed salmon bleeding to death, their gills in tatters. At one monitoring site on the Cowlitz River, below its confluence with the Toutle, mortality rates for juvenile chinook salmon remained at 100 percent for several days after the eruption.

Fortunately, migrating fish such as salmon, steelhead, and sea-run cutthroat travel up to forty miles a day to spend part of their lives in the ocean. Born in freshwater streams, they travel hundreds of miles to the Pacific Ocean to become adults, then return to the streams of their birth to spawn. Before the eruption, the Toutle was home to winter-run and summer-run fish of many different ages. Consequently, some of the Toutle River's fish were at sea on May 18. These survivors, on their return run up the Columbia River, stayed away from the pallid currents where the Cowlitz, burdened with the Toutle's mud, emptied into the Columbia. Sensitive to water temperatures, some returning salmon probably detected an increase in warmth in the Toutle, whose tree-stripped banks exposed its currents to hot sun. Salmon and steelhead also have a keen sense of smell that helps them locate the streams of their birth. Many survivors, confronting the Cowlitz River's strange-smelling, warm currents, abandoned their age-old spawning grounds and journeyed up other Columbia River tributaries instead. One such river was the Kalama. During the summer of 1980, nearly 9,000 steelhead were caught by anglers on the Kalama—almost twice as many as had been caught before.

Some juvenile fish also survived the river's ashy drainages. Exactly one month after the May 18 eruption, Bob Lucas, a biologist who first began monitoring the Toutle's runs in 1976 for the Washington Department of Fish and Wildlife, found juvenile steelhead and coho salmon in Devils Creek, a tributary of the Green River. But even more surprising was a discovery on the same day that young steelhead and cutthroat were alive in Elk Creek, which flowed well inside the blast zone. Two months later Lucas came upon an even more startling discovery. As he and another biologist monitored the

North Fork itself, he heard himself shouting. There, leaping out of the ash-clogged water, was nothing less than an adult summer steelhead. A few steps later another adult splashed above the gray surface. It, too, was somehow navigating the world's most heavily silted, sun-exposed river. To this day, Lucas isn't quite sure how the fish survived.

Eventually, even more steelhead swam up the Cowlitz and entered the Toutle, enduring the glasslike ash that eroded their gills with each intake of water. But even for these hardy fish the river posed a new problem, a problem more permanent than ash or warm water: the dam.

In late 1980, concern for both downstream communities and commercial navigation on the mud-choked Columbia prompted the U.S. Army Corps of Engineers to construct a dam on each of the Toutle's forks. It was hoped that the debris dams would trap sediment and prevent flooding. But both dams failed under heavy rains, and eventually the South Fork dam was breached by the Corps to help the fish return upstream. By 1983, wild winter-run steelhead were spawning in the South Fork. On the North Fork, however, a bigger and stronger dam was being planned even as its old dam was being repaired. As these plans were being laid, anadromous fish were once again returning to the North Fork. In May 1984, young adult steelhead were found in Hoffstadt Creek, upstream from the old 1980 dam. But by 1989 the North Fork's runs were confronting their new obstacle: the new $60 million SRS. The mile-long wall blocked the fishes' migration route and inundated their spawning beds upstream.

I wanted to see that wall. So Celeste and I walked a short path through a dark, fern-edged forest to reach a deserted viewing platform that faced the valley. Spread out before us lay a mile-long, grassy slope, under which ran the concrete, steel-reinforced wall. As rain struck the backs of our legs and tapped our shoulders, my eyes ran the length of the wall to the spillway—a gray, 400-foot-wide ramp that looked like an oversized millrace. The spillway ran roughly fifty feet lower than the huge, 184-foot-high wall, which was catching debris sent down from the volcano. According to the Corps, the accumulating silt will fill the upstream pool by 2035. When that happens, the spillway will become the river's permanent channel. But there are no precise plans for the upstream pool, where the steelheads' spawning beds once lay. According to the Corps, by 2035 it will contain 258 million cubic yards of debris.

Posted next to us on the viewing platform was a brown metal sign that showed fish being poured through a funnel into the tank of a semi truck. We were near the "fish-collection facility," where the North Fork's steelhead are caught downstream and trucked upstream to spawn. But it isn't clear that the baby fish can survive the dam on their way down, which includes a 915-foot plunge through the dam's pipes.

On that day, despite the trucking efforts, steelhead had yet to re-establish themselves on the North Fork. Lucas had observed some limited spawning above the dam, but the North Fork's fish populations were still down dramatically from pre-eruption totals. In contrast, the dam-free South Fork contained runs that were already topping pre-eruption levels.

After monitoring the fish for more than a decade, Lucas retired from the Washington Fish and Game Department in 1993, but was still keeping an eye on the river. He had nothing but respect for its old inhabitants, the salmon and steelhead, and the volcano that rose over them all. The mountain had reinforced his perception that "although we think we can do better, the best thing to do is stand back and let natural processes occur."

As Celeste and I walked back to the parking lot, I hoped that some of Lucas's optimism would rub off on me. Would the walled valley ever again possess its abundant salmon and trout? Would native plants and animals ever return here? I took heart as my eyes wandered over a cover of sword ferns beyond the chain-link fence. The rain-bent fronds shone a dark green. Water dripped from each frond's tip. Like pearly everlasting, here was a tough species reappearing in the volcano's shadow. But unlike pearly everlasting, the moisture-loving ferns relied on shady forest ground—ground that was hard to come by in the logged and blast-scrubbed valley. These ferns, however, were thriving.

In fact, sword ferns had formed the foundation of a small but prosperous industry along the Toutle for almost a hundred years. Wagon loads of fronds were first harvested here at the turn of the century. And it had been a short autumn day like ours, forty years ago, when the well-known naturalist Edwin Way Teale sped up the old Spirit Lake Highway with a logging truck riding his rear bumper. He had come hundreds of miles to join the fern gatherers, who were hard at work picking evergreens for national holiday distribution. Teale accompanied two gatherers on a short expedition halfway up the valley to milepost 25, only a few miles east from where the dam's wall now soared. There, in the deep shade of the forested valley, the East Coast writer was astounded at what he saw:

> The forest closed around us, a forest of giants such as I had never entered before. We paused beside a stump, furry with moss and moldering away. It seemed, in the dim forest light, as big as a cabin. I gazed at the massive trunks of spruce and fir and hemlock. Soaring up and up, they appeared to lean together in their great height. The tops of some of them were 150 feet above us.

Standing amid alder trees, which he did not recognize because of their 100-foot height, Teale learned from one of his companions,

Orlo Stephens, the names of strange plants he had never seen: licorice fern, devil's club, and a fungus called *Cordyceps myrmecophila,* which fed on dead ants. He stood motionless to hear the whistle of a bird he loved: the varied thrush. Meanwhile, the pickers bundled fronds into piles of twenty-six to take to the Fern Barn in Castle Rock. There, the greens would be refrigerated and shipped hundreds of miles to florists across the nation.

Half a century later, the fern-picking business was alive and well, as Celeste and I had discovered earlier that day when we stopped at the old Fern Barn in Castle Rock. Outside, an old cracked mural of the volcano still hung over the barn's front doors. Inside, the cold air was perfumed with cedar, moss, and fir branches. As rain drummed on the roof, two women in red sweaters and gloves were hard at work loading fronds into cardboard boxes. Norma Fleming was the current owner's mother; her sister Lorna Goldsby was managing the Fern Barn when the volcano erupted.

With hundreds of acres of forests coated with sticky, gritty ash, the fall 1980 fern harvest was a disaster. To make wreaths for Christmas, Goldsby purchased a power washer and hired crews round the clock to shower off the powdery bits of mountain, ground finer than sand. Over the next few years, the business recovered as the valley itself recovered—at the slow pace of nature. Now, more than a decade later, Goldsby believed the ash had acted as a fertilizer. Her observation echoed centuries of stories about volcanic ash. Unlike wood ash, volcanic ash is not a product of combustion but of pulverization; it is rock that has exploded apart rather than burned. Low in nitrogen and capable of suffocating plants, these dustlike particles nonetheless help nourish the soil. The ancient Greek geographer Strabo noted that ash from Vesuvius and Etna helped produce roots that were so good for fattening sheep the animals sometimes choked on them. Loowit's ash, it seemed, also now helped rather than hindered the conifers and ferns.

When Teale traveled through the Pacific Northwest in 1952, he arrived just in time to watch the last salmon jump over the Columbia's dam-doomed Celilo Falls. Perhaps he wouldn't be surprised to know that where he once stood by the Toutle a dam now sprawled. But at least the sword ferns he had admired were still unfurling their fronds through rain and sun.

We left all green things behind as we traveled 2,000 feet up the last stretch of highway straight into a cloud. Snowflakes collided with raindrops on the windshield. We hugged the wake of a snow-plow clearing the way to Coldwater Ridge, where the first winter snows were piled one foot deep. Six miles away, the dusk-darkened volcano was barely discernible. But atmospheric light glanced off the snowy hills of the valley below to illuminate the tiny profiles of isolated firs and stumps, and among them, a slow-moving bull elk. It strolled in front of us, then picked its way downhill. On such a cold day, with the grasses buried under snow and the hunting season drawing to a close, the elk wasn't about to be bothered by humans. A full herd wasn't far behind. Soon our solitary car, already enveloped by dusk and clouds, was enveloped by elk.

So the elk had returned to the Toutle, and downriver the sword ferns were thick and green. Perhaps the fish would follow. For this was an unpredictable valley. Whether destruction came in the form of a boiling mudflow from the east, or as an army of chainsaws from the west, or as a massive dam smack in the river's midsection, the valley's organisms swung back like a tree trying to right itself in the wind.

Cabinless, we felt a little like the North Fork's fish, whose spawning beds lay buried. On any wintry evening before the eruption, we would have built a fire, made hot chocolate, and settled in for the night.

As the elk left us behind, Celeste swung the car around. This time, in the dwindling light, we would be traveling with the river— out, away from the mountain. It was the direction Spirit Lake's coho salmon once took, swimming all the way from Harmony Creek on the lake's east shore to the Columbia River's wide bar and beyond. Like the salmon, we knew the way by heart and counted on the day when we could return. For the most dramatic change along the Toutle still lay ahead of us—a mysterious thing called the debris avalanche. We would have to wait until spring to see it, this thing that had swallowed the cabin—and the upper Toutle—whole.

The Debris Avalanche

Every force has its form.

—Shaker Saying

The day Celeste and I visited the debris avalanche, seven months after our autumn drive up the Toutle, the words of Heraclitus kept tumbling through my head. The Greek philosopher had it figured out more than 2,000 years ago. Believing that fire was the prime mover of nature, he recognized that nothing was truly stable: it was the uniformity of motion that created the illusion of stability. "You cannot step twice into the same river," he wrote. He was more than accurate: just west of Spirit Lake, you can't step into the same river, period. What were once the headwaters of the Toutle are now hummocks of broken mountain. There simply isn't any river to step into at all.

It took me years to comprehend this. The first time I saw the debris avalanche I did not know what it was. I was eighteen years old, and the volcano had erupted the day before. Like millions of other television viewers, I watched Mount St. Helens explode and collapse on one news station, then watched it explode and collapse on another. I stared at hundreds of images time and again, never understanding them. Neither television screen nor printed photo offered spatial dimensions. The volcano kept exploding into nowhere—indefinitely. For days and months it kept appearing whole, at 8:32 A.M. and 20 seconds, only to burst like a sporulating mushroom against the flat glass of the television.

But the day I visited the debris avalanche I finally understood Heraclitus and fire. I understood how volcanoes bloom on the Earth's crust like so many bunches of scarlet paintbrush. Thousands of miles below our feet is fire. The planet's core is a furnace; we survive on a thin, cool peel. And that peel is cracked, its tectonic plates adrift like ice floes, rubbing against each other for hundreds of miles. When one tectonic plate shoves another plate under itself, the lower plate melts, and its molten rock surges upward to become a volcano. In this neighborhood, the small oceanic Juan de Fuca plate is being forced under the bigger continental North American plate in a process called subduction. All along the Northwest coast, sixty to eighty miles beneath the Earth's surface, magma is seeping under the American plate, rising in cracks we know as the Cascade volcanoes. Loowit is just one in a 1,000-mile-long chain of volcanoes, from Lassen Peak in northern California to Mount Garibaldi in British Columbia. And that chain is but a fraction of the Ring of Fire circling the Pacific Ocean. Nothing is stable. A displaced river is but a tiny grain of sand dislodged. And the living things it buries? Even smaller.

As Celeste and I stood on the Pumice Plain's western edge, a few miles north of Loowit's crater rim and a mile west of Spirit Lake, I stared unblinking under a patchwork sky of sun and cumuli at the start of the avalanche's lumpy, fourteen-mile-long path down the Toutle River valley. We were positioned at the head of the largest landslide ever seen by human eyes. I thought of the television images shown after the eruption. Unlike that May day long ago when I watched unbelieving, now I knew exactly where the volcano had cascaded. In the lower-right corner of every television and newspaper image of the collapsing mountain was a tiny home doomed to receive the onslaught of that giant gray wave.

In the iffy June weather, I tried to recall the details of that tiny home and its furry inhabitants. In my mind's eye a small, brush-covered hump of earth emerged. The forest behind the hump was striped with green sunlight and coal-gray shadows as the morning sun penetrated the understory between each trunk. The hump itself was cluttered with fresh-cut twigs. Beavers.

Perhaps their lodge was shaken apart as chunks of glacier ice and exploding rock rumbled toward them. Perhaps the quaking forest itself collapsed trunk by trunk upon them. Or the river, sloshing in a hundred vortices as the earth slammed into it, flooded their den with a churning wall of water. Did they drown or were they buried alive? Did they die slowly or immediately? By replaying this morbid sequence of disasters as I stood at the head of the debris avalanche, I allowed myself to die with the beavers. A strange imagining, but I had known them for just two summers—enough time to grow curious about their vegetarian habits and fond of their aquatic ways.

The beavers' dam lay downstream from a small bridge at mile-post 45 on Highway 504. The concrete bridge had been built in 1938 and spanned a placid stretch of the North Fork, only a mile upstream from where I had watched fingerlings swim in the shadows. On this simple, two-lane structure my older sister Terese and I stood looking out over the translucent water one summer afternoon in 1978, when a V-shaped wake behind a small brown head advanced steadily toward us. The adult beaver glanced up at us, then continued to swim upstream toward Spirit Lake, passing directly under us. We ran to the other side: there was the brown head again, followed by the broad flat paddle of tail. This occasion marked the first time I had ever seen a wild beaver, though I had lived all of my sixteen years in Oregon, the self-acclaimed Beaver State, and had attended a high school called Beaverton.

As Terese and I learned to look for signs, we came to see that this stretch of riverfront property clearly belonged to the largest rodent in North America. Alder, cottonwood, maple, willow—all of these deciduous trees grew along the North Fork, supplying the fifty-pound animals with more than they could eat. Nibbled twigs, stumps, and at least one sturdy dam: all were evidence of *Castor canadensis*, whose formidable regenerating teeth were once observed by historian Elliott Coues to hack down a poplar on the Upper Missouri River that was nine feet in circumference. As we came to understand the beavers' daily schedule, Terese and I eventually happened upon their lodge. Not far from the 1938 bridge, we walked down a dirt road that was slowly being reclaimed by the forest. This shaded path was the old 1903 road, which had been abandoned. We tiptoed to an inconspicuous pile of branches, not so different from any other brushy hump of streambank. But once we stepped quietly on top, the twiggy, muddy mound began to squeak and rustle. For as much as we had tried to arrive silently, the baby beavers knew we were there.

The North Fork's beavers were members of a species that once roamed over all of wooded North America. Unlike its European cousin, *Castor fiber*, which is extinct in most countries except

Norway, the North American beaver has survived two centuries of being bludgeoned, dynamited, and drowned to death. Although I grew up wide-eyed at the haunted-house stories my father told us, as a native Oregonian I had never heard the gruesome bedtime story called beaver trapping. Eighteenth- and nineteenth-century trappers caught their prey by placing rock-weighted traps underwater near the beavers' "landings," where the animals hauled trees into the water. The trappers then coated a twig with castoreum, a strong-smelling secretion from the beaver's own genitals, and hung it above the water where the trap was submerged. Attracted to the castoreum, the beaver tried to eat the twig but was instead bitten by the trap. In its panic the animal dove to the bottom of the pool, dragging the rock-weighted trap with it. There, unable to resurface, it drowned. Trappers also broke holes in the beavers' dams and fastened their steel traps just below the hole. When the beavers rushed to repair the leaking dam, their tiny front paws or—better yet for the trapper—their strong hind legs would be snatched by the trap.

This treachery began in the 1700s to satisfy the demand for beaver-lined hats, a fashion craze among upper-class European men. As beavers were depleted in the northeast, trappers moved west. From 1820 to 1830 the main thrust of the British-owned Hudson's Bay Company was to eliminate every beaver south of the Columbia to discourage American trappers from crossing the Rockies. The campaign ended when it became apparent that the Oregon Territory was going to be settled anyway by wagon trains of pioneers. By 1859 the nearly beaverless Beaver State had been incorporated into the United States.

The North Fork's beavers had escaped centuries of trapping to thrive near the volcano, but the day I walked the debris avalanche I was certain that it would be a matter of decades—if not centuries—before they returned to the valley. A different kind of dam from those of the beavers had blocked the North Fork—the collapsed mountain. And because the U.S. Army Corps of Engineers created an artificial drainage for Spirit Lake to prevent flooding downstream, the North Fork no longer began at the lake's southwestern corner, as it had for centuries. I looked for a river and saw nothing but mountain. Where would the beavers swim?

Celeste and I walked to where miniature mountains of mud, pumice, and other volcanic rock stretched for miles. We had no idea where we were, where the cabin was, or what lay on top of it. Only later did I learn that the earth covering these mounds was the remnant of a mudflow that had swept the area in 1982. It formed a thin skin on several layers of geologic flesh. Geologist C. Dan Miller of the U.S. Geological Survey dissected the layers of flesh for me one day soon after our June hike, when I visited him in his Vancouver office.

Miller was a member of the USGS team headed by Dwight Crandell and Donal Mullineaux that monitored the volcano before it erupted. Mount St. Helens was the young geologist's first assignment. He arrived at Spirit Lake in 1974 and camped on the south shore for several summers. When the mountain became active in March 1980, Miller became part of the hazards-assessment team that tried to forecast what the mountain was going to do. With Crandell, Mullineaux, and colleague Rick Hoblitt, Miller established the Geological Survey's observatory posts (Coldwater I and Coldwater II), then set to work trying to determine which rivers and towns were at risk from mudflows, ashfall, and other threats. If it hadn't been for two faulty cameras that needed repairing in Portland, he would have died at Mount St. Helens the morning of May 18. He was returning north on Interstate 5 when he saw the mushroom cloud on the horizon.

After the May 18 eruption, Miller and his colleagues spent the
entire summer hiking across the new land left by the volcano's blast
and debris avalanche. It required months of study to piece together
the order of events for May 18—what came out of the volcano and
when. Much of that first summer was devoted to understanding the
pyroclastic surge and lateral blast. The likelihood of a lateral explosion had been underestimated by the USGS; that Loowit might
erupt sideways was hardly considered at all. Now, lateral blasts and
debris avalanches are common factors the geologists consider in
assessing volcanic dangers. As the head of a USGS team of experts
who evaluate volcanic hazards worldwide, Miller still relies on
knowledge gained at Mount St. Helens. By hiking across the same
area on which Celeste and I were standing, Miller had come to
understand exactly how the mountain had burst sideways.

I asked him what now lay on top of the beaver den, barely a half-
mile from my family's cabin. He sketched each volcanic action on a
piece of paper. By the time the sketch was complete, five stripes lay
across the paper. The first stripe was the lateral blast—the mountain's initial surge of explosive gases and shattered rock. Then the
debris avalanche—or collapsing north flank—swept over and left
rocks, trees, and mud hundreds of feet thick. Then, as the blast
overtook the avalanche, the blast fragments swept over the area
again. Then, over the next several hours, pyroclastic flows roared
through and deposited layers of buff-colored pumice several feet
thick. Finally, over the next two years, mudflows sporadically
flushed the area with gray, syrupy water.

It seemed to me that this mountainous blockage impounding
Spirit Lake was characteristic of Loowit's terrain—a heap of contradictions. What had been low in elevation was now high; what had
been water was now rock; what had been living was now dead; what
had been shaded was now sunny. The secrecy of the dark forest had

been replaced by the announcement of vistas, and the small beaver den that had once hid its inhabitants from predators was destroyed by a mountain whose interior movements were hidden to humans. One of the smallest natural dams on earth was replaced by one of the largest. Heraclitus, again and again.

That day on the avalanche, Celeste and I tried in vain to navigate our way through the remodeled land. Storm clouds clumped over our heads. We looked north at Spirit Lake, uninviting and strange compared to what its banks once looked like. We looked for the river in vain. We felt like a pair of beetles whose log had bounced downhill. So this was the Toutle! It wasn't that I wanted things to be the way they were before the eruption. I simply wanted to be able to recognize some small ridge or curve. One landmark was all I asked for. One small landmark.

"I used to sit by the Toutle every time I visited the mountain," Celeste said, "even in winter, when there was deep snow. It was the place I always thought about when I was in school. I told myself that I could always go there, that it would always be there."

Like Celeste, I had had my own favorite place on the river—a big round pool framed by fallen logs. And I, too, had believed that it would exist forever, that I could always return to it regardless of my own life's unpredictable turns. In summer I watched the fish and caddisflies. In winter I could see how deep the snowpack was by how much snow had piled on the logs. That big round pool was now fading in my memory like the beaver den.

"If someone told me tomorrow that the mountain had erupted and the Toutle was suddenly flowing here again, I would believe it in a minute," I said. Reality was fabulous, Thoreau had said. Stability was an illusion.

Only a few days after the beavers were buried beneath the avalanche and the Toutle's course was rearranged, ecologist Virginia

Dale visited the area as a member of the first group of biologists to view the blast zone. She flew by helicopter over the gray, steaming hummocks that had somersaulted down from Loowit's summit. Fumaroles sent up puffs of gas; ash swirled in pockets; no living thing could be seen. Intrigued by the lifeless land, Dale wanted to see how long it would take for new plants to appear on the avalanche's unstable flanks. Her study would become one of the longest continuous research projects in the blast zone.

Dale first mapped out two large areas on the avalanche. The upper area ran between Castle and Coldwater Lakes, only a few miles west from where Celeste and I stood. The lower area lay even farther west, near the toe of the avalanche. In each area she flagged large circular plots roughly 800 feet wide and placed them 165 feet apart. In the middle of each plot she sank wood frames meshed with mosquito netting, then smeared the netting with car grease. These "sticky seed traps" would help her determine which kinds of plants would be the first to disperse their seeds over the brand-new ground. Two years after her first helicopter ride, nearly one hundred traps dotted the avalanche's humps and valleys.

One of the first things Dale discovered was that although the avalanche began as one volcanic action, it was hardly simple terrain. Composed of different kinds of rock from the volcano's many eruptions, the fourteen-mile-long landslide is subject to erosive rains, steady winds, intense sun, and other forces that have sculpted it into a world of diverse miniature habitats. While one acre of avalanche might remain dry and barren for years, another might contain several ponds in its lumpy depressions. Yet another might be carved by the river's frequent floods, dried by sun, then flooded again.

Where Celeste and I stood, hardly a wisp of a plant could be seen. We were on the avalanche's upper reaches. Here, no life had survived the landslide. That meant that Dale could watch plants return to perfectly barren land. Ecologists call this process "primary succession"—the appearance and change of living things over time on a previously lifeless surface. Primary succession is hard to study because disturbances to ecosystems are often only partially destructive. For instance, while a forest fire will destroy certain plants and animals, hundreds of organisms will survive in the soil alone. A fire is therefore a type of secondary succession, where survivors spring back. But with the debris avalanche, hundreds of tons of new rock from inside the volcano were suddenly transformed into the valley floor. The old valley floor—with its beavers, fish, minks, trees, worms, squirrels, birds, and flowers—was buried so deep (an average of 150 feet) it was no longer viable or ecologically related to the new surface.

Nonetheless, by hiking across the avalanche the first two summers after the eruption, Dale discovered that the first plants to grow had resprouted from root and sucker fragments. In a random event Heraclitus would have loved, these mutilated plants had been catapulted down the landslide to land on or near the surface of the slide as it came to rest. Some were wedged in the roots of conifers, where parts of the old forest soil still clung. These early colonizers included broadleaf lupine, willow, horsetail, Canadian thistle, salmonberry, blackberry, and pearly everlasting. Some pioneers also arrived as seeds blown in from neighboring clearcuts. If these seeds managed to land on moist ground or were trapped against the earth by spiderwebs, they germinated. And if they received enough water, they grew into adults that likewise dispersed more seeds. Alongside these pioneers, one wildflower in particular conquered the avalanche in the first few years following the eruption: fireweed.

Known for its quick appearance after forest fires, *Epilobium angus-tifolium* could just as easily have been named avalanche weed for its colonization of avalanches throughout the Cascades. Like pearly everlasting, the tough perennial thrives in sunny, exposed areas, from low-elevation valleys to 4,000-foot ridges. However, unlike everlasting, fireweed is not only more attractive to most people, with its bright pink flowers, it is also useful. Bears, elk, and bees all find fireweed delectable. Honey from fireweed-pollinating bees is sold in markets, and Russians make tea out of dried fireweed leaves. Some Washington tribes have used the plant medicinally and have taken advantage of its downy seeds. Each fall, the plants produce a blizzard of snowy, featherlike plumes to transport their seeds. These plumes—long white hairs that emanate from the tiny seeds like silken barbs of goose down—were harvested by some Cascade tribes to stuff blankets.

Dale found that fireweed's plumes were critical to its early success. In 1981, she compared fireweed's seed-dispersing ability to that of the avalanche's three other most common plants that year—Canadian thistle, sow-thistle, and wood groundsel. By counting seeds and analyzing the ratio of each species' seed diameter to its plume size, Dale found that fireweed's plumes were proportionately much larger than those of groundsel or thistle seeds. As a consequence, fireweed's seeds were transported farther, and the flower was ten times more abundant than its competitors.

But fireweed's heyday was soon over. While visiting her lower plots in 1984, Dale noticed that the sandy hummocks were dotted with blond spears dangling bushy, seed-heavy heads. Grasses had arrived. And in other areas, low bunches of green herbs brightened the ground with yellow and white flowers. Peas and clovers. Even a conifer seedling or two poked its foot-high stem out of the mountain's old flanks. Unfortunately, some of the newcomers were not indigenous to the area. And Dale soon discovered that some of the non-native species were spreading westward at a rapid pace, disseminated by winds as well as by grazing elk that scattered the seeds in their droppings. These exotic invaders were changing the lower avalanche's vegetation considerably. One flower in particular, a small pea called bird's-foot trefoil, was preventing the valley's native conifers from taking hold. A European perennial, bird's-foot trefoil is a hardy, five-leaved legume that can cover barren land quickly. Dale found that in some places so much trefoil had seeded in that there was little ground left for the trees.

The pea and its exotic cohort were the result of a fall 1980 aerial seeding by the U.S. Soil Conservation Service. Worried about erosion and conifer recovery, the service seeded 6,000 acres on the west end of the avalanche with eight different species of legumes and grasses, of which only two were native. The agency had hoped that the plants—including white clover, perennial ryegrass, orchard grass, and fescue—would stabilize the avalanche's loose soil and help the conifers seed in. But the seeding failed. During heavy rains, many of the seeds washed into canyons along with the ash. And in addition to the damage the pea had caused, the introduced grasses attracted hungry mice, whose soaring populations gnawed the bark off conifer seedlings, killing half of the trees in Dale's lower plots until hawks and coyotes stabilized the rodents' irruption.

But then, like a cresting wave in Heraclitus' river, the non-natives subsided. When Dale visited her plots in 1994, she found that the grasses and legumes had diminished, and, instead, native trees like willow and red alder were gaining ground. The plant ecologist speculated that the alder would play an important role in the avalanche's future since it adds nutrients to the soil through nitrogen-fixing bacteria on its roots. The bacteria convert nitrogen from a gas into organic ammonium, a fertilizer. Dale realized from this that the greatest lesson learned at Mount St. Helens was that nature takes care of itself.

An afternoon wind swept up the valley. Rain was on the way, but we didn't want to leave. Celeste was lost in her dreams of the Toutle, and I dreamed that the beavers had returned. I pretended to see them, pretended they had crept back up the river. But instead it seemed that wherever I went I was outrunning an avalanche, counting the things consumed in its wake. Beavers, fish, flowers, trees. Skyscrapers—what were those? Roads, towns, dams, power lines: nothing Loowit couldn't demolish in a minute. The town of Castle Rock was built atop an old mudflow. The city of Tacoma was built upon one of Mount Rainier's old flows. How many cities have been buried by volcanoes in this century alone? Saint Pierre, Heimaey, Armero, Shimbara City, Fukae Town. How many Cascade volcanoes do geologists consider hazardous? Mount Baker, Glacier Peak, Mount Rainier, Mount Adams, Mount Hood, Mount Jefferson, Mount Shasta, Lassen Peak—and Mount St. Helens. Some scientists even think that a volcanic eruption in Siberia 250 million years ago may have caused the extinction of the dinosaurs, as well as 70 percent of all land species. And I was once fond of a bunch of beavers. I once thought I could live at a place called Spirit Lake!

We stood at the head of the avalanche until the wind whipped up a light rain. Clouds descended upon the crater. We looked for wildflowers but saw none. Whatever life grew around us was dwarfed by the mammoth crater and lumps of broken mountain. As we trudged six miles back to Windy Ridge, the wind stiffened into a cold, steady wave that never ebbed. Rain hammered against our legs and dripped from the cuffs of our jackets. Zippered against the weather, we marched heads bowed, fighting nature tooth and nail.

The Spillover

Then shall you think fit to flee
in panic and yield
place to the divine event.

—Unknown Roman poet describing an eruption of Etna

When the volcano spills over, how far do you run? And once it has buried everything, do you dare return? Or, like a plugged creek, are some things sealed for good?

The day I visited Jim Lund in the Mojave Desert, the Joshua trees were in bloom. It was only February, a few months before our trip to the avalanche, when snow still shrouded the Spirit Lake wilderness. But down here every Joshua tree already bore a huge cluster of pale flowers at the end of each spiky branch. An entire forest of the giant, thorny green candles brandished their petaled torches to the cloudless blue sky. My elbow rested on the warm metal sill of the car window as I raced along empty roads shaded only by occasional raptor wings. Unfamiliar with the desert, I had underestimated my travel time and was late beyond belief. The sun was already overhead and hot.

What on earth was Jim Lund doing in a place like this? By the time I met him in 1977, Jim had lived in his Spirit Lake cabin for years, surviving ten-foot snows, winter winds, and the lake's interminable rains. Apart from Harry Truman, the proprietor of Mount St. Helens Lodge who became famous when he refused to leave Spirit Lake before the eruption, Jim was the only permanent, year-round resident I knew at the lake. As a logger he had walked the wet woods of western Washington most of his life. And like his father, Spirit Lake's first game warden, Jim knew the ridges around Mount St. Helens like the back of his hand. He had hiked and fished all over the backcountry, foraged for mushrooms and hunted grouse on the Toutle, and knew the history of the place as if he had been born there.

So what was he doing in the hot, dry Mojave?

"Arthritis," his wife, Pauline, had said over the phone. I had trouble believing it. The Jim Lund I knew could strum a guitar like a fiend. Not even his own deafness impeded his playing; he had learned to play on his father's antique Swede guitar before he lost his hearing during an illness in his teens. On rainy afternoons he used to entertain us for hours, singing folk songs fast and loud. One afternoon I walked over to the Lunds' cabin to reciprocate and play their small spinet piano. Jim shouted that he loved one piece by Mendelssohn because he felt the music vibrate in the air as my hands traveled the keys.

I pressed down harder on the gas pedal. I wasn't sure whether I would recognize him after so many years, but even so, I knew Jim well enough to figure that it wasn't just arthritis that had pushed him south. The wily outdoorsman was simply one in a long line of people who had been forced to make their peace with the volcano or stand in its shadow and die. For centuries the volcano had attracted and repelled, attracted and repelled. Old Loowit had long fingers that either beckoned or pushed, depending on which moment you happened to be standing on the shores of Spirit Lake. Jim had lived through several decades of peaceful beckoning and was now enduring a long finger push that had landed him in the desert, hundreds of miles away.

The last time I had seen Jim was on a tranquil winter day in January, only a few months before the eruption. We had waved to each other with the friendly nonchalance of neighbors as we passed each other at some distance in the snow. Then the confusion after the eruption had swallowed him up so completely he might as well have been dead. To track him down in the desert had required a certain amount of effort, including several long-distance phone calls and two letters returned due to an incorrect address. It was as though the volcano had shattered its human settlements faster than a gunshot scattering a flock of geese. But unlike the flock of geese, the tiny community that had made up Spirit Lake would never be pieced together again.

It wasn't the first time such a thing had happened. When Loowit exploded in 1500 B.C. with its largest known eruption, the sky rained down six feet of pumice and ash over many miles. Local tribes fishing on the Lewis River had had the choice of waiting there to die or escaping as fast as they could. From research done by archaeologists, it appears that the ancient people chose the latter. One fishing camp excavated by researchers Rick McClure, Cheryl Mack, David Brauner, and Loren Davis showed fragments of chipped obsidian and fish scales, but no human skeletons. Like Jim, the native people had escaped, but the volcano's continuing eruptions caused them to abandon their camps for good. McClure and his colleagues found that the Lewis River fishing camp had remained uninhabited for 1,500 years. More striking, it wasn't the only abandoned camp. After excavating more than twenty sites around the volcano, McClure found that time and again the native inhabitants fled Loowit for safer places to hunt elk and pick huckleberries. As far back as 8,000 years ago—perhaps even 10,000—a pattern of volcanic-induced abandonment had begun.

For the ancient inhabitants the long finger pushing them away had been showers of pumice the size of pinecones and sky-blackening, suffocating ash. For Jim and my family, it was something called the Spillover. Celeste and I first saw it at close range on our hike to the debris avalanche. The sight of it filled us with dismay: How could a place so loved and familiar become so strange?

Named by geologists, the Spillover marks the site where the avalanching mountain and its initial pyroclastic flow of searing gases and rock swept over the unnamed 1,100-foot ridge where the unnamed creek flowed past our cabin. But this was of little consequence to the collapsing mountain, which roared up the ridge much faster than the little creek flowed down. Speeding away from the summit at 155 to 180 miles per hour, the chaotic mass of skyrocketing debris lunged up the ridge and topped it—hence the name Spillover. By the time the steaming materials came to rest on either side of the ridge, the creek was gone, along with the Lunds' spinet piano, my family's yellow canoe, and every other thing in front of the ridge, both living and inanimate.

As I drove through the desert it dawned on me that, like my family, Jim had drunk from the unnamed creek for years. Perhaps he knew something about its name and origin.

I turned off the highway onto a single-lane, unpaved road. The rental car's tires shifted like skis through the soft desert sand. A car was approaching, so I pulled over. The other car pulled up and stopped.

"Thought maybe you got lost," the tan face said with a grin. Then the grin broke into a laugh. "Boy, that sure is a red car!"

The laugh included a dark-colored front tooth—the incisor Jim had carved himself out of jade. It had stayed in place for years, solid as the smile that disclosed it.

We parked the cars in the driveway in front of the small, one-story house. Jim wore a short-brimmed cotton hat, white shirt, and jeans. I couldn't recall whether he had always worn glasses. He had them now, but he looked the same as I remembered him—a slender man with a huge smile.

"Give your old Uncle Jim a hug," he said, and showed me to the front door. The front of the house was covered with a long veranda littered with assorted patio chairs. As we approached, an Irish setter, tail wagging, licked Jim's hand.

"This is Red," he explained. "My new Red. You remember my other Irish setter. The old Red died a while back. This one minds better, but he's just as bad at cards. Can't deal. His thumb comes up too far. No good at card playing *a-tall*." The words flowed in a slow, accented English, as though he savored each vowel before letting it go. It was the music of someone who relished the pleasure of talking, even if he couldn't hear himself speak.

The new Red came over and sniffed my shoes, then offered his head for petting. Inside, Pauline sat in a chair at the kitchen table. She had been suffering for years with diabetes. Her short, fine hair had gone completely white, but her face looked the same—round and friendly. She offered me a seat while Jim asked whether I wanted a pop or some beer. It was dark and cool inside—the kind of shade people seek in a sun-fierce climate. As Red sat quietly by,

I took a few gulps of soda to wash down the desert dust. Then the three of us began to talk about the lake.

Jim's father, John "Chickaloon" Lund, came to Spirit Lake in 1947 as a trapper, hunting coyotes, bobcats, cougars, skunks, and other animals then deemed troublesome by the Washington Department of Fish and Wildlife. By 1951 he was promoted from trapping to protecting, an occupation he greatly preferred. He worked as a game warden at Spirit Lake for the next twenty-five years, checking fishing licenses and chasing poachers like Harry Truman. Having arrived at Spirit Lake in the 1920s, Truman had built his two-story, mint-green lodge in the late 1930s and had lived there, bourbon and cola in hand, until the eruption, carrying on alone after the death of his wife in 1975. The innkeeper became nationally known when he refused to abandon his lodge during the spring of 1980. Chickaloon Lund never caught Truman poaching, but after a while it no longer mattered; the two became close friends. Chickaloon died in 1976, a few months before my parents bought our cabin. His nickname, given to him in Alaska during the Great Depression, lived on after his death. In my family we often referred to Mount St. Helens as Chickaloon's Mountain, though we had never met the man himself.

The first time Jim saw Spirit Lake was in 1947, when he accompanied his father to the lake in an old green 1937 Pontiac. At that time, few people had heard of the deep, cold lake at the base of Mount St. Helens. What trails existed in the backcountry had been blazed for horses. For Jim, the lake's steep, forested basin was irresistible; he was fifteen years old and ready to "run ridges" in the wild. He learned about the land from his father, whose job it was to canvass every inch of it. Back home in Castle Rock he worked summers cutting trees for his uncle, who owned a logging operation. Then, after graduating from high school, he paid his rent by working in sawmills along the Columbia River. He continued working on and off for his uncle until 1964, when his deafness became a serious disability. "But that didn't last long. I couldn't just sit around and wait to win the lottery. So I wound up right back in the woods again!"

By the time my family met Jim, he had retired from logging for good and was settled in at Spirit Lake with Pauline. The couple lived in a small cabin Jim had framed out of hand-hewn timbers from an old barn on Umiker Road, down along the Toutle. Jim had dismantled the barn to salvage the straight-grained beams. The sturdy, weathered cabin stood fifty yards south of my family's A-frame and was the only visible building between our cabin and the mountain. Jim and Pauline were planning to spend the rest of their lives in their small rustic castle, living simply and getting by. Jim loved to take Red to the backcountry lakes to go fishing. Pauline swam at Duck Bay with her own small dog cradled in her arms. The two went morel-hunting and coyote-watching down on the Toutle. They picked huckleberries in their backyard and chased bears off the porch. In the fall, they stood near Truman's lodge to watch the coho salmon run.

Then, all of a sudden it seemed, Jim's Irish setter was growling at earthquakes. At night the nails would squeak in the old barn boards that made up the cabin, and Red would stand snarling over Jim's sleeping body to protect his master from the spooks shaking the house. As the cabin wiggled back and forth and Red circled angrily, Jim would wake to see the mountain erupting outside his bedroom window.

While Jim and Red endured the earthquakes, Pauline stayed "on the outside" that spring to petition the authorities to allow them to remain at Spirit Lake. The couple saw no reason why Truman was permitted to remain in his lodge while they were forced from their own primary residence.

By the eve of the eruption the Lunds had been kept out of their house for more than a month. They had fought the authorities and lost. When property owners were allowed past roadblocks on May 17 to retrieve belongings, Jim and Pauline brought in groceries instead, stacking canned food for Jim and Red so that he could stay to further protest the roadblock. But the deputy sheriff told the two they had to evacuate along with the others. In her haste, Pauline forgot their marriage license and photographs.

"The sheriff said, 'It's time to go home now,' " Pauline recalled. "And I said, 'This *is* my home, Phil.' And he said, 'Tomorrow, Pauline. Come back tomorrow.' "

So the couple said good-bye to their friend Bob Kasewetter, who owned a small cabin nearby. A scientist from Portland, Bob had obtained a research permit that allowed him to remain in his cabin. Within fifteen hours of Jim's and Pauline's farewell, the signed permit would be a death certificate. The Lunds were heading up to the mountain the next morning with a box of Presto logs and a twelve-volt battery for Bob when the volcano exploded.

"I can still see Bob's face as if it were yesterday," Jim told me, thinking about his friend. "He's got that grin on that he always wore."

In all of nature, it is perhaps only human will that resists the path of least resistance. When the mountain avalanched into the foot of the ridge where the cabins lay, the saddle with its unnamed creek deflected the fluidized earth like a solitary dike stopping a tsunami. Blocked by the ridge, the gurgling, steaming mass of mountain curved west at 180 miles per hour down the Toutle River valley to form the debris avalanche. The mountain had followed the path of least resistance. But the unnamed ridge paid dearly for its deflection. In the folds of the ridge, where the unnamed creek once flowed, an estimated 600 feet of debris piled up—the deepest deposit in the entire avalanche.

And still the mountain spilled that spring day, perhaps just about the time Jim and Pauline turned their car around at Silver Lake after seeing the ash plume. As most of the broken north flank collapsed westward, a glowing hot cloud of superheated materials from the innermost portion of the north slope flew toward the saddle. Unlike the initial landslide, composed of material from the well-known "bulge" near Goat Rocks, this viscous mass originated deeper inside the mountain and contained pulverized rocks. A concoction of powdered dacite and andesite mixed with steam and explosive gases, the mass crested the saddle at 600 miles per hour and roared into the valley of South Coldwater Creek, leaving behind a trail of debris 150 feet deep.

Even if Jim and Pauline had won their fight to stay on the mountain, it would have made little difference to the Spillover. Two more corpses would have hardly affected its gigantic shape at all. The laws of physics had already determined that the speeding mass of mountain would overtop the ridge as quickly as blood spills from a deep gash.

A part of me understood why Jim would want to confront the mountain in his own way, on his own terms, even if it meant dying under those heavy barn boards. The risk he faced was different from the glamour-seeking risks of the hundreds of trespassers who crept close to the active volcano for a cheap thrill. Instead it was the impulse of someone who had established a long dialogue with the mountain over decades, and who could not conceive of a future in which that dialogue would end—except by death.

The native fishermen on the Lewis River had their own long tradition of oral history that told them to stay away from Loowit. For

Jim and Pauline, it was the federal government. Soon after the eruption, the Lunds' property, along with all other individual private property within the proposed monument, was condemned as worthless. Angry over the loss of their land, the couple sued the government for a fair land trade and received $2,000 minus attorney fees. The government seemed to be echoing the mountain's message: Stay away.

Six years after the volcano spilled over their cabin, Jim and Pauline packed up and headed south to California. Their second home was constructed of stone rather than wood. Jim had kept it simple and dark, like an adobe. Proud of his work, he asked if I wanted to have a look around. As we walked outside, I couldn't help but notice that the couple's camper still wore its old Washington license plates.

"She still wants to head up north," Jim said with a wink. "That old camper still has a mind to go home."

We wandered around the backyard, where Jim had built a stone barbecue and outdoor bathtub. Tiny red flowers dotted his garden. The dry heat made the straight black stalks of telephone poles squiggle in the distance. I would have to leave soon if I wanted to cross the desert before dark.

"When I die, don't bury me here," he confided before I left. "Send me back to Castle Rock. I might have to push up daisies down there in Hades with some of those old logger friends of mine. But I'd go back and do it all over again. Spirit Lake was the highlight of my life." He repeated the last sentence as though it were a refrain.

Did those ancient fishermen on the Lewis also live with the memory of Loowit sharp in their minds? Did they, too, grieve over a murderous land that had sent them packing? How did they reconcile their love of a land they had to leave?

As I headed for the car, I asked Jim if he knew whether the creek behind the cabin had ever had a name.

He frowned. "I never heard anybody say there was a name on it. But that was a pretty good creek that came down there, all spring-fed. Did you ever go up to the head of it, where the spring started?" he asked in his slow, melodic way.

"No," I said, shaking my head. "I never did."

Everlasting: Summer

T he taste of windblown ash is on the tongue. The dry bracts
of pearly everlasting now reign. Clouds of flowers brighten
the slope where Harmony Creek tumbles in a green riparian ribbon.
A wind stirs the flowers, then subsides. It is late August, a dry
moment before the September rains.

I grasp a sprig in my hand. At the tip of each beady flower is
a tiny mustard-yellow puff surrounded by bracts unfolding like
miniature garlic husks. I crush one bead: the bracts crumple with
the soft rustle of paper. There, upon my fingers, are the seeds—
enough to claim the edges of a meadow, or, in another year, an
entire plain. I have unlocked the wildflower's treasure. Its secrets
are mine—until the wind rises again, and the seeds are blown
from my open palm.

How can a bloom no bigger than the tip of an index finger hold
so many seeds? I sit down for a moment, high above the Harmony
basin, to dissect one everlasting blossom seed by seed. It contains
sixty-three brown threads, each one one-eighth of an inch long.
Radiating from the base of each thread are seven plumes, thin as
spider's silk. I watch how the plumes bend outward like a fountain,
spreading open and downward into a parachute to catch my
slightest exhalation. Then I measure the empty plate from which
each plumed seed came: one-sixteenth of an inch in diameter.
Sixty-three seeds on the head of a pin! Plumes no longer than an
eyelash to travel miles by wind!

In earlier days, botanists placed one pearly everlasting bead
under a microscope and, finding its plateful of florets, called it
a "composite" flowerhead. Then they placed the wildflower into
one of the largest, most diverse families of flowering plants in
the world: the Compositae family, or, as it is now called, the Aster-
aceae family. Named after one of its members, the aster, this
family contains plants that possess composite or multiflowered
blossoms. Instead of just one flower and seed pod to rely upon,
composites—including sunflowers, dandelions, and daisies—bear
several flowers on a "disk" or "ray."

The tough little seeds blown from my palm could not belong
to a more appropriate family. Totaling roughly 21,000 species
worldwide, composites are prolific plants that grow almost everywhere. Their habitat ranges from low-elevation streambanks to
high-elevation desert brush. In North America alone, several hundred species flourish; in the Pacific Northwest, many are considered
weeds—such as tansy and thistle, which were introduced from
Europe over a century ago. These unwanted invaders are found
along roadsides with native composites such as yarrow, goldenrod,
groundsel, aster, and, of course, pearly everlasting.

I pause to count the flowerheads on one small clump of everlasting. It displays fourteen stems, each ending in clusters of
approximately seventy-five flowerheads, which in turn contain
roughly sixty-five seeds each. If every wind-dispersed seed germi-
nates from this one small plant, 68,250 new individual plants
will be produced in one summer. Or the plant might choose to
reproduce without any seeds at all. Pearly everlasting's rhizomes—
modified underground stems shooting sideways rather than up—
enable it to propagate without even flowering. No wonder it is
one of the most common everlasting plants in the world. Not only
does it reproduce with abandon, it adapts to whatever terrain it
inhabits, leading botanists to create varieties. Anaphalis margaritacea var. subalpina is a slightly smaller mountainous variety; A.
margaritacea var. revoluta bears slightly narrower leaves and
was identified near Mount Adams; and A. margaritacea var. occi-
dentalis prefers coastal bluffs from Alaska to California.

Which variety just flew from my palm? Revoluta? Will it, in turn,
evolve to become specific to the blast zone?

Before the eruption, no endemic plants—species unique to a
certain area—were found on Loowit. In fact, every other Washington peak possessed endemic plants except Mount St. Helens,
which regularly wiped out its inventory of plants and animals
with eruptions. Perhaps pearly everlasting encoded the survival of
volcanic eruptions into its everyday genes long ago and no blast
zone variety—such as Anaphalis margaritacea var. spiritensus—

will ever be found. Given that the flower has existed for millions
of years, in contrast to the volcano's mere 40,000, pearly everlasting has probably endured catastrophes far greater than the
1980 eruption.

I smile to think that the wildflower is older than the volcano.
For all of the volcano's dramatic, earth-shattering displays, it is
the herbaceous thing that endures.

Botanists theorize that composites originated as a family some
time after the break-up of the mother continent, Pangaea, 200 million years ago. Some even believe that it was plate tectonics—the
drifting of the continents away from Pangaea into their present-
day positions—that contributed to the explosive growth and distribution of composites around the world. Long before Loowit rose
up, pearly everlasting was riding the earth's plates like a white bug
skipping over a group of slowly dispersing rafts. Its present-day
distribution reflects this ancient passage: the montane wildflower
blooms on sunny mountain slopes as far away as Taiwan as well
as on the Cascade volcanoes.

But I would like to think that the lateral blast was something
new for pearly everlasting. Geologists believe that the sideways
eruption was unprecedented in Loowit's history. So perhaps pearly
everlasting's colonization of such a vast area as the blast zone is
at least a new challenge for the aggressive wildflower.

On the slopes above Harmony Creek the wind lifts the everlasting seeds from hundreds of flowers. The air is littered with tiny
white specks that drift overhead like a massive hatch of midges.
Some spiral upward, as though they will never land. Never before
have I seen one flower claim this place so thoroughly. How strange
compared to the dark, diverse forest that once grew here.

Few botanists visited the mature forest that once shaded the
hill where I now stand. Only a handful of plant surveys were conducted at Mount St. Helens before 1980—and those were carried
out mostly at timberline. In fact, no plant inventory exists for
the slopes that form the Spirit Lake basin. But I remember the
everlasting flowers I once gathered at Harmony Falls Lodge. And

*I remember this ridge plunging into the water below me. It was
once dry land, and I once walked there.*

Arranging small bouquets for the lodge's dining-room tables
was one of my tasks the summer I worked at Harmony Falls. I
was responsible for picking fresh flowers for the dinner guests who
arrived each night at the lodge. No one commented about the
flowers, being more attentive to the chicken or roast beef steaming
in front of them, but I didn't care. The finished bouquets were
incidental to my principal goal: wandering in the woods near the
lodge. There, I was certain to find pearly everlasting, fireweed,
lupine, and foxglove. Introduced from Britain, foxglove had "natu-
ralized" around Spirit Lake; I grew up thinking it was a Cascade
wildflower.

At other times I discovered purple penstemon, white yarrow,
pink pedicularis, or rosy bleedingheart. The deep duff under the
old hemlocks and firs was obscured by hundreds of bunchberry
dogwood flowers hatching their tiny red berries, or the three flat
leaves of deerfoot vanillaleaf. Everywhere were flowers whose
names skipped across my tongue: trefoil foamflower, twisted-stalk,
alumroot, trillium, pipsissewa. One afternoon I sat beside Harmony
Creek to watch the drunkenlike swagger of a mist-rustled monkeyflower. Its bright-yellow petals swung to and fro as cool updrafts
from the creek toyed with its stem. The slope above the lodge was
where I first recognized the little white bells of salal, hanging above
a winding trail of pink twinflowers. On slow afternoons I strayed
from my task to sit for a few minutes in a wet, mossy grotto where
maidenhair ferns grew. There I crushed a vanillaleaf to inhale its
spice, and touched the single peacock-blue berry of a queencup
bead lily, enchanting and poisonous.

By late August many spring bloomers like the bead lily had gone
to seed. Pearly everlasting was one of the few flowers I found suitable for bouquets. Even on the lodge's shaded, old-growth property
it persisted, claiming a warm patch of sunlight along the trail to
one of the cabins or near the beach. By September, the month of
highest seed production at Mount St. Helens, Harmony Falls Lodge

*was shutting down in 1979 after the busiest summer it had ever
known. No vases needed filling, but just the same, pearly everlasting abided by the lakeshore, scattering its seeds like dust for
a summer that would come again, but not to the lodge.*

*I stand here now, open-palmed above Harmony Creek, where
I once gathered flowers like a young miser. But for the summer
progeny of a prolific wildflower, I would not know where I was.
Is that water or mud below me? No, it is a mile-wide raft of logs
floating flat as corpses.*

Do not be fooled by this place, *I want to tell people who walk
here now.* This place hoards its secrets, buries them deep, lights
them on fire, plunges them down to watery depths where no
light shines.

THE LAKE

Duck Bay

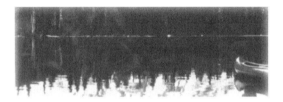

A field of water betrays the spirit that is in the air.

—Henry David Thoreau

The summer before the May 18 eruption my brother Bernie swam every day at Duck Bay, at the lake's southeastern corner. After finishing work each day he threw himself into his old pick-up, ambled down to the Duck Bay parking lot, then dove off the wooden boat dock into Spirit Lake's freezing water. Regardless of the weather, he would swim to a white buoy fifty yards offshore. Sometimes a family of mergansers, ducklings tailgating their mother, bristled at his presence. But mostly he had the wooded cove to himself, white-pumice beach and all.

At twenty-one years old, Bernie worked as the campground's firewood concessionaire to earn money for school. Felling snags for firewood was fatiguing and dangerous, but it allowed him to live in the cabin, climb the mountain, trade jokes with Jim Lund, and swim in the lake all summer. On rainy days I thought he was half-crazy: there he swam, arms flapping, wet brown head bobbing, while all around him raindrops dimpled the lake's surface and white caps frothed in the distance. Perhaps he needed to prove something. Bernie nearly died at Spirit Lake in 1977 from a head injury he incurred at timberline. If not for Jim Lund driving eighty miles an hour down the Spirit Lake Highway to the Longview Hospital, my brother would have bled to death from a fracture behind his right ear. For weeks he sat bandaged and memory-less, hands shaking, at our family's house in Portland. Perhaps the waters of Duck Bay accelerated his healing the following summer, when his memory returned to him bit by bit. I like to think that he swam for the pure love of it—in a place that now itself swims underwater.

For Duck Bay is a drowned place. No trail can take you there. Like the rest of the pre-eruption shoreline it has been swallowed up—consumed by a broken mountain and bloated lake. Its trees, which once hid the mountain from view, are now hidden under mudflows and lake water. Its boat launch, wooden dock, and buoy are gone. The very topography that made Duck Bay a cove has been erased. Today, the only way for my brother to reach Duck Bay is by memory.

Having faced death, no doubt my brother felt a certain alliance with Spirit Lake. Long before places like Duck Bay vanished, the lake had earned a reputation as a haunted place, a place for the dead. It was a spirit-lake, a body of water that was not a body but a ghost. For centuries its cemetery depths had hoarded logs and lost corpses. According to native traditions, its vast waters echoed with the moans of the dead. Some scientists believed the moans were the sound the wind made as it whistled inside the steep basin. But such was the apprehension of nineteenth-century indigenous people that no one traveled to Spirit Lake. The Klickitats foraged for huckleberries at Mount Adams and left the lake's overburdened bushes alone. The Cowlitz Indians conducted their vision quests for *tamanawas*, or divine medicine, at the mountain but left Spirit Lake to its shrieks and moans.

In the last century native stories have risen up from the lake like so many leaping trout—stories of supernatural beings and demons of dread. One native story tells of "a race of man-stealing giants" who lived above timberline. Leaving an unpleasant scent wherever they went, the giants whistled before attacking lodges where people slept. They stole salmon and even sleeping people. The kidnapped victims would wake in the morning and not know where they were. But perhaps the most well-known story of Spirit Lake tells of the Seatco, who were neither fully human nor animal. Outcasts from various tribes, the Seatco would murder twelve Indians every time one of their own was killed. Clever and elusive, they could mimic the call of "any bird, the sound of the wind in the trees, the cries of wild beasts." It was their presence, perhaps, that accounted for the sound of waterfalls where there were no waterfalls.

One of the people who heard these stories was Paul Kane, a nineteenth-century painter. Born in Ireland in 1810, Kane emigrated to Canada as a young man. In 1847 he traveled west to record native life in the Pacific Northwest. In March of that year, he arrived at the Lewis River and wanted to explore Mount St. Helens, but could persuade no one to escort him. In his journal entry for March 26 he wrote:

> *This mountain [Mount St. Helens] has never been visited by either Whites or Indians; the latter assert that it is inhabited by a race of beings of a different species, who are cannibals, and whom they hold in great dread. . . . These superstitions are taken*

*from the statement of a man who, they say, went to the mountain
with another, and escaped the fate of his companion, who was
eaten by the "skoo-cooms"—or evil genii. I offered a considerable
bribe to any Indian who would accompany me in its exploration,
but could not find one hardy enough to venture.*

With the coming of white people, the legends escalated into a
widespread belief that Bigfoot inhabited the area. In 1924, a story
of apes attacking a group of miners on Loowit's east side led to the
naming of Ape Canyon. Five miners heard a shrill whistle each
evening, followed by another whistle from a distant ridge. They also
came upon large tracks beside creek beds. One night, they woke to
"a tremendous thud" and the sound of "a great number of feet
trampling over a pile of unused shakes." One miner grabbed a
pistol, the others their rifles. Squinting through holes, the miners
saw three "mountain devils" who threw rocks at the cabin "and
danced and screamed" while the miners shot back. In the morning,
one miner shot one of the creatures, whose body fell into a deep
gorge. They reported the incident to the forest ranger, who climbed
down to the floor of the canyon. He found nothing—not even an
upturned stone.

Flocks of journalists arrived at Spirit Lake to hunt the "great
hairy apes." But depending on whom reporters questioned, the apes
were either Bigfoot or an elaborate hoax created by mischievous
Forest Service personnel, who made the footprints using huge,
wooden contraptions strapped to their feet like sandals. According
to some, excitement died down when trackers realized that the huge
footprints were of the same right foot. Years after the event, *Red
American* editor Gorg Totsi claimed that the apes were the Selahtik
Indians, a fierce tribe living like animals in the Cascades. By 1969,
officials in Skamania County had passed an ordinance forbidding
the killing of Bigfoot. Even the eruption failed to extinguish the

legend. In August 1980, a Forest Service employee discovered a large print on a trail near Packwood Lake, forty miles northwest of the volcano. Bigfoot trackers took this discovery as evidence that the mysterious animal had survived the blast. In his book *Where Bigfoot Walks*, naturalist Robert Michael Pyle tells of his own post-eruption tracking of Bigfoot east of Spirit Lake. According to Pyle, the legend of Sasquatch—if not the animal itself—persists in Loowit's shadow, although the creature's habitat has been greatly diminished by logging and development.

In contrast to the ape stories, other native tales focused on the lake itself. One described a demon whose hand spanned the entire lake. The demon could swallow fishermen whole, canoe and all. In one version, the demon was a giant fish with the head of a bear. In a second, an elk ghost lured a hunter to the lake, then plunged underwater. The hunter followed the elk—a phantasm created by the demon—and disappeared beneath the cold, dark water.

Certain physical phenomena may have contributed to the lake's eerie reputation and name. The moans could well have been the result of ice melting in the spring, which groaned and whistled as it broke into chunks. Several eyewitnesses attested to such sounds. The huge demon's hand could have been one of the many old-growth snags that lay at the bottom of the lake. Released suddenly from the bottom as the ice melted, these skyrocketing snags were observed by various winter caretakers as they shot up through the ice as if from nowhere.

The huge demon's hand could also have had its origin in one particular phenomenon—the lake's windless wave. Observed by different people on different occasions, the wave would appear without wind, lap on the shore, and cease as mysteriously as it had begun. Retired Forest Service ranger Chuck Tonn witnessed the windless wave. As the campground supervisor from 1969 until the eruption, Tonn lived in a Forest Service cabin only a few hundred yards west of Duck Bay. He and several other Forest Service employees watched the wave form in the center of the lake and sweep south toward them on several occasions.

Having known Chuck Tonn briefly at Spirit Lake, I visited him and his wife, Karen Jacobsen, in Olympia soon after I caught up with Jim Lund. Chuck and Karen met at Spirit Lake in 1978, when Tonn hired Jacobsen as a backcountry ranger. After the eruption, Tonn supervised the Mount St. Helens Visitor Center for a decade, then transferred to New Mexico. At the time I visited them in March 1994 he had retired, officially ending a professional acquaintance with Spirit Lake that had spanned more than two decades. He no longer had the beard I remembered, and his brown hair had grayed a little. Their daughter, Laurel, was eleven—too young to recall the eruption of the mountain where her parents had met.

Not a superstitious person, Tonn described the windless wave matter-of-factly: "The lake would be really calm, with no boats or wind, and then all of a sudden the wave would come across and lap on the shore. The explanation given to me was that the warming of the water in the spring caused the lake to roll over, like an upwelling, but I never had it proven."

In fact, lake turnover is common in mountain lakes. Lakes that experience summer warming and winter freezing undergo an overturn in autumn and spring, when the water rotates in a circle. The circular turning equalizes the lake's water temperatures, which tend to stratify in layers. Turnover helps bring nutrients from the bottom to the surface, and likewise flushes oxygen to the lake's depths. The turning occurs because in winter slightly warmer water tends to be trapped on the lake bottom, allowing fish and other organisms to hibernate under the ice. But in summer the reverse occurs: the surface layer (called the epilimnion) is warm, while five feet down the water cools dramatically at the thermocline to have a cold bottom, or hypolimnion. Any swimmer who dove into the pre-eruption lake in August experienced its dramatic thermocline. The water was warm at shoulder-level only to cool to ice at a swimmer's toes.

Spring turnover could well have caused the windless wave. During the equinoxes the warm water trapped on a lake bottom rises, disturbing the lake's surface. Tonn recalled seeing the wave after spring thaw—during May, June, and early July. The wave happened at any time of day, but was most noticeable at dawn or in the evening, when the lake's powerful winds had died down.

My brother Bernie also witnessed the windless wave in late spring. He believes that geothermal springs under the lake caused sudden spurts of warm water to rise quickly to the surface, creating the wave. My brother's hypothesis is supported by Tonn's observation of the wave always forming in the same place—in the middle of the lake, between Eagle Point and Harmony Falls—before it lapped against the shore near Duck Bay.

Whether it was due to turnover or geothermal activity, the windless wave has most likely disappeared since the eruption. Without its forests, Spirit Lake no longer freezes every winter as it once did, and the geothermal springs my brother believed lay deep on the lake's bottom have had ample opportunities to release their heat. In fact, since the eruption, geothermal springs *have* been discovered by scientists near what was once Duck Bay.

Like the windless wave, the legend that Spirit Lake swallowed its dead was also more fact than fiction. During the twentieth century, despite frequent drownings at Spirit Lake, few corpses were recovered. One drowning was recorded by Retlaw Haynes, who summered at Spirit Lake from 1922 to 1979. According to Haynes, a man named Mr. Teeters, who leased a cabin on the lake in the early 1920s, disappeared from his boat while fishing one morning in

1924. Haynes' sister rowed out to Teeters' boat only to discover it empty and the fisherman's hat floating on the water. No other evidence was found. Tonn, too, recalled a drowning as recent as 1977. The male victim's corpse could not be located even after Skamania County rescue personnel dragged the lake's depths for hours.

Why were the bodies never recovered? Because Spirit Lake was— and is—large, deep, and cold. Before the eruption, Spirit was two and one-half miles long, with 1,300 acres of surface area. Even in summer, icy water beneath the thermocline acted as a refrigerant on a descending victim and prohibited gases from forming inside— gases that usually cause a corpse to rise and float. When people drown in water as cold as that of Spirit Lake, the body sinks to the bottom of the lake, where it may or may not decay, depending on scavengers. According to one of the few underwater surveys conducted at Spirit Lake, no benthic (bottom-dwelling) animals existed in the lake. Even trout had to be stocked yearly to maintain a resident fish population in the exceptionally pure water. That means that, at the least, the bottom of Spirit Lake, which lay 184 feet below the surface before the eruption, still harbors skeletons buried in mud. And, in its coldest depths—those least affected by the eruption—it may even contain preserved corpses in fishing gear and swimsuits.

Given all the things I did at Spirit Lake, I should have been more afraid of drowning there. I canoed, sailed, and boated around the lake for hours. I often swam with Bernie at Duck Bay, racing him to the buoy. As a child I tiptoed onto shoreline logs and floated for more than two miles from Bear Cove to the south shore on a flimsy raft. As a teenager I swam a half-mile across the lake from the campground to Eagle Point, and for more than a mile from Harmony Falls Lodge to the Boy Scout camp. Sometimes I swam so long I lost my equilibrium when I returned to dry land. But I can recall only once when I experienced a fear of drowning.

One August night at Harmony Falls, before the eruption, Laura Bernard and I decided to skinny-dip in the lake after a long sauna. Wary of guests, we ran barefoot, at top speed, from the lodge's old boathouse, where Laura's husband, David, had built the sauna, to the lake. We crashed into the shallows laughing. The lake's sun-warmed waters had cooled to ice. Its intense clarity, so remarkable during the day, was invisible after sundown: darkness turned Spirit Lake black. Unused to the lake's opacity, I swam out a few feet. I was treading ink, blinded by water that during the day carried light into its depths for thirty feet. I could see neither below nor beside me, not even my own submerged body. Involuntarily I turned toward the shore. Then Laura and I floated motionless on our backs in the shallows, eyes open to stars, lungs full of night air. Water filled my ears with a silence that hummed. I stretched my arms across the lake. Cold water encircled my rib cage. Drowning at that moment seemed like a dream.

What frequently frightened me was something that had already drowned. On any sunny day they could be seen erupting from the lake's tranquil expanse: not Bigfoot, not demons, not fish with the head of a bear. I was frightened of snags.

My sister Celeste and I shared the same irrational horror of snags. It was an inconvenient phobia because snags were unavoidable at Spirit Lake. For several yards offshore long black stubs of logs broke the surface at odd angles. Some towered straight up like pillars, others jutted at 45-degree angles like the sorry masts of abandoned ships. Celeste and I looked at each other in sympathetic dread when we swam near them. The most horrifying one was near Duck Bay. The black, branchless trunk plummeted down so far it disappeared in the icy depths. The jagged top reared like a huge coal-faced fish, but did not break the surface. It stood there, frozen, a foot below.

According to a map drawn by botanist Donald B. Lawrence, the snags I found so anxiety-producing had drowned in approximately A.D. 1500. In 1958, Lawrence, one of Spirit Lake's few pre-eruption botanists, recorded one hemlock snag in front of the south-shore campground rooted under fifty-eight feet of water. A fir snag near the YMCA camp broke the surface above ninety-six feet of water. Lawrence believed that both trees had drowned during an eruption that dammed the Toutle River valley, thereby raising the lake's surface sixty feet. If Lawrence was right, the snags had remained in the lake for nearly 500 years.

These drowned beings were in fact landmarks commemorating the lake's violent birth. According to geologists Dwight Crandell and Donal Mullineaux, Spirit Lake was dammed during one of Loowit's major eruptive phases, from 1200 to 800 B.C. At that time, Mount Mazama had already collapsed to form Crater Lake, and Mount Rainier had also erupted with a mudflow that buried the land upon which present-day Puyallup now stands. All along the West Coast, salmon-fishing tribes were well established; on the other side of the world, the Assyrian culture was at its zenith. During these four centuries, as mudflows fanned north and west of the mountain, the headwaters of the North Fork of the Toutle were blocked, and the steep valleys directly south of Mount Margaret filled with water. The snags' message was clear: Spirit Lake was not simply a lake that happened to exist at the base of a mountain; it was a lake *created* by the mountain.

But why were the snags upright? Why did they not lie prostrate on the bottom? Shoreline burial—submergence of a lake's shoreline—is common among lakes vulnerable to volcanic flows. Mudflows in particular can bury a lake's bottom, raising its level, which in turn drowns the standing trees along its shores. Perhaps some of the snags were drowned in place and remained standing for 500 years. But not all of the snags in the lake today are so easily explained.

During the May 18, 1980 eruption, the same avalanche that buried the beaver dam, our cabin, and the unnamed creek, slammed into Spirit Lake so hard it traveled straight through the lake to Bear Cove and caused an enormous wave to crash up the steep ridges forming the lake's basin. Some geologists hypothesized that Spirit Lake was displaced entirely when it sloshed north. If ever a huge demon's hand stretched across the lake, the monstrous May 18 wave was it. Scientists estimated that the wave crested 500 to 600 feet up the lake basin. As it washed back down, so did every fir, hemlock, cedar, cottonwood, and alder in the surrounding forest.

What was the sound of such a wave? Was it like the low clapping of Spirit Lake's gentle surf on a calm day? The slap of its windless wave? Or the ancient songs of the Seatco? One winter evening I sat beside a stormy Pacific Ocean and imagined the sound of the monstrous wave. I heard the mountain catapult itself toward the south shore, jawing in a thousand rockslides as it chewed up 600-year-old firs. Then the lake explodes, leaping out of its basin like a giant, terrified cat. In some places, it consumes the forest in one smooth, choreographed roll—a solid roar. In other places, the water is shunted backwards, twirled, then returned, log-heavy, to its roiling basin. Was it the noise of a hundred stormy oceans? Could the crack of a branch or the crash of a trunk be discerned? Perhaps, as with the native legends, water could have been heard where there were no waterfalls.

No one will ever hear the sound of the monstrous wave. But this is known for certain: when the lake curled back into itself, it was a turbid swamp of boiling water, mud, pumice, dead animals, and trees. A giant log raft drifted over most of the water. On top of the logs lay a foot of ash. The entire lake looked like land, not water. Two days after the eruption, geologist Don Swanson landed in a helicopter on the lakeshore. He thought at first the lake had disappeared, evaporated, or been buried. Then he dug down and found water—or something like water. As a "collection basin," the term some researchers give to lakes, Spirit Lake was its own tree museum. And the liquid itself was a steaming, toxic mix of chemicals never before known to scientists. Three days after the eruption, researchers recorded temperatures of 626 degrees Fahrenheit ten feet below the surface of the south shore. Six days after the eruption, the entire lake still steamed. Underwater gas vents, as well as bacteria feasting on dead matter, caused the surface to bubble for months. Perhaps most significantly, the lake's outlet—the North Fork of the Toutle—was plugged by the debris avalanche. Spirit Lake was locked in its basin. The unusually pure water was transformed into a black, stagnant, tree-jammed stinkbath. Scientists flying over the lake could hardly breathe due to the horrible odor.

Douglas Larson was one of those scientists. As a limnologist, or scientist who studies inland bodies of water, Larson began observing Spirit Lake even as the media were using words like "dead" and "gone" to describe it. Having written his doctoral dissertation on Crater Lake, Larson was well acquainted with the chemistry of volcanic lakes. But post-eruption Spirit Lake was something he had never seen before. He visited the lake in September 1980 as an employee of the U.S. Army Corps of Engineers and was awestruck at the sight before him. Still bubbling from putrefaction, the lake water was 104 degrees Fahrenheit and choked with debris. No sign of life was apparent. In fact, Spirit Lake was anoxic—entirely devoid of oxygen. Its oxygen had been consumed during the month following the eruption by aerobic bacteria that had gorged themselves on the lake's sudden influx of organic debris, including the massive log raft. Larson and other limnologists hypothesized that by July the aerobic bacteria had proliferated to such a degree they had sucked all the oxygen out of the lake and, as a consequence, died. With no oxygen, the lake's biochemistry had become a volcanic soup of reduced elements such as iron, manganese, and sulfur. Hydrogen sulfide vapors emanated from areas that once smelled of hemlock and fir. As if that weren't toxic enough, the lake also became saturated with metals—including mercury, lead, arsenic, and cadmium—and was steeped in phosphates thirty-three times higher than pre-eruption levels, which made it highly alkaline. As a consequence of anoxia, Spirit Lake could support only primitive life-forms such as anaerobic bacteria and certain protozoans that do not need oxygen to survive. Before the autumn rains arrived, Larson and others recorded concentrations of bacteria in Spirit Lake that were unprecedented in the field of environmental microbiology. True to its ghostly reputation, Spirit Lake was neither dead nor alive. Its opaque, chemically enriched waters were inhabited by life-forms associated with the beginning of life on Earth and, as Larson discovered, illness and death.

While Larson was sampling Spirit and other blast zone lakes in 1980, he fell sick with a strange respiratory ailment worse than any flu he had ever experienced. Several other blast zone scientists as well as a photographer for *National Geographic* also became ill with similar symptoms—high fever, cough, weakness. The illness became known as "Red Zone Fever" and remained undiagnosed. Larson and other researchers believed that the illness was in fact a mild form of Legionnaires' disease because they found, along with anaerobic bacteria, significant numbers of pathogenic forms of *Legionella* throughout Spirit Lake, Coldwater Lake, and the Toutle's North Fork. Other pathogens included *Klebsiella pneumoniae.* Two entirely new strains of *Legionella* were discovered and named *sainthelensis* and *spiritensis*.

As Larson recovered from his illness, so, too, did the lake, following a seasonal influx of rainwater from autumn storms that pounded its watershed in November 1980. The fresh, oxygenated water temporarily revived the lake, although in the absence of green plankton the lake's organisms remained nonphotosynthetic and microbial for two years. After steadily improving over the winter, the lake nonetheless suffered a chemical setback the following summer when it was again depleted of oxygen. Then autumn rains diluted it for a second time, and by the summer of 1982 Spirit Lake was slowly clearing and cooling, although it still harbored elevated populations of pathogens.

Larson monitored Spirit Lake closely until 1986, and he remains convinced that Spirit Lake posed a health threat for several years. With fellow researcher Michael Glass, Larson produced a report documenting the area's health hazards. Published by the U.S. Army Corps of Engineers, the report, *Spirit Lake, Mount St. Helens, Washington: Limnological and Bacteriological Investigations,* was largely ignored by the Forest Service, whose top officials believed that the bacteria posed no problem to the public, since access to the lake was restricted. To this day, the only path blazed to the shoreline is the Harmony Trail, on the lake's eastern shore. Since the report was published in 1987, no cases of illnesses have been recorded at Spirit Lake, although another potential health threat—a brain-eating amoeba called *Naeglaria fowleri*—was discovered by two other scientists near Spirit Lake's geothermal springs that same year. The geothermal vents have replaced Duck Bay's white-pumice beach with slimy algal mats, tepid water, and *Naeglaria*.

Like *Legionella* and *Klebsiella, Naeglaria fowleri* requires warm water to survive. Found in swimming pools, ditches, bathtubs, ponds, and other freshwater places, *Naeglaria* is considered ubiquitous. It has caused the deaths of 150 people worldwide, as opposed to *Legionella*'s infection of 125,000 people in the United States annually. But its method of attack is unforgettable. While the *Legionella* bacterium attacks humans' white blood cells and can be stopped with the antibiotic erythromycin, *Naeglaria*'s course usually proves fatal: it enters a swimmer's nose, travels to the brain, then kills the swimmer within three to twenty-one days by feasting on nerve tissue. The victim suffers high fever, delirium, and seizures before lapsing into a coma and dying.

Bacteria weren't the only things on Larson's mind while he was sampling Spirit Lake. There were, of course, the logs. Traveling out from the south shore for deep-water samples, Larson found that he often had to fight off a log raft that seemed to have a mind of its own. The raft would drift from one end of the lake to the other in minutes, depending on winds. Submerged snags hidden in the muddy, uncharted waters also proved dangerous; there was simply no way to see them. Larson lost two Army Corps boats to the renegade raft. The first—a nineteen-foot-long fiberglass cabin cruiser—became unserviceable when logs gashed a five-foot-long split toward its bow. The second—a twenty-six-foot-long, steel-hulled survey vessel—had even been equipped with a customized cage to protect its propeller. But it too suffered leaks, and one autumn day it stalled in the middle of the log raft and began to take on water. Alone and a half-mile from shore, Larson radioed for help. With a helicopter to escort him, he managed to reverse the boat and drive it back to shallow water. Forty-five minutes later the boat sank in the south shore's mud. The following spring it was airlifted out, never to return.

During the same years that Larson was trying to avoid the lake's logs, Harold Coffin was trying to get as close to them as possible.

A Washington native, Coffin had undertaken postdoctoral training in geology and paleontology to round out his doctoral studies in invertebrate zoology. At the time of the eruption he was employed at the Geoscience Research Institute in California. When he heard the news about Spirit Lake he became curious about its trees. Here was an entire forest—root wads, bark, and all—displaced into a lake. He had studied Yellowstone's buried petrified forests and wanted to confirm a hypothesis about their origins.

In September 1982, Coffin and scuba divers James McMillan and James White waded out into the lake's log raft while it huddled against the south shore. Sulfurous fumes rose from fumaroles behind them, and steam billowed out of the crater. Their legs were immersed in water dark as coffee. Upon diving into the log-infused mixture, McMillan and White found that at fifteen feet down they could see nothing: the turbid water blocked all incoming sunlight. In vain the divers tried to photograph submerged trees. When they backed far enough away, the stump was no longer visible, so they had to be satisfied with shots of roots or trunks only. The partial pictures disappointed Coffin: he had come to Spirit Lake to prove a point about buried trees.

Coffin believed that Yellowstone's buried, petrified forests were allochthonous—transported by a force (flood, landslide, etc.)—rather than grown and rooted in place. There was some evidence to support his hypothesis. First, the roots of some of Yellowstone's erect stumps were abruptly broken. Second, no animal fossils had been found among the trees. And third, trace elements in the ash covering the trees were similar throughout all the layers of forest, suggesting that the entire area had been laid down within a year, rather than grown in place.

Although it was undetermined whether Yellowstone's forests were displaced, Coffin knew for certain that Spirit Lake's trees were allochthonous; they had been transported by the monstrous wave. But he wanted to confirm that the drowned trees were capable of floating upright. If the trees floated vertically, in the same position as they had grown, they would then settle upright on the lake floor, and geologists hundreds of years from now would think the trees had grown there, in place. Coffin knew of many instances of floating vertical snags, including Puget Sound's deadheads, which escape from timber rafts and hover in many places just below the surface. Crater Lake, too, has an upright snag called the "Old Man of The Lake," which has floated for three decades.

When Coffin visited Spirit Lake he confirmed that, yes indeed, the lake was full of vertically floating snags. He returned several times during the next three years to study them, circling the log raft in a row boat. He found that some of the snags protruded above surface; others hovered only inches from the lake bottom, their root wads barely touching. The divers pushed some submerged vertical snags so that they were horizontal. But each bounced back with the light touch of a hand to float like an upright tree. Coffin also noticed that at Eagle Point, at the center of the lake's north shore, some snags had become grounded, their roots settling into the new lake bottom. To the casual observer, it looked as though they had grown there.

Coffin also discerned that although the raft's Pacific silver fir, noble fir, and hemlock trees had sunk to the bottom, the Douglas-firs were still floating. Why? And where were all the cedars? A forester helped him solve the cedar mystery. Most of the brittle cedar logs did not survive the blast intact; instead, they lay in fragments all around the lake. But the forester wasn't sure why the true firs had sunk and the Douglas-firs continued to float.

According to Monument Scientist Peter Frenzen, true firs have thinner bark and therefore sink faster than Douglas-firs. Frenzen also believes that the Douglas-fir logs were larger than the other trees, requiring more absorption of water to sink. The fast-growing Douglas-firs were probably the largest trees in Spirit Lake's pre-eruption forest because they were older, having seeded in before the hemlocks and true firs.

On one of his last visits, Coffin and his assistants ventured out onto Spirit Lake with side-scan sonar equipment to estimate the number of submerged snags hidden in the lake. Traversing the water near Duck Bay, Eagle Point, and from Donnybrook to Harmony Falls, Coffin covered 0.79 percent of the lake bottom. The torpedo-like sonar machine, sending out echoes behind the boat, located 154 vertical trees and 95 prostrate logs. A conservative projection for the entire lake indicated that Spirit Lake may have contained roughly 31,000 submerged trees soon after the eruption—in addition to the thousands of logs drifting willy-nilly in the raft.

Coffin's research at Spirit Lake confirmed his suspicions about Yellowstone's petrified forests. Since 1985 he has lacked funds to continue his work at Mount St. Helens, but returns yearly to watch the raft, now one-half to two-thirds the size it was after the eruption. He predicts that the raft will remain on the lake for many more years, drifting to and fro on the winds.

Snags, demons, pathogens, dreams. For centuries Spirit Lake frightened the Cowlitz and the Klickitat. And today? Who is not afraid of Spirit Lake today?

In 1982 a national state of emergency was declared at Spirit Lake. Scientists, public officials, residents, and engineers were so afraid of the lake they requested federal money to pump its rising waters. Prompted by research done by the U.S. Geological Survey, the Army Corps of Engineers believed that the plugged lake— which had almost doubled in size since the eruption—was a serious threat to downstream communities. One report warned that a forty-foot wall of water could crash through Castle Rock and Longview. To deal with this threat, construction crews—complete with tractors, bulldozers, and temporary buildings—established a village-size camp on Spirit Lake's south shore and spent three years pumping the lake around the clock, at 5,400 gallons a second. The water was siphoned into a stilling basin, which drained into the Toutle via a five-foot-wide pipe that ran for two-thirds of a mile. Then, in 1984, the Corps of Engineers began its permanent solution: a $13 million artificial tunnel. With a giant snakelike machine that bored through eighty feet of rock a day, the Corps gouged a hole through Spirit Lake's west wall. Completed in May 1985, the 1.6-mile-long tunnel now keeps Spirit Lake at 3,440 feet by draining water into South Coldwater Creek.

The new tunnel is a far cry from the old wooden dam that once regulated Spirit Lake. Built out of logs in 1910 by prospector Henry Waldo Coe, the little dam kept Spirit Lake's water five feet higher than its natural depth during the first few decades after it was constructed. Then, as it began to decay, it turned into a loose raft of aging logs near the lake's outlet. The decrepit dam persisted as a ramshackle testament to the prospector's ambitions. In contrast, the Corps' 11.5-foot-wide drainpipe—along with fifty-foot floodgates—remains a billion-dollar concrete testament to the public's long-term fear of Spirit Lake. That the lake could eventually find its own natural outlet is unthinkable to individuals, agencies, and corporations living more than fifty miles away.

What, then, are harmless snags? Entire towns are afraid of drowning in Spirit Lake. It is a lake that seems to have no bottom, no borders, no predictable course of collection. With the lake seemingly poised to flood downstream towns such as Longview, in the minds of the authorities it has become a body of water that could kill a person even if that person were nowhere near its basin.

The summer before the eruption, I slept most nights directly above the lake. In front of the boathouse at Harmony Falls Lodge stood a large, square diving tower made of sun-grayed cedar and fir. Its platform sat atop four pillars—barkless tree trunks—that rose approximately fifteen feet out of the sharp slope of the shore. Accessed by a simple ladder anchored in pumice, the eighty-square-foot platform was walled in by a short fence of two-foot-tall slats spaced about eight inches apart. A diving board jutted from the northwest corner of the platform at a 45-degree angle. Although it was called "the diving tower," the tall platform was used more frequently as a sunbathing deck than for diving. At night it became my roofless bedroom, a bearproof loft suspended between two vast expanses: Spirit Lake's black surface and the alpine sky, crowded with a wilderness of stars.

Some nights I slept inside the lodge, in my small bedroom above the dining hall. One night indoors, a packrat crashed into my metal honeypot. I fumbled in the dark for a match, but by the time I had lit the kerosene lantern it had gone, along with one of my pens. On several other nights the attic's resident pine marten scampered back and forth for hours, hunting the hoarding packrats. But mostly I slept outside on the tower's worn planks, drifting off as the temperature of the night air plummeted and galaxies began to appear in clouds at a time. Sometimes I fell asleep late, or awoke in the middle of moonless nights. Then, in the immense darkness untroubled by even a single light around the shore, I could discern objects only by stellar absences—by where stars were not. The forests on the opposite bank could not be distinguished, nor could the trees rising above the lodge, nor could the lodge itself. The white pumice beach could be guessed at in faint outlines. The mountain's profile—vivid by day—was discernible only as a starless triangle.

On those moonless nights, the one world on fire was the night sky itself, an ocean of lights above my sleeping bag. Its silent weightlessness bore down on me, stamping out the night's occasional sounds. Perhaps a deer crunched the pumice beach below. Perhaps the giant cottonwood near the lodge's kitchen glimpsed a draft in its hundreds of leaves. But no waves lapped the shore beneath my body. All noise faded, tiny and incidental to the tremendous silence of the crashing Perseid meteorites, Ursa Major, the river of milk from our own galaxy. If I leaned over the diving tower's railing during those dark hours, that same bright ocean glowed back from the water. I was a pumice stone lodged between them. What terrifying marriage of sky and water had I fallen into? Miser of a lake, to hoard each night so many stars! But it is a lake of spirits in the land of the dead, a fire-born body of water reflecting back its own explosive genesis. Who can say how many candles it must gather to itself?

According to physicists, the iron in the hemoglobin of our blood is star dust; we carry the vestiges of old supernovas in our cells. We careen round the sun at 22,000 miles per hour, with 200 billion stars for neighbors in our galaxy alone. On this little island, each of us wanders the world with troubles tucked under our consciousness and dreams hoisted high above the day's chatty events. We hoard them unknowingly, thinking them forgotten. But they lie protected and still, immune to passing traffic, doors opening and closing, the distant bark of an unseen dog. I sleep inside most nights, in cities lost to the stars. But I know how acres of lake water stretch black and frozen, and how, one summer, if I could have walked on water I would have strolled the stars.

The South Shore

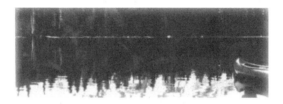

Sweet berries ripen in the wilderness.

—Wallace Stevens

The day Celeste and I hiked to the south shore, I fought to recall my earliest encounter with Spirit Lake. Cumulus clouds raced overhead, playing hide-and-seek with the bare land. A few days had elapsed since our trip to the debris avalanche, and here we were again, hiking the Truman Trail amid boulders and scraped hills. I closed my eyes to forget the landscape in front of me—the mudflows, crater, and ash. The bald ridges surrounding Spirit Lake burned with an aggressive fluorescence that threatened to blanch the dim candle of their forested past. So I blinded myself for a moment to remember the vanished land.

As I trolled my memory, I found that my earliest remembrance was not of the water itself but of its effect on my skin.

One August afternoon long ago, when I was seven or eight years old, I walked a gravel road from the lakeshore to my family's campsite with my entire body tingling. The icy lake had left its cold imprint on my water-taut skin. Barefoot and sniffling, I tiptoed to avoid the road's gravel, which nibbled at the balls of my feet. Because my family had camped far from shore, the barefoot walk took forever. Not that I minded: patches of sunlight eased my goosebumps as I wound my way through a forest of gigantic trees and ripe huckleberries. I plucked a handful of the sour-sweet beads and popped them into my mouth. Tart juice squirted onto my tongue as the skins ruptured; tiny seeds lodged in my teeth. I wandered through woodsmoke rising from a departed camper's smoldering fire, then the warm humus-heavy air again. Before I knew it I was back at camp, the lake's chill gone from my skin and my fingertips stained with purple berry blood.

Nine different species of huckleberries grow in the Pacific Northwest, or twelve if you count all berries, such as cranberries, in the *Vaccinium* genus. But as far as I remember, only three or four graced the forest that stretched from Spirit Lake's south shore to timberline, where the berries were considered the best. The least numerous species was the red huckleberry, whose luminous orbs blinked like red beacons in the forest's shade. My family did not harvest the red berries. Instead, we focused on the more abundant species that made up the understory: oval-leaved huckleberry, black huckleberry, and Alaska huckleberry. The Cascades blueberry, with its Latin name *deliciosum,* also poked a branch or two from the forest's berry thicket. Its large, black berries were the biggest and sweetest. Perhaps it was this species my brother Bernie picked along the old 100 Road, where the Windy Ridge parking lot now stands.

The berries were so large, he claimed, he had to roll them down Highway 504 to take them to our cabin.

Devoured raw in summer, huckleberries were feasted upon year-round in my family, rationed out from the freezer in mid-winter for my mother's Sunday pancakes and weekday pies. When she wasn't cleaning up after nine children, my mother also baked muffins and turnovers with the berries. And somewhere between August camping and getting us ready for school she made jam—sweet huckleberry jam, tucked away in odd-shaped, recycled jars from the previous summer's canning. Years after the eruption, Bernie happened upon one such jar in the basement of my parents' house. Stuck in a dark corner, the dusty container had gone unnoticed for years. "Spirit Lake Jam 1979" the label read. He ran up to the kitchen to unscrew the lid. But the wax seal had leaked air, and the jam was fermented.

Harvesting huckleberries in the south-shore forest was not without certain dangers. As I explored the woods for that perfect berry bush, I thought continuously of other pickers—berry-lovers with big claws. My inexperienced suburban imagination had black bears everywhere, napping behind fallen logs, grazing on high slopes, sniffing my scent downwind. It didn't matter that black bears were largely herbivores. It seemed that everyone in my family except me had a bear story to tell. Even my sister Jeanine, who preferred high heels to hiking boots, had encountered a black bear. But the lake's bears were rarely seen during the day, although they were regular night visitors. Before the Forest Service installed bearproof dumpsters, hungry bears would patrol each campground loop to knock over the old-fashioned metal garbage cans. By 11 P.M. loud *kabooms* could be heard, as the bears made their way along each road, trashing cans. First, a distant *kaboom*. That meant that you were camped in loop A, and the bear was in loop D. Then, a little closer. *Kaboom.* A little closer still. *Boom. Kaboom.* He was now in Loop B.

Then the final *KABOOM!* as the bear reached the can closest to the tent. That was when you heard the terrifying, exciting sounds as it lapped up the garbage—the heavy half-cow, half-pig snort.

The south shore contained other mysteries besides bears. Not only did fallen logs crisscross the ground, but ancient tree wells lay hidden everywhere. The wells were formed by trees that had been buried alive in pumice and then had decayed away. Obscured by fallen branches and pale-green tufts of lichen, some of the wells were deep enough to swallow a four-foot-tall child. The Forest Service continually warned campers of the wells, but every now and then someone would discover a new one, along with a sprained ankle. A brochure for the "Ancient Forest" exhibit behind the visitor center stated that the "numerous" wells were "a hazard to off-path travel." To a child who played daily in the Ancient Forest the warning was ominous. For that reason, I never ran at top speed in the forest on the south shore. The earth had secrets there—treeless pockets that wanted you to fill the space of their vanished trunks.

Like Spirit Lake's snags, the tree wells were remnants of Loowit's A.D. 1500 eruption, when pumice was ejected as far away as the Cowlitz River and north of the town of Randle. The eruption's airborne pumice is evidence of the fact that, as forest ecologist Jerry Franklin explained to me, "Soils fall from the sky in the Pacific Northwest." A nationally known ecologist, Franklin first visited Spirit Lake in 1947 on a family picnic trip and returned two decades later to conduct fieldwork for his doctoral dissertation. It was while digging holes for his research that he discovered that the soil textbooks he respected—published on the East Coast—offered no clue as to what he was seeing. That was when he realized that in the Northwest "Soils either fall from the sky, or they roll down a hillside, or wash into rivers and streams. Deep soils, in general, have not formed in place." And the most extraordinary source for such soil has been volcanic tephra, which offers trees a deep mantle to take root in, and in which moisture can be stored.

The south shore's "mantle" was, in fact, quite deep—created not only by the 1500 eruption but by an even more recent one, around 1802. Donald Lawrence measured the 1802 pumice layer to be eight feet deep at timberline. A few miles downslope, some stumps where I picked huckleberries with my sisters were in fact the crowns of buried snags—the tops of trees whose trunks disappeared in pumice and mud. Even as I piled berries high in my pail, the ground I walked on was announcing its story of burial and regrowth. In fact, these violent disturbances were partly why sweet berries grew on the south shore. Smoothed by mudflows, the shore contained no steep, north-facing ridges, so sunlight combed the entire forest. And, according to Lawrence, a young forest dating from the mountain's 1802 eruption was still advancing up Loowit's northern slope toward its "true" timberline or climatological limit, at 6,500 feet. It was this eighty-year-old forest that contained the largest berries. As any picker knows, Cascade huckleberries thrive in open areas at about 2,000–5,000 feet in elevation. Once a forest matures and its canopy completely darkens the forest floor, the huckleberries disappear from its understory. The Klickitat living east of Loowit knew this and burned their berry fields to keep harvests high.

At Spirit Lake, far more huckleberries grew in the south-shore understory than even in nearby areas like Bear Cove, which had escaped the A.D. 1500 mudflows. The south-shore forest had also most recently been battered by Hurricane Frieda, the strongest storm on record for the Northwest. Known as the Columbus Day Storm of 1962, the hurricane slashed through the Spirit Lake basin with eighty-five-mile-per-hour gusts. The storm tore down so many trees on Harry Truman's land at the lake outlet it created a meadow. Western hemlocks, common in Spirit Lake's mid-elevation montane forest, were especially susceptible to the gusts. Although their shallow roots readily soaked up surface moisture, during the 1962 storm the huge hemlocks could cling to little more than pumice— and consequently were uprooted. One of the most familiar sights in the south-shore forest was an uprooted hemlock, its massive, spiderwebbed root wad crammed with pumice. But what spelled destruction for mature trees meant sunlight and space for the berries. Even Highway 504, with its sunny swath winding up to timberline, was itself encouragement for the bushes; much of the best picking was within sight of the road.

By the time I explored the south shore, munching on berries and dancing on logs, a new forest had grown up and camouflaged the 500-year-old eruption. Besides the droopy-headed western hemlocks, other conifers branched overhead, obscuring the volcano from view. A colonizer of avalanche tracks, Alaska cedar punctuated the forest with weeping branches that, as naturalist Donald Peattie described them, looked "weighted with snows" even in summer. Also known as yellow cedar because its inner wood is a warm yellow, the slow-growing cedar could not yet have reached maturity on the 500-year-old flows: Alaska cedar lives at least 1,000 years. Jim Lund lined his cabin with Alaska cedar because its aromatic wood is rot resistant. At Harmony Falls, Alaska cedar was used to repair old cabins.

Another tree common to Spirit Lake was found to be so "lovely" to the nineteenth-century botanist David Douglas he dubbed it *Abies amabilis*. Known today as Pacific silver fir, the conical evergreen is often found with another true fir named by Douglas and recognized as the largest native fir in North America—the noble (*Abies nobilis*, now *procera*). For some campers, western hemlocks and silver firs typified Spirit Lake's pre-eruption forest. Others recall standing under huge nobles and Douglas-firs near the south-shore campground.

As a child I did not realize that these trees, in terms of geologic processes, made up what was essentially a young forest sprouting in the lap of a mountain whose slopes shook regularly like the fur of a wet dog trying to get dry. For as mammoth as it was, the south-shore forest was like a daisy blooming in front of a stoked furnace.

On March 26, 1980, the day before Loowit broke its 123-year dormancy, Chuck Tonn and his future wife, Karen, spent one of their last days together at the south-shore campground. Earthquakes had begun six days earlier. On March 21, twenty-four hours after the first earthquake, Tonn was laying out a new cross-country ski trail at timberline when the second earthquake struck. By March 26, the two rangers were packing up small things and heading out. All around them green trees swayed, silver snags shook, and buildings trembled. Before they left, they tried to evacuate Harry Truman, whose lodge was close by. They tried again in April, when they visited Spirit Lake one last time. Tonn has a tape of that last conversation with Truman. In the background, glasses are tinkling incessantly.

How could Truman leave? Having lived at Spirit Lake for fifty years, the old bootlegger was as rooted to the south shore as one of its 500-year-old hemlocks. His lodge and fifty acres of sun-filled meadows were officially owned by Burlington Northern Railroad, but in reality Truman was as territorial about his grounds as any landowner. Nonetheless, during those spring days, Truman's roots—like those of the old hemlocks—wiggled in pumice that shook like loose popcorn. Then the entire forest—huckleberries, hemlocks, and all—disappeared beneath the unfurling volcano. Tonn believes that Truman was probably asleep in his bed the morning of May 18 and never knew what hit him. But the day I visited the new south shore, I couldn't help thinking that Harry Truman had heard the mountain long before he died. The trees alone would have sung out their collective death as they collapsed upon each other. The deafening roar of the advancing mountain would have spelled out, over and over again, what fifty years meant to a 40,000-year-old volcano.

As Celeste and I hiked to the new south shore that June day, memories of the old forest seemed like obsolete road maps. Not a single trace of the old forest could be seen. Certainly in terms of Loowit's history this most recent inundation was profound. The A.D. 1500 mudflows had only partially buried the lake's trees. Now those same trees had vanished. I squinted as the sun's rays exploded through the cumuli for a moment—intense rays undisturbed by any overhanging branch or crown. Never before did I hate so much sunlight, even as a crack between clouds.

The treeless expanse reminded me of the one place I never liked much before the eruption: the Plains of Abraham, on the volcano's east side. There, hardly any flowers bloomed. What few trees grew there were stunted. It was only behind haystack-size boulders that a person could find any shade. A hostile place. Ugly. Its razed surfaces repulsed me; its boulders were oppressive. After hiking there a few times, I avoided it completely. Why bother?

Because now the Plains of Abraham were everywhere. The same volcanism that had made me curse the plains had transformed Loowit's north slopes into a gray, rocky plain. The area where we now hiked had been subjected to every one of the volcano's forces on May 18: the earthquakes, landslide, pyroclastic flows, mudflows, and ashfall. The swollen lake, its bottom raised by the avalanching mountain, ballooned 200 feet over the old south shore. Truman's lodge, the campground, and Duck Bay were no longer beside the lake but in it.

It made me dizzy to consider the intricate layering of land that had happened in so short a time, so violently, over a forest that I knew at the level of a huckleberry. I felt an odd disbelief. Physically, there I was, between the volcano and the lake, but it didn't make sense that I was approaching the south shore, where I had once watched rough-skinned newts float orange-belly down in the shallows. This was not the place where I had leaned back against a massive log and dug my sandals into wet pumice while the pale orange sunset faded to blue over the lake's dusk-dark ridges. The puzzle pieces didn't fit. *That's Spirit Lake,* I repeated to myself. Within minutes we would even be at its shore.

Turning our backs on the crater, we stepped gingerly down a gravely dry wash and hiked a mile toward the water. No huckleberries, no bears, no hemlocks, no tree wells, no Toutle Creek. Just rocks and a few wildflowers. By the time we reached the shore, massive old-growth torsos, busted and crumpled atop each other, were strewn everywhere, cast up like detritus on the sandy shore. Even on their sides they were wider than we were tall, their girth exceeding our puny human height.

On our left, a distant steel-gray square marked the Corps of Engineers' tunnel on the lake's west shore—the place where Spirit Lake was bled, gallon by gallon. Out on the water, the log raft bunched up at the lake's east arm, near Harmony Falls. Close by, a few wispy willows and cattails sprang from marshy seeps. A cold spring wind knocked the cattails together as cumulus clouds bumped against the backcountry's ridges. The smell of humus and woodsmoke had been replaced by something brackish, as though we were beside a salt marsh at low tide.

"What are cattails doing here?" I asked Celeste, who was staring out over the water.

"I don't know," she said, in a monotone. "I'm trying to get my bearings."

She was gazing at a little island piled high with gray logs. The island marked the general vicinity of Truman's lodge. It sat like a marooned battleship about a half-mile from shore. Like the debris avalanche that had demolished the Toutle, the jutting piece of land was one of the volcano's many earthen fingers.

I found myself laughing an odd little laugh. "What would you have said if in 1979 someone planted you here and claimed, 'This is Spirit Lake.' Would you have believed them?"

"No," Celeste said, her eyes still on the island. "I would have laughed."

"We would have laughed," I said, nodding.

"Just like we laughed at . . . " She paused, so I finished her sentence.

". . . all the predictions of volcanic eruptions."

She turned to me slowly. "There were never any islands in Spirit Lake."

"Or cattails," I answered. "Or horsetails. Or marshy seeps."

Celeste moaned. "Look. There's a snag."

Earlier that day I had asked Celeste if she had ever had any dreams of Spirit Lake. In fact, she had experienced recurring dreams and nightmares just like mine. Her dreams of the pre-eruption forest were calming and colorful, the post-eruption nightmares disturbing. In one, she was alone on the lake in our family's bright-yellow canoe, and, as in my dreams, the lake was radioactive.

As we stood on the south shore that day, Celeste couldn't stop looking for fragments of that bright-yellow canoe or some other sign of pre-eruption life. She wanted to identify something that would tell her that she was once part of the land, had swum and slept and walked here before, that the logs around us were once a standing forest.

"But what's more disturbing," she asked after a while, "the fact that there aren't any signs, or the possibility that there could be? It might be worse to come upon some object that told you that life was once entirely different here. Imagine a yellow canoe drifting across the lake *now*."

The lake water lapped against the bellies of the old logs. The sound—such a familiar one from pre-eruption days—made me look straight into the lake. The scene turned my stomach. The water was fairly clear but something near it seemed to stink, or perhaps it was the water itself—the faint brine odor of stagnant water. The water along the chocolaty-gray shore was unbelievably shallow— like a tidal flat stretching for miles. Upon the soft lake bottom flourished a field of grassy water plants. If there was anything I found more troubling than snags it was aquatic plants that grabbed at your ankles as you swam. I bent down to touch the water. For as cool as the day seemed, the shallow water was tepid—a disturbing temperature for a high mountain lake. Where was the icy temperature of its past?

"I used to swim here thinking I was a part of this lake," Celeste said. "I used to dive into the water and look up without wiping my eyes. The first thing I would see was the mountain. It was so beautiful, so close."

I stood next to her, silent. The memory was identical to mine.

Bear Cove

Some places are forever afternoon.

—Richard Hugo

oes first, to baptize my appetite for ice. Then the whole body at once—thighs, torso, forearms, shoulders, neck, head. Pain flashes to my fingertips. I gasp, then wipe my face with both palms. *I can stay here.* I gasp again. *No problem.* A rivulet of ice water trickles down from hair to shoulder blades as I gaze up at a blue sliver of sky rough-edged by evergreen branches. Gray-trunked trees are everywhere. Some have fallen across the creek, others stand 200 feet tall along the steep west ridge. Old-man's-beard lichen brightens the drab bark of each with its minty strands.

Disencumbered of clothes I become part of the moss-banked pool. My soles press against a soft bottom of sand. Within a minute I am breathing easily, extending one arm along the surface. It waves back at me like a branch caught by the current. Now, again, under. Again, a deep draught of the forest. If not for the sunlight I would fail in this bathing game, but it is sunny at Bear Creek this summer afternoon.

I am submerged in a small, rocky pool my sisters and I call the Bath Tub. There is also the Swimming Pool—a large, deep area dammed by logs—higher up the creek. There, a person can actually swim a little. The Swimming Pool is the largest basin in Bear Creek. It is also easy to access. A path carved out of the forest's deep humus winds up from Bear Cove's beach at the lake's northwestern tip and through the campground to end at the Swimming Pool. The needle-duff path is so soft I can sprint along it in bare feet.

Although it is more difficult to reach, the Bath Tub is well worth the journey across rotted logs and salmonberry vines. Obscured by a lush island tangled with devil's club and coltsfoot, it is further hidden by a fallen log. Yellow monkeyflowers droop over the water here, along with maidenhair ferns fluttering in the draft produced by the falling stream.

No one bathes here but my sisters and me. Bordered by steep, forested ridges to the east, west, and north, Bear Creek is warmed little by the sun. Sunlight strikes the Bath Tub for an hour at most each day. Compared to the bright pumice beach back at the lakeshore, there is too much damp shade here to make this a popular swimming hole, and the water is simply too cold.

But that is why I like it. The cold ignites each nerve ending, sending my skin to flame. If I hug myself to keep warm I feel colder. So I open my body to the current—feeling muscles tighten into a steady ache. My heart thumps against my ribs, chronicling each sensation. I cup the water in my hands and shower my face, licking the drops from my lips.

But what is this? A soft splash behind me. I wheel round to face— within two feet and swimming straight for me—a small black-nosed, whisker-cheeked otter. It is so close I can reach out and touch it. A slight cry escapes me. The otter pup glances up. Our eyes meet. Then in a flash it swings around 180 degrees and snakes back up the island's mossy bank, where its mother waits. For a moment I glimpse the glistening brown fur on the backs of mother and baby as they slink through the brush. Then both are gone. "Wait!" I shout to the salmonberry bushes. How could it be that of all creatures it is a harmless otter that frightens me? A baby otter, no less, who mistook me for a tree.

Perhaps it had not yet gained its complete eyesight. North American river otters are born blind and remain helpless for six weeks. During that time, and until they are six months old, their mother teaches them to swim. Was that what I had interrupted? A swimming lesson? Such lessons may be the origin of what makes otters resemble humans: they love to play. As soon as the pups are able swimmers, they are out cavorting with their parents and siblings, frolicking in waves and along riverbanks. Families construct slides in mud or snow and slip down them—on their bellies, limbs loose at their sides—time after time. A gentle shove with their hind feet propels them on their way.

If I had known how to look for signs of otter, perhaps I would not have been so surprised by my visitor. Being territorial, river otters mark their grounds with "spraints"—fishy, green scat strategically placed on logs and rocks near the water. They also have easy-to-identify tracks: alongside the five-toed, webbed footprint is the slide mark of the long tail. River otters have both webbed and clawed feet because they often travel overland at night, sometimes up to sixty miles. Like urchin-eating sea otters, they belong to a mostly terrestrial suborder of carnivores called *Fissipedia*. These flesh-eating land mammals (including bears, dogs, raccoons, and cats) have slightly different teeth from marine carnivores and possess claws. The otter's webbed claws are an exception.

Although they're classified as land animals, nearly everything about otters bespeaks an aquatic lifestyle. A nictitating membrane protects their eyes; their luxurious fur keeps them warm underwater; and they dine more on amphibians, crayfish, and small fish than they do on rodents and insects. Even the word otter sounds like *water*. It is not a coincidence: the two words share etymological roots in *hydra;* in ancient Greece, otters were called water snakes.

Living up to fourteen years, river otters are members of the weasel family *(Mustelidae)*. Like other short-legged mustelids at Spirit Lake—such as martens, minks, fishers, weasels, and wolverines—river otters are elusive fur-bearing mammals that have proved vulnerable to trapping, logging, pollution, and development. Apart from parasites, the only known enemy of the river otter is *Homo sapiens.* Although they were not as hard hit during the eighteenth-century rush for furs as their saltwater cousins, the sea otters, river otters were a valuable commodity in European markets until the early part of the twentieth century. Historical records in London show that during the 1800s alone, 1.5 million river otters were imported from North America, along with 3 million minks, 3 million sables, 500,000 skunks, 100,000 wolverines, and 25,000 sea otters, whose numbers had already declined precipitously. The German immigrant John Jacob Astor was one of the barons of the Northwest fur trade. From his home in New York, Astor organized two expeditions west, and by 1811 one of the expeditions had established a fur-trading station at the mouth of the Columbia River, which became known as Astoria. Today, although the fur trade has diminished, mustelids remain a rare sight, although some river otters have adapted themselves to saltwater and thrive in Puget Sound.

At Spirit Lake, river otters were not seen much in the early part of the twentieth century but were a common sight by the 1970s. One August day in 1978 Celeste, Terese, and I camped at Cedar Creek, on the east shore of Spirit Lake. After a night of bear stories and laughter, we rose at daybreak to sit quietly by the glassy lake. As I read to Terese from a remarkable book I had discovered called *Leaves of Grass*, I was interrupted by some splashing offshore. Four otters—parents and babies—were fishing for breakfast in the small cove. They had seen us before we saw them. To our delight, they crawled onto logs, dove, and swam with no sign that they were bothered by us or Walt Whitman, even though we were only a few yards away. Then, materializing in a flash out of the faint dawn sky, a great blue heron swooped down and landed in the cove's shoals. It stood on one leg, not ten feet from the four brown shadows. Within moments the fishing competitors recognized one another, and soon the heron was working the wind with its huge wings, and the family, likewise perturbed, swam in the opposite direction of the heron's low *garronk.*

Far across the lake from Cedar Creek but probably only a short stroll for the frisky family, Bear Cove was an otter paradise. Voles peeped out from the damp forest sod. Fingerlings slipped through the creek. Alders shaded the mouth of Bear Creek, so an otter could swim, protected, straight from Spirit Lake into the creek's deep-forest shade. Perhaps most significantly, no trail or road accessed Bear Cove, so day-use picnickers had to arrive by boat, and most of them left by dark. As a result, forest animals dominated Bear Cove. It was there that I encountered most of the wildlife I ever saw at Spirit Lake—woodpeckers, squirrels, fish, rodents. And it was far back in the cove's dark forest, while I was walking back from Bear Creek one afternoon, that I heard a blood-curdling scream.

Bear? Cougar? Sasquatch? Certainly not an otter. The loudest sound an otter makes is a chuckle as it nuzzles its young. Sounding not at all human, the half-shriek, half-roar had me sprinting within seconds for Bear Cove's sunny, populated beach. If the scream had come from any other direction I would have thought it a game, since by the time I was twelve my older brothers had played so many tricks on me that I was wiser than my years in the cruel-hoax department. But the scream came from up the ridge, where no trail existed.

Like the vast seventeenth-century North American wilderness that lapped up against the pilgrims' huts at Plymouth Rock, Bear Cove's forest seemed to my twelve-year-old mind endless, mysterious, and dangerous. No matter that the ancient conifers met a clearcut four miles north. The trees that made up Bear Cove's forest seemed darker, damper, older, and taller than any other trees at Spirit Lake. Entering the forest there was like entering a green high-ceilinged cavern that had no end. Even the vegetation was different. Instead of the south shore's cheery bunchberry dogwood—a wild-flower that tolerates sun—oxalis obscured every inch of Bear Cove's forest floor with its enormous cloverlike leaves, tart as a lemon. With their tiny white flowers, foamflower and star-flowered Solomon's seal sent up pinpricks of light near black roots and decaying logs. Tucked in this forest was the Forest Service's small campground, complete with heavy-beamed picnic tables and an outhouse or two. Ten or so campsites had been carved out of the dark forested plateau that rose gently from the flat shore. A few hundred yards from the beach the forest rose sharply as the north-west ridge of the lake basin shot up toward the Dome, elevation 5,707 feet.

According to Forest Service ranger Chuck Tonn, one of Bear Cove's noble firs was in the process of being measured at the time of the eruption because Forest Service personnel believed it may have been the largest ever found, both in height and width. A pocket of huge nobles stood in the center of the cove, but one in particular was enormous. Tonn recalled that it was 100 feet just to the first limb. Certain it would challenge the record, the Forest Service had begun to measure it the summer before the eruption. Then it was blown away.

To outdistance its neighbors would have been no small feat for the noble. The tallest noble firs in the world are found in the Pacific Northwest—all of them at the foot of volcanoes. The same volcanic soil that allows logging operations to flourish despite erosion-promoting clearcutting practices also enables the centuries-old nobles to poke their crowns higher than any other on the planet.

From the description Tonn gave of Bear Cove's noble fir, it couldn't have been very far from where I myself sprinted that afternoon long ago when I heard the scream. But I never took note of the giant tree. At the time I dashed through the woods, cedars and hemlocks were the only evergreens I could distinguish with confidence, conifer identification not being a required subject in school. To this day I am surprised by how few adults can identify the cone-bearing trees outside their houses or shading their offices. One person I know refers to all conifers as "pines," thereby ignoring the Northwest's most common conifer, the Douglas-fir, or true firs, such as the noble. Once, as I passed through a security gate at the Spokane Airport, I asked the guard what sort of pines were growing in the area. From the air I had seen small, lovely stands greening the hills. "Oh, who knows?" the friendly woman answered. "You know, it's funny, they call Washington the 'Evergreen State,' but all we have is pines."

So while I still hear the scream charging through Bear Cove's trees, I have no memory of its giant noble—the true mystery of the cove.

Three years after I heard the scream, it took a fair portion of my courage to camp out under the stars one night at Bear Cove. To commemorate a midsummer's full moon, Terese and I canoed over to the cove at dusk to sleep on its beach. We spread our bags out under the bright moon that illuminated the snow-tipped summit across the shore. I had purchased a maroon sleeping bag with money from my first job making tacos at a fast-food restaurant, and the full-moon outing was one of my first nights to see if its goose down worked. The lake was silent, the woods were still, and I tried to sleep, but that earlier scream filled my ears. After what seemed like hours, I drifted off into uncomfortable dreams. Then, as the pumice beach glimmered faintly with blue moonglow, I woke to the dark profile of a furry animal on my sleeping bag and another scrambling past my head: curious mice come to feed. Haunted cove indeed.

On that May day in 1980, when Loowit discarded its northwestern flank like a flap of rotted plywood in a hurricane, part of the volcano rolled so hard into the south shore it continued straight through the lake for a mile, coming to rest only after it had been stopped by the ridge where I heard the scream. The result was a double entombment: Bear Cove was not only interred under the debris avalanche, it was submerged under the lake.

Where Bear Cove's huge nobles once soared, tall mounds of black and red rock now lie in discrete pyramids, as though placed in some secret arrangement. The gravely pyramids—sections of the airborne mountain—rise from a flat plain of ash that has trickled down from the surrounding slopes. Little islands of the same red and black rock jut out from the new cove's shores. These are the tombstones for the Bath Tub, the myopic baby otter, and the mysterious noble fir.

As Celeste and I stood on the south shore, on that June day of cattails and clouds, I scanned the distant north shore for Bear Creek, to see where and how it tumbled into the new cove. But it was too far away. And the longer I looked, the farther away the cove seemed—almost as if the creek were an abstraction. I failed to see any connection between the view in front of me and the cove of my memory. Worse still, that high-ceilinged cavern of old-growth seemed to elude me. I thought of the huge noble that I would never see. How many other plants and animals had Bear Cove once sheltered? Did Pacific giant salamanders once nap there, lying like branches at the bottom of the creek? Did corydalis droop its lacy leaves and purplish-pink flowers over a rotting log? Surely hungry water ouzels worked the creek in the afternoon. Why did I never remark on the energetic gray bird as it dove into the creek's falls? How did I never notice it swimming underwater while I bathed? Perhaps no ouzel visited the creek. But how would I ever know now?

Houses burn, ancestors emigrate, empires crash, dust settles on the dead. Why should Bear Cove be any different? It has undergone a transformation—why resist that? Because we are born, like otters, eyes closed, dreaming of a land of enchantment. And when we wake to a worldly place, we struggle for the rest of our lives to glimpse the dream behind those shuttered eyes. It is a strange predicament: happy blindness and desirous sight. To this day, otters have yet to return to Spirit Lake. But if I close my eyes, I glimpse Bear Creek again, tripping down branch-clogged gullies. I step into one of its pools: cold still, to the point of pain.

Eagle Point

Only the birds can cast off their shadows.

—Vladimir Nabokov

That June day, Celeste and I paused beside the cattails to assess for ourselves how high Spirit Lake had risen since the eruption. Two hundred feet was the going estimate, but what did that really mean? Most of the shoreline around the lake was so different we failed to gain any perspective on where the old lake level lay. Bear Cove was too far away to see its submerged beach; the campground and Truman's lodge were gone. It was only by looking at Eagle Point that we understood how high the new lake was.

Located across from the south shore, Eagle Point jutted out from the center of the lake's north shore to separate the lake's east arm from its west, thereby creating the lake's characteristic U-shape. Although most people referred to the shape as a horseshoe, I preferred to see it as a giant bird: Bear Cove lay at one wing tip, the Portland YMCA at the other, with Eagle Point marking the massive bird's head.

Before the eruption, no road or trail traveled to Eagle Point. The only way into the small cove created by Eagle Point's dented tip was by water. Years before the eruption someone had tied a heavy rope around a fir tree there. Celeste and I often swam or canoed to the cove, along with our siblings Elizabeth and Michael, and swung out over the lake to enjoy a spectacular view of the mountain. Since the rope was tied high above the shore, the drop was considerable— perhaps eight to ten feet. The split-second sensation of flying was absolute: on a clear day, we would soar out over the blue water that contained the mountain in its reflection. Then, just as the swinger let go of the rope's knot, two things would loom: mountain and mountain. One was at eye level; the other below, reflected in the lake's surface. Time after time each of us dove into the mountain, destroying it with a shout and a splash.

Now, it seemed, it was the cove that was destroyed. Not only were the rope swing and fir drowned but Eagle Point itself was flooded; only the very tip of the high ridge remained. We stared at the ridgetop as one might look at the crown of a drowning victim's head. Our adolescent fear of snags claimed us again: Spirit Lake was a flood that would never recede.

Long ago someone had once seen an eagle at Eagle Point, hence the name. Before the eruption I had seen many birds near the point, but never an eagle. Instead, ospreys nested there atop snags in large nests of braided branches, and it was near Eagle Point that I saw my first great blue heron, soaring overhead like an airborne ocean liner. I was thirteen years old and had never seen such a huge bird. I thought it had escaped from the tropics. The wingspan alone was at least eight feet. The air whistled on the downbeat of each wing flap. I was certain I had seen something rare and mysterious, so I paddled as fast as lightning to the south shore and ran to the little office that served as Spirit Lake's visitor center. There, out of breath, I learned that I had just seen a common resident of the Pacific Northwest, a regular summer inhabitant at Spirit Lake. Sure enough, the more I ventured around the lake, the more herons I saw each summer, plunging their yellow-dagger beaks into the shallows for trout. I hung back in the trees, trying not to disturb them as they fished. The lake was so calm some mornings I discovered that when herons walked the shallows I could watch both heron *and* its reflection. But herons in flight forced me to choose which to admire: the huge bird or its reflection. Once I tried to remain as motionless as a heron hunting just at the water's edge. It required a patience beyond my squirmy adolescence. Nonetheless, the suspended moment between the heron's frozen pause and strike was something I wanted to inhabit—a timelessness loaded with intention.

That day, as we looked across the lake at the new Eagle Point, I realized that I had yet to see a heron anywhere in the blast zone. I realized this because scattered at our feet were the green, tubular droppings of a large bird. I didn't recognize them but half-hoped they might belong to a heron. I later found out that they were the traces of a flock of Canada geese that had taken up residence on the south shore during the last few years. It seemed bizarre to me— geese and no herons. Mergansers, mallards, and loons had made up the pre-eruption lake's waterfowl, not geese. But as I talked with Forest Service ecologist Charlie Crisafulli about the blast zone's new birds, I realized that the Canada geese were only the beginning of a strange new community the lake had never seen before.

Having conducted bird surveys at Spirit Lake since 1981, Crisafulli became surprised a decade after the eruption by what he was observing. The rocky, windswept plain that now reached from the south shore to the volcano was so varied in habitat it was attracting striking combinations of birds. The area was now home to a mix of species never before observed on the western slope of the Cascades. Rock wrens, horned larks, and killdeer had flown in to breed near the lake. The community resembled something out of the Great Basin—not the forested Cascades. In addition, Crisafulli found that the south shore's fierce winds, rocky surfaces, and extreme temperatures mimicked an alpine environment, inviting such mountain dwellers as gray-crowned rosy finches and water pipits. At the same time, its wildflower meadows were attracting lower-elevation species such as Savannah sparrows and meadowlarks, and the willow-lined creeks lured song sparrows and yellow warblers.

It all sounded unbelievable to me. The south shore seemed so barren the day Celeste and I visited it even the goose droppings had looked out of place. Accustomed to the sight of eagles, ospreys, and herons at the lake, I had trouble imagining horned larks and Savannah sparrows flitting above the pumice as though it were a prairie. It seemed even stranger when one considered that the forested lake had once harbored northern spotted owls.

Before the eruption, spotted owls were frequently observed at Donnybrook, on the east shore. Chuck Tonn saw his first spotted owl there around 1975. Tonn had accompanied wildlife biologist Ernie Garcia into the campground one night, while Garcia was conducting some of the first spotted owl surveys on national forest land. The biologist called to a pair of nesting owls and they flew to the log right beside the two men. It was also at Donnybrook that camper Sam White nearly lost part of his scalp to an owl. White was exploring the ridge behind Donnybrook one evening when he was hit on the back of the head by a pair of talons. The talons probably belonged to an aggressive great horned owl rather than its peaceful spotted cousin, but the bird disappeared before White could discern the species or the reason for its attack.

Like Eagle Point, Donnybrook was now flooded. And like the rest of the blast zone, the dark forest had been replaced by sunny expanses. Perhaps it wasn't so unbelievable. The new colonizers were simply following their own instinct for open plains, in the same way that spotted owls sought out the shelter of old conifers.

Crisafulli had also seen red-winged blackbirds along the south shore, gurgling their intricate melodies among the cattails I had found so out of place. More striking still, the south shore's geo-thermal vents had created algae-rich waters that pleased ducks such as mallards, cinnamon teals, and green-winged teals. One mallard was found in a small patch of lupines, sitting on a nest containing eleven eggs. Water-loving birds such as spotted sandpipers were also now flitting over the lake. Water, returning plants, few humans—what more could a shorebird want? Crisafulli believes that random events—such as a single pair of birds flying over the lake—could have been the start of the unexpected colonizations. Some birds may have been blown off their migratory route by storms and others may have been dispersing to find new nesting sites when they happened upon the big, uninhabited lake. Seeing a habitat below that suited them, they circled to land, then stayed to breed.

The ecologist had even spotted Vaux's swifts—birds that are usually associated with old-growth forests—in the blast zone's sunny "blowdown," where entire forests lay sideways. The swifts led Crisafulli to speculate that snags may be the critical habitat feature for the birds, rather than the entire old-growth forest.

After more than a decade of watching such birds, the ecologist discovered an emerging pattern of succession: it was the quickly changing vegetation in the blast zone that lured new species of birds. In the first decade, ground- and cavity-nesters swept in. These birds, including dark-eyed juncos, mountain bluebirds, hairy woodpeckers, and flickers, nest and forage on the ground or in snags. Because snags are abundant in the national monument, these birds were still common more than a decade later. Then, as the area began to green up, other species swooped in. As with the willow-bordered creeks flowing into the south shore, bright-green riparian areas throughout the blast zone began to attract migrating flocks from far away. Foliage-gleaning, insectivorous birds such as flycatchers and warblers arrived, lured by the taller, bushier vegetation. The neotropical migrants feasting among the waving stands of twenty-foot-tall cottonwoods included willow flycatchers, MacGillivray's warblers, yellow warblers, and orange-crowned warblers.

Predators, too, were now common. Kestrels and screech owls were nesting well inside the monument, and red-tailed hawks, ospreys, bald eagles, golden eagles, and ravens were spiraling above the blast zone's lakes and streams. It was not inconceivable that a person might even spot an eagle above the old drowned point, reviving the pre-eruption name.

Crisafulli had even seen great blue herons feeding along Clearwater Creek, at the blast zone's eastern edge, and at Obscurity Lake, high in the backcountry. Perhaps it was only a matter of time before they returned to Spirit Lake. When they did, I hoped to be there. I had loved Eagle Point's rope swing but was now ready to pawn its memory for the sweeping shadows of a living heron's wings over the lake. My desire to see the great gray bird stayed with me long after our south shore hike. I held the anticipated moment inside me the same way I had once tried to imitate the bird's frozen pose. To my surprise, this time I found that I possessed the patience to wait.

Harmony Falls

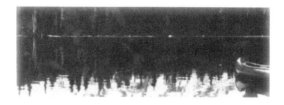

I have kept high moments.
They go round and round in me.

—Carl Sandburg

The summer Celeste and I visited the south shore, I received a brief note from Laura Bernard saying she wanted to see Spirit Lake again. I perused the card surprised. Laura hadn't visited the lake since 1979. At the time of the eruption, she was twenty-eight years old and had spent nearly every summer of her life at Harmony Falls, on the lake's eastern shore. She had operated Harmony Falls Lodge with her husband, David Berry, for six years. They had two children, Sam and Dylan, who grew from babies to little boys during those years. But after the eruption she had avoided the entire area as though a volcano named

Mount St. Helens had never existed. In fact, I had the impression that she didn't care if she ever saw the lake again.

I knew of others like Laura, who preferred to keep their memories intact. Not only did they not want to see the volcanic aftermath, they also didn't want to know that two paved roads now accessed the backcountry, or that a $12 million building and parking lot had been built at Coldwater Ridge, or that millions of cars entered the blast zone each summer. There were enough stories in the newspaper for them to know that the eruption had dumped more than ash and pumice on the land: it had rained down notoriety. The beloved and little-known mountain was now a world-famous volcano. I knew how Laura felt, particularly after a couple from New Jersey asked me which was the quickest way to drive to the top of Mount St. Helens. "You can't *drive* to the summit," I told the husband, who was on the last day of his vacation and in a hurry. "It's a five-hour climb and you need a permit. But you can take an interesting hike through Lava Canyon."

"I just want to drive to the top of Mount St. Helens," he replied politely, "You know, like at that crater in Hawaii."

Part of me wanted Laura to stay away, to preserve the chasm the eruption had caused in all of our lives. But now, it seemed, not only did she want to see the lake again, she wanted me to escort her. We would camp together over a weekend: Laura would be the cook and I would be her blast zone guide. Having hiked down the Harmony Trail on some of my early visits, I had already seen the area where Harmony Falls Lodge once stood. And so things would be reversed: long ago it had been Laura who introduced me to the lodge, now I would return the favor by reacquainting her with her past—or what was left of it.

Blazed a few years after the eruption, the Harmony Trail begins high up on the eastern ridge bordering Spirit Lake and wanders for a mile down to the lakeshore. From my previous hikes down the trail I knew that everything Laura once cherished was gone: the kitchen where she had cooked hundreds of meals; the diving tower where we had sunbathed on sleepy afternoons; the eight rustic cabins, each with its restored wood cookstove; the docks, boat house, sauna, forest paths, cedars, cottonwoods, elderberry trees, pumice beach, you name it. Logs lay scattered there like so many beached bones. The most I had stumbled upon to tell me that something had once existed at Harmony was a bent railroad spike sticking out of a log. But worst of all was the crushing silence at the end of the trail—a silence so complete it sucked memories into its void like a black hole. Only people who had stood at Harmony Falls before the eruption could understand the horrible tranquility: the 100-foot waterfall itself was gone.

Its absent crash made you wince. Before the eruption, Harmony Falls was the largest waterfall at Spirit Lake—a waterfall that announced its presence in a distant *wshhhhhhhh* long before you actually set eyes on it. No doubt Harmony Falls was one of the reasons local tribes told stories of hearing waterfalls where there were none. Roaring down through the conifers, Harmony Creek surged in a wide wave over a high blue-black cliff, ran flat for a few feet, then surged again to the right over a smaller cliff into a broad, shallow pool before tumbling through a grove of cottonwoods into the lake. Mist from the crashing water rose like steam into the giant hemlocks and firs. Some of the tiny droplets also landed on eyelashes, cheeks, lips. Sometimes your eyes rested on a brown waterlogged branch or yellow monkeyflower, but mostly they were consumed by white water, black rock, and green moss. And as with all shapes of falling water, if you kept your eyes in one place, it was a stationary noun, a *waterfall*; but if you followed one particular splash from upper cliff to lower cliff to basin, Harmony Falls became a verb in the hillside—drifting, cresting, sprinkling, eddying, leaving you behind on the bridge.

When I first visited Harmony Falls I was nine years old, and there was no bridge. Hikers had to pick their way across if they wanted to continue along Trail 211. My father had brought Celeste, Elizabeth, and me on a "big" hike to the falls. More thirsty than tired, we cupped the water and drank it. Then I drew back from the tremendous boom. That it should *always* fall—that same huge sound winter and summer, day and night—disturbed me, but in a pleasant way. I was glad to know that it fell always. *Harmony Falls,* I thought to myself: *Does that mean that the falls are harmony, or that harmony is falling?*

Now there were no falls, no moss, no bridge. It seemed an odd honor to be the person to acquaint Laura with so much destruction. Other friends or family could just as well have accompanied her. But I was glad that she had asked me. Each time I had visited the blast zone I had thought of her. In fact, it was impossible for me to separate Laura Julia Bernard from Harmony Falls. Our friendship had begun as a product of a place, hovering there like the music we had once hummed under our breath as we worked.

Laura hired me to work at Harmony Falls Lodge because I had drawn a picture of the lake on the back of a letter I had written asking for a job. She usually hired cousins or friends, due to the close living quarters, but she risked hiring a stranger, she told me later, because she sensed we had something in common: the lake inked in black across the envelope's flap. When I arrived in early June, Laura hugged me on the boat dock as though we had always known each other, then escorted me to my bedroom above the lodge's dining hall and left me to get settled in. As I unpacked my things, her seven-year-old son Sam swung against the metal foot-board of my quilt-covered twin bed, chatting away, then dashed off in a red-headed blaze to show me his own room, next to mine. Before I left my narrow room with its small desk and plain wood chair, I gazed out its single window. Between the fir and cedar branches the lake stretched like a giant blue plateau, claiming every inch of window that wasn't first claimed by the green and gray of the trees. I sat down at the little desk facing the window and considered my own small square of blue. Then Sam's voice skipped through the wall. *Hey, come here, I want to show you something!*

Harmony Falls Lodge began as a mining camp owned by Henry Waldo Coe in the early 1900s. The miners ate their meals in a small lodge near the waterfall and rented cabins for their families. Vacationers also rented the cabins—that was how Laura's mother, Julia Schauffler Bernard, first visited the lake around 1930 at the age of five. She remembered the lodge as "very very dark." Among the coal-grained shadows the little girl was served a big slice of huckleberry pie. About the same time she had her first encounter with Jack Nelson, the energetic outdoorsman who ran the lodge for twenty-five years. The friendly storyteller regaled Laura's mother and other wide-eyed children with stories of the lake's great hairy apes as he sat beside a large campfire with a flashlight under his chin.

Nelson rebuilt Harmony Falls Lodge in the early 1930s and leased the six-acre waterfront property from Coe with the plan to operate a summer resort with his wife, Tressa, and her sister Ruby. Together the three of them made Harmony Falls into a one-of-a-kind rustic resort, with no cars, televisions, or phones. By the time Nelson died in the 1950s, he had made a name for himself as well as for the cedar-shingled lodge.

With its pitched roof, slatted windows, and gabled entryway framing a large, primitive front door, Harmony Falls Lodge was a handsome mountain inn. Constructed of local materials, the two-story lodge had sunk over the years into its soft pumice-humus slope like a comfortable, aging beast. Pummeled by winter storms and inhabited only in summer, the small wooden lodge was always one season away from being claimed by the forest. Each spring Laura and David spent long days cleaning chipmunk scat out of kitchen bins, soldering broken pipes, and replacing cracked windows. Steps creaked, floors sloped slightly, even the furniture carried the dust of decades long past. The paneled walls were taken from the forest; the front-door handle was a curved branch; the roof gathered fir cones and lichen; the foundation was made of stumps. The floor of the dining hall announced its stumpy underpinning: the tightly tied wood floor curved up and over each stump like a cotton cloth over a loaf of rising bread dough. If you dropped a pencil on the floor, it rolled for a while until it encountered the slope of another stump, then rolled back.

The wood cabins were similarly funky. Tucked into forested pockets around the lodge, the cedar-shaked cabins had gathered funny little names during the 1930s and 1940s: Eagle's Roost, Harmony Hums, Harmony Fails, Melody Hut, Paddle Inn, Shangri-La, Gov'ners Mansion, Tree Top, Malarkey, and Lookout. By the time I worked there, heavy snows, falling trees, and a fire had destroyed a few, and Laura's husband, David, had rebuilt two.

With his quiet air and long stride, David Berry seemed as though he had always belonged at Harmony Falls. David knew every kink and crack, as well as every kind of conifer that grew on the ridge. But his air of assurance was probably just the small daily joy of being alive; David had survived Vietnam. By the time I met him, he spoke of life in the army as a bad but distant dream, embracing the wild earth around the falls as his permanent home. His hands bore calluses from the axes and hammers he wielded to keep the place up and running. When he wasn't repairing something, he ferried guests across the lake as his predecessor Jack Nelson had done, cigarette and coffee mug in hand, although the boat had changed. Nelson had relied on two old, steel lifeboats, the *Tressa* and the *Ruby*. Of the two, the *Ruby* was still used and was freshly repainted in 1979. But Laura and David had invested in a smaller boat called the *Loon*, and it was mostly in this sturdy aluminum boat that David traversed the lake, the lapel of his wool jacket turned up against the lake's chill winds and his blond hair momentarily obscuring his blue-gray eyes.

David and Laura hired other workers to tackle the countless odd chores the resort business demanded. During the summer of 1979 we totaled five: Todd was David's right-hand man, reroofing cabins and cutting firewood; Mark "ran buckets," a euphemism for cleaning the outhouses; Lainie helped Laura maintain the lodge's reputation for homemade huckleberry pie and bread; and Alexcia and I worked as a team to clean cabins, set and wait tables, prepare salads, and wash dishes.

Alexcia and I began our day with mops, soap, and fresh rolls of toilet paper. Housekeeping was easy because each cabin had its own rustic character and view of the lake. Paddle Inn had a peacock-blue enamel cookstove and high ceiling. Shangri-La had two spacious floors, a central staircase, and yellow-cedar beams. Melody Hut was dark and tiny. My least favorite was Eagle's Roost, the only electric cabin. Vacationers staying at Eagle's Roost invariably brought hair dryers or electric razors that caused the lodge's primitive electrical system to overload. Generated by a Pelton wheel driven by the falls, the lodge's electricity stopped almost daily due to branches stuck in the wheel or a hair dryer surreptitiously plugged into Eagle Roost's wall. At night it wasn't a problem, since the Pelton wheel was shut off. Then, kerosene lamps were lit, casting flying shadows along the lodge's dark-wood walls.

As we cleaned cabins and washed dishes, I came to the conclusion that Alexcia was one of the most exotic people I had ever met.

Only a couple of years older than me, she had already thrown away
her birth name for the name Alexcia and had smoked so much mar-
ijuana she'd renounced it completely. If that wasn't exotic enough,
she was from a faraway state called Missouri and was an accom-
plished spelunker. In one cave, she told us, her group had come
upon the skeleton of a saber-toothed tiger. Soft-spoken with long
sandy hair and glasses, she reminded me of a forest faerie, someone
who might vanish at the drop of a leaf. In fact, she did just that
soon after the eruption. The last time I saw Alexcia was in Portland
around 1982. She had become a survivalist and was planning to
move to Seattle, where her group was preparing for World War III.

Todd, too, slipped out of my life, along with the oatmeal-brown
sweater he wore early mornings as he ferried departing guests across
the lake. Lost to the eruption, the thick-spun sweater smelled of
woodsmoke and wool. He wore it on cold nights as we sat together
on the diving tower, talking late into the evening about incidental
things. By the end of the summer, rooms changed hues depending
on whether he strolled into them. We remained together for three
years, traveling to Montana a month after the eruption to work in
Glacier National Park. There, we hoped, no news of Mount St.
Helens would reach us. Eventually I left for France, and though
Todd with his enduring sense of humor tried to lure me back with
baguettes and Brie, I stayed abroad until he grew tired of waiting.

In the same way that Todd and Alexcia were more than just co-
workers to me, Laura was more of a sister than a boss. Laura and I
had attended the same high school and were fond of the same
books. Laura played the guitar; I played the piano. Even more fortuitous was the fact that she and David had lugged a secondhand
piano from the Longview Goodwill all the way across the lake. It
was an old, dilapidated upright that hugged a back wall of the
lodge's dark lobby. With several ivories missing and a G note below

middle C that wouldn't play, it was a tired, out-of-tune creature, cowering under the staircase that led to the crew's bedrooms. But by the end of the summer I no longer noticed its infirmities. Perhaps it was Laura's guitar that camouflaged the discordance, or her smoky-nightclub voice singing *Wrap your arms around me like a circle round the sun.* Most evenings the two of us would harmonize on old blues and folk songs while uphill, behind the lodge, the waterfall crashed its own harmony in the dark. As I learned during the lodge's annual Malarkey Week in August, we were part of a tradition that went back decades. The corporation of Portland families that had bought Harmony Falls Lodge after Nelson died was loaded with singers, strummers, hand-clappers, foot-stompers, and hummers.

It came as no surprise to me that Laura would describe our mutual disbelief at the lodge's destruction in musical terms. "Crayteeana," her voice sang cheerfully through the phone, "I'll believe the lodge is gone when I see that old piano come floating across the lake!"

A few days after the eruption a pilot who knew David and Laura flew over Spirit Lake and saw something floating in the water. It was the lodge's white propane tank, caught among the logs like a bloated corpse.

Along with the lodge went the rest of Laura's life. Within a year of the eruption her marriage collapsed in a heap like the volcano itself. I sat open-mouthed over a cup of coffee at the Otis Cafe near Neskowin when she announced that she was leaving David. "You can't leave David," I stammered, more to preserve the few crumbs I had left of Spirit Lake's permanence than out of concern for her. But within months Laura had packed up and moved from her winter home on the Oregon coast to Seattle, where she found a job waitressing near Pike Place Market. One night she and her two young sons camped outside in the backyard of her tiny house in the middle of the city. "Listen to that! You can hear the ocean from here!" Sam said. "No!" Dylan, said, "It's the waterfall!" Laura lacked the courage to tell them it was the white noise of the freeway. "Yeah," she said. "Isn't it beautiful."

Our own friendship ebbed when I graduated from college and moved to France. We sent occasional letters but rarely saw one another. During that time, we both ricocheted from one relationship to another, trying on men like so many different pairs of shoes. After a few years on her own, she remarried, and things seemed lively, at least from the way she described them in letters. But then one sunny Sunday in 1986 I called Todd from a phone booth in Paris and learned that Laura had experienced a nervous breakdown. It was as though the mountain had erupted again, spewing ash across the Atlantic. I stepped out of the phone booth onto a crowded boulevard and wiped the tears away with my sleeve. Laura hospitalized? It didn't make sense. I was the moody one, the dark-dressed expatriate afraid of going insane. Laura was the strong one, the one who could slaughter a chicken if she had to and bleed it dry.

That summer I flew home for a month and visited Laura in Seattle. She had spent eight weeks in the hospital and was managing fairly well without medication. The doctors had prescribed antidepressants but she had refused to take them. "No way were they going to keep me on that stuff," she told me one evening from across a restaurant table where we toasted our friendship over a bottle of champagne. "Who wants to live without emotion?"

As we kept in touch over the next few years, Laura seemed to recover in the same hardy way pearly everlasting was reclaiming the mountain. At the time of our blast zone trip she had met a dark-haired man named Michael whose children were also grown and who loved the waters of Puget Sound.

We chose a weekend in September for our reunion. With Laura driving south from Seattle, we met several miles north and west of Spirit Lake, at the junction of Interstate 5 and Highway 12, where she had parked her 1973 green pick-up truck. In an empty parking lot she opened the truck's canopy to show me where she had stashed enough food and firewood for a cross-continent journey, not to mention her smiling chocolate labrador, Java, whose entire back half was lost in a fierce wag. We drove in morning sun along the clearcut-ravaged Cowlitz River valley north of Spirit Lake to Iron Creek Campground on the Cispus River. In a small grove of old-growth firs we reserved a campsite for the night and parked the Lizard, as Laura called her truck. Then we drove in my mother's small car up Highway 26, which entered the blast zone from the north. I knew the curvy road would end at a panorama of acres of standing dead trees untouched by logging operations. I had planned the trip so that those hills would be the first thing Laura would see of the blast zone: the distant snags' prickly-gray fur.

As we drove south through the Quartz Creek valley, the one-lane road curled through thick stands of old-growth and second-growth firs. We climbed slowly through delicious green shade flickering with robin-sized birds—varied thrushes. I had grown fond of them over the course of my blast zone hikes and considered their presence a good omen. As the car made one final turn around a moss-covered cliff, I smiled across the seat at Laura. "Here we are," I said. "Welcome to the blast zone."

I expected her to be full of *ooohs* and *aaahs*. Instead she sat quietly, gazing at the acres of silver snags.

"Explain to me where we are," she said. "I don't know where I am."

"You're in an area you probably never explored before the eruption," I told her. "This would be the distant backcountry, accessible by horse or maybe a logging road." We were at the northern edge of the blast zone, still roughly an hour's drive from Spirit Lake and its familiar ridges.

We stopped at Ryan Lake for lunch. While Laura pulled out two submarine sandwiches from her neighborhood deli, I laid out my blast zone map. As we ate the sandwiches, I tried to explain the blast zone's varying degrees of alteration: the scorch zone, the blow-down zone, and the lake. The map meant almost nothing to Laura, who was taking it all in by sight, scanning Ryan Lake for signs of life. Its surface disturbed by a single coot, the flat blue pool was ringed by a riot of logs. The tangled, dead trees lay everywhere, from the distant hills to our feet. Fireweed rose like pink vapors from the prostrate timber, releasing its white-plumed seeds on the wind. Swallows swung above. Laura sat, silent. Then she looked at the map again.

"How come it just says 'Harmony' there?" she asked, pointing to the little Forest Service icon designating a viewpoint. "Why doesn't it say 'Harmony Falls'?"

"Well, the Forest Service renamed it," I answered.

"Why?"

I was sideswiped by her unfamiliarity with the blast zone's scale of change. I had to remind myself that fifteen summers had passed since Laura had set foot at Spirit Lake.

"Well you know, Laura, the falls are gone."

She rolled her eyes. "They could have at least kept the name."

We continued to Meta Lake and the Miners' rusted car, an old sedan that had been destroyed by the eruption. There, Laura first noticed the number of vehicles on the road. "What are all these people doing here?" she asked. I explained that it was an ordinary day at the Mount St. Helens National Volcanic Monument, which now attracted 4 million tourists annually.

"Everybody out of my room!" she mock-shouted in a soft laugh to passersby toting cameras toward the fenced-in car. I had experienced the same sort of territorial response. What had seemed so personal before the eruption was now wide open and public.

We could have stopped at several more places, but I drove on straight to Harmony, or Harmony Falls, as Laura wanted to call it. *Might as well get it over with,* I thought. We pulled up to the rock wall lining the little parking lot and hopped out of the car. I expected Laura to become sad immediately, but instead she mumbled the same thing I did when I first saw Spirit Lake after the eruption.

"I have no idea where I am," she said, smiling her quintessential smile. "I don't know what I'm looking at."

"That's the Dome there, in the backcountry, straight across the lake to the west," I tried to explain. "And there's the lake below. It doesn't look like the lake because of the logs, but that's water, not land, below us."

She still didn't know where she was. Like most pre-eruption residents, the only way she had ever visited Spirit Lake was by Highway 504, from the west, but here we were arriving from the east. I tried to orient her in reference to the lodge. "We're on the ridge way up behind the falls," I said. "The ridge that makes up the east side of the lake basin, where the old 100 Road ran." But we might as well have been on Mars for all that Laura's face told. It was an expression I had never seen—not in the face of her divorce or any other obstacle she had encountered during what she called her "volcanic years." She looked as though someone had just told her a joke that wasn't funny, and she was searching for its humor.

With Java tugging at her leash, we started down the Harmony Trail as the afternoon sun bleached the log raft white on the lake below. I pointed out Harmony Creek's green ribbon on our right, winding its way down to the mud-flattened basin. On our left, wildflowers that had been protected by the ridge during the eruption were finishing blooming. Alders lined the trail like a bushy wall. About a quarter of a mile down we stopped beneath a cliff dripping with springwater. The cliff reminded me of the little grotto I used to visit above the lodge. Nowhere else along the Harmony Trail did the vegetation so resemble the former forest floor. This earth was, in fact, a moist vestige of the original forest. Moss and algae hung off the wet, black walls. Ferns flourished. Cool air emanated from the seep like a refrigerator door opened in a desert. Laura took off her baseball cap and tilted her head toward the necklace of falling droplets. Then she opened her mouth, letting the water trickle down the sides of her jaw.

"Delicious," she said, as she wiped her eyes and brushed away her long brown hair. "Aren't you going to try some, Crayteeana?" I placed my forehead under the trickle and let the water pool in my mouth before swallowing. The icy thread was as cold as I remembered the falls to be.

We followed the trail down the ridge and across the barren plain known as the Harmony Basin. No plants were growing in the ash-filled valley, except for an occasional tuft of pearly everlasting or willow. The basin was also devoid of logs. The monstrous wave of May 18 had pushed the falling trees of the forest flat against the ridge, or yanked them into the lake as it returned.

We reached the shore, where the log raft bumped against the mouth of Harmony Creek. The tumbling creek had poked a hole in the raft by swirling the logs outward as it entered the lake. Behind us, higher up, the creek splashed over pale-peach boulders, filling little pools and feeding a chartreuse moss that brightened the rocks. Yellow monkeyflowers waved in the breeze near the creek's lush banks.

"Look, there's part of the falls!" Laura exclaimed.

"No, Laura, we're too high up for that to be even the top of the falls."

"But there's a little waterfall there."

To help orient Laura we concentrated on the lake itself, where the Mount Margaret backcountry still sat with its pre-eruption topography. At least those peaks hadn't been rearranged. But the lake was so different only certain views reminded Laura of sitting on the lodge's dock, with its postcard view. She recognized the base of the mountain, and the ridge to its left where lightning had struck in the first part of the century. That ridge was now named Windy. But the distance to the south shore seemed endless, and even the stretch we once swam from Harmony to the Boy Scout camp looked unbelievably far. Before the eruption it was roughly a mile, now it seemed like two. I relived the same overwhelming sense of submergence Celeste and I had experienced at the south shore three months earlier. The lake was like a continual dream of drowning.

We sat for an hour on Harmony's new pumice beach—a small flat area at the end of the trail. The sun warmed our faces the same way it had all those afternoons we had sunbathed on the diving tower. Hikers came down the trail, then departed, like other hikers who had visited the lodge on warm afternoons. A strong breeze came off the lake and ruffled our T-shirts. "A familiar wind," Laura said, recognizing it as the same one that blew years ago while the crew sipped cocktails before dinner.

So the sun and wind hadn't changed. But I thought of the strange light that had once existed on this side of the lake. I had experienced it in only a few places since the eruption. I called it "liquid light" because it was light that moved like water. It occurred each afternoon at Harmony Falls as the sun traveled west over the lake. The slanted rays struck Spirit Lake's surface, then bounced off the water at an angle to illuminate the undersides of the conifers' branches, backlighting them with the lake's watery reflection. When the wind churned up the lake or an otter swam near the shore, the liquid light rippled on the underside of each bough. That the branches were moving was just an illusion: it was only the reflected sunlight trilling upon the shaded green.

Liquid light was not unique to Harmony Falls. Any shady branch along a body of water is subject to such a phenomenon if the angle of the sun is right. Usually, light is refracted in water, making it blue or green depending on which wavelengths are absorbed. But when light falls at a particular angle—the "critical angle of reflection," according to scientists—it is bounced off the water's surface rather than absorbed. At Harmony Falls, bright white light was reflected off the lake every sunny afternoon of summer and was thrown into the trees like mist. The result was an extravagance of water-light, an overabundance of blacklit boughs. Perhaps residents subjected to the aurora borealis yawn in the face of such repetitive drama; liquid light at Harmony Falls was one such extraordinary, everyday thing.

Today, no fluttering light occurred for one simple reason: the trees were in the wrong place. They now made up the giant raft that littered the lake, and they absorbed the sunlight before it could strike the water's surface. And even on those few days when the raft was far away, floating in the lake's west arm, still no liquid light would be found on the eastern shore: there was no standing forest to catch the reflected rays and let them dance on its dark palette of branches.

As Laura sat in silence, I scanned the lake for signs of fish. The last time I had hiked the Harmony Trail I had been dumbfounded by the silver semicircle of trout flashing out of the lake. I had stood open-mouthed at the sight, since Spirit Lake's stocked trout had been cooked by the eruption. I later learned that some wild rainbow trout had mysteriously worked their way into the lake. There were suspicions that someone had illegally dumped the fish, but the Washington State Department of Fish and Wildlife tested the genes of two fish and announced that they were indeed wild and had probably made their way naturally into the lake. Soon afterwards the department closed the lake to fishing. I was glad to hear of the closure, since not only did I hope the trout would attract other fishers, such as otters and herons, but it seemed that recreational activities like fishing, boating, and swimming no longer belonged at Spirit Lake. The volcano had shown us that it wanted the lake for its own.

"Man was only borrowing a little time up here," Laura said. "I always felt that I was being allowed by the grace of God to be at this lake. The mountain was just claiming back her territory. I know what it means to self-destruct and start over. Sometimes you have to blow up to save yourself. I'm proud of the mountain for refusing to allow the encroachment that was happening up here, the logging and everything. She took it all back."

The sun was dropping over the Toutle River valley as we started up the trail. With the wind pushing at our backs we talked about the lake's vanished community, its camps and lodges, and the people we knew. Laura asked about Jim Lund. I told her that I had visited him in the desert.

"Does he still have that jade tooth?" she wanted to know. "He used to take out that old jade tooth and show it to me," she laughed. I told her how I would have liked to have met Jack Nelson, and Ruby, whose name I had painted that summer in red letters on the hull of the old lifeboat. It seemed to me that so many people who knew a lake even more wild than the one we knew were gone: Retlaw Haynes, whose family's cabin had preceded the campground; Franz Nilsson, who had been fond of the alpine wildflowers and ptarmigans; Lige Coalman, the mountaineer; Laura's great-grandmother, who had tied up her skirt in front of her as she stooped over the lake to catch tiny trout in a milk bottle for Laura's mother, then five years old. These, too, were the wild souls wandering Spirit Lake.

I thought of other spirits haunting the lake—the two people Laura and I never became because of an eruption. The crew had already been lined up for the summer of 1980, and I had planned to return. Would we have become better friends than we were? Would Laura have divorced David? Even she once admitted that their marriage had worked in some way at Harmony but not beyond it. And what would have become of me? At seventeen I had plans to make Spirit Lake my permanent home after I graduated from high school. How would I have gotten by? Perhaps I would not have gone to France or even college. But it never happened, never could have happened, although it seemed easy to fill up that parallel life with details, a plot, even a conclusion. It was as though I possessed yet another twin—not better, not worse, just untried, unlived. She was my own private lake ghost, treading the years 200 feet down, playing an old upright piano with missing keys.

As Laura and I talked about the volcanic roller coaster we'd both ridden, I asked her if she had ever dreamed of Spirit Lake. "Plenty of times," she answered.

I stared at her. "What sort of dreams?"

Like Celeste, Laura had experienced nightmares like mine. However, unlike my recurring dreams, which wandered all over the lake, Laura's dreams always took place at Harmony Falls, and she dreamed of the eruption itself—trees on fire, buildings collapsing, her own voice screaming, *get out!* In other dreams, everything blurred in slow motion as the mountain began to erupt. In those dreams, too, she heard her own voice screaming to people to leave. That was when I realized that Laura, Celeste, and I had probably suffered some sort of post-traumatic stress disorder. If so, we had suffered through the same illness at the same time, unaware.

From what I had learned regarding the psychological effects of the eruption, we weren't alone. Sleep disturbances, depression, even a man who hijacked a bus near Portland—all had been documented as human responses to the volcano. In a study begun in 1981, psychiatrists found that survivors of the 1980 eruption suffered from three distinct disorders—generalized anxiety, major depression, and post-traumatic stress—which the researchers collectively called the Mount St. Helens Disorders. The psychiatrists interviewed 1,000 people and determined that those who experienced major residence damage, a loss of $5,000 or more, or a death in the family due to the eruption were eleven times more likely to suffer from the disorders than members of a control group unaffected by the eruption. The disorders included several symptoms: shakiness, sweating, racing heart, loss of appetite, insomnia, survivor guilt, recurrent nightmares, and thoughts of death. Women were particularly susceptible: twice as many women in the "high exposure" group displayed symptoms as men.

We returned to the car. I decided to head for Bear Meadow, a few miles northeast, where Laura would see a different edge of the blast zone before the sun went down. We swung in and out of hairpin turns swoozier than swells on the Pacific. Snags lined the right side of the road. As we looked about, a tiny bird darted from out of nowhere, sweeping past the windshield. Its feathers glowed so brightly it looked like a flying blue lightbulb.

"What was that?" Laura gasped, as if she had seen a ghost.

"A mountain bluebird," I answered. "The first I've ever seen."

We paused briefly at Bear Meadow, haunted by the unearthly blue of the little bird's wings. The crater steamed in the distance. I had just enough time to show Laura one last place—a pumice-powdered grove just outside the blast zone that smelled and looked like Spirit Lake's old forest. A creek ran through it, and there were three cedars on a hill there that cast a single shadow if the light was right. We were too late to experience the shadow, but I wanted Laura to walk among the huckleberries anyway. I wanted her to re-enter Harmony just one more time, through a different door.

We stopped the car, got out, and stepped into the trail-less forest among ripe huckleberries. The cool air smelled of moss and earth and firs. Our shoes pressed silently against dead needles and pumice. We strolled a short distance until we were out of sight of the road.

A long high whistle broke over the cedars and firs. Then another, even higher. "Varied thrush," I whispered to Laura, whose eyes scanned the tops of the trees. Yet another call trilled among the boughs like the ascending notes of a flute. Was that the call of a hermit thrush? A birding acquaintance had told me about them. Hermit thrushes were one of his favorite birds because of their intricate calls. I looked for the singer but could discern nothing in the deepening dusk. But the dueling music drifted over our heads, as though the birds were right above. Long note. High. And then the other's dizzying escalation—like watery notes as a small glass filled.

We headed back to Iron Creek Campground, where that night Laura would break out her guitar, and the two of us would sip red wine and sing and fall asleep under the stars as the Cispus River shushed along. Laura would share a new song with me, a ballad she had discovered by folksinger Phil Ochs, a Greenwich Village anti-war hero who committed suicide in 1976. Entitled "Changes," the song lilted along for several verses, including one that stayed with me for days:

The world's spinning madly,
it drifts in the dark,
swings through a hollow of haze,
a race around the stars,
a journey through the universe ablaze
with changes.

Even as we pulled into the campground Laura must have had the song in her mind as a gift she would present after making dinner. As the dusk turned to darkness, the car rolled quietly among the 200-foot-tall trees. Laura tried in the failing light to catch up with the day's events. For all that she had seen, she couldn't forget the neon blue of that solitary mountain bluebird. She gazed out the passenger window, perhaps hoping to see it again.

"I wonder what I will dream of now," she said.

Windy Ridge

In the House of Blue Water,
There I enter.

—Navajo night chant

I t was windy as hell and cold the evening I sat alone on
one of Windy Ridge's west-facing humps, high above the
new Duck Bay. A few days had passed since my trip with
Laura, and other visitors had departed with the rain. On my left,
a solid wall of thunderheads descended over the crater. On my
right, the backcountry was lost in fog. The lake alone escaped the
low storm.

Anchored like a solitary stump, I let the wind push against my
face and shoulders. It was a duel of no consequence, a tug-of-war
the wind would eventually win, but still I leaned into the gusts as
the storm closed in. It was a pleasant resistance, fighting the wind

the same way I had fought for years an old stubborn feeling: the sense that Spirit Lake had abandoned me.

What a notion, I thought, to be abandoned by a place. It was the mobile animal that abandoned a place, not vice versa. And yet even at that moment I felt that the lake had failed me, rolled up its tents and—poof! But no, there it was below, sprawling in lead-gray gaps between the storm-pushed clouds.

How like the lake to be the thing existing *between* the nomad clouds. Spirit Lake was what remained between Loowit's eruptions: it was the suspended moment between the volcano's violent events; the watery consequence; the fluid afterthought; the lull. It was here before and would remain tomorrow, a lying chimera. If I fell in love with this scene now it would disappear next year. If I fell in love with clear water it would turn black. If I accepted black water it would run clear again. Spooky lake! Lake of smoke and mirrors— to disappear and stay in one place!

A black bird lifted off from a snag far below me. It was a raven, swinging out over what was once Donnybrook Campground, or maybe Cedar Creek. With such vast changes caused by the eruption, I could only approximate. But why would it matter? This was not a landscape of certainty. People who fell in love with Spirit Lake fell in love with uncertainty—the land not as a period but as a question mark, a riddle, a query from the belly of the earth. A volcano like Loowit was nothing but a collection of secrets. Was it dormant or extinct? If dormant, when would it erupt again? How large an eruption? Which way? How many dead?

But it was the lake, not the volcano, that had first taught me such uncertainty. From the time I was seven I had dreamed of returning to Spirit Lake each summer, asking myself each winter *when?* It was this lake that had first taught me the adult art of remembering and the practice of desire—how to sketch the outline of a beloved thing when it was absent, how to gather it in my arms though it was air. I grew old beyond my years for the love of this lake, swamped by too much beauty too early in life, water that was too clear.

As I sat on the rain-pocked log the raven circled back, flapping downslope. My eyes followed its arrowlike course, then fell on the portion of lake behind its wings. It was an island—a tiny, log-ringed island I had never seen before. Was it part of some high ground that had escaped inundation? Or the tip of one of the many mud and pyroclastic flows that had buried Duck Bay?

It was far away, maybe 700 feet down—but I found myself drawn to it like a hawk plunging for a vole. I wanted to scramble down and crash into the water to reach its perfectly round shape. The impulse seemed strange. Why dive into Spirit Lake from such a height? Why swim in this lake at all? It was windy, cold, and cloudy. Who would want to dive into this lake in the rain?

And yet I could not stop wishing I could swim to the little island. I imagined climbing over its logs, standing in its middle, hugging my ribs to fight off the cold. Its center suddenly seemed to be the center of the great loneliness of the blast zone—the reason I could never be a tourist passing through. If I could reach the island, I thought, perhaps I could plunge the knife through the heart of my loss. Maybe I would drown.

But who would want to die in Spirit Lake? Even in the worst of my nightmares I did not die by drowning in the lake.

No, it was a matter of ashes. As I sat above Duck Bay in the wind I realized that I wanted to have my ashes scattered over the lake. It was not a death wish but a longing for communion—a desire to be a part of the land indefinitely, like the raven.

Because that little log-ringed island down there was green, green, green.

Everlasting: Autumn

Damp winds, burst pods, rusted sedges, black wood: autumn has come to the blast zone. The tiny, yellow lights at the center of each pearly everlasting blossom have been extinguished; the dingy bracts now cup a dark-brown core. Rain has glued the blooms together. No seeds will float from those tight beads today. And even as the flowerheads droop in gummy clumps the plants are dying upright, stiffening into dirty skeletons, losing the green in their leaves the way the stems first rose—from the ground up.

The bracts, too, have died the way they first appeared: closed, hugging each other. Water compels them so. The bracts fold for wetness, then open for sun. If time-lapsed photography recorded an everlasting blossom over several days, it would show a flower-head that opened and closed its bracts the same way humans flap back and forth doing jumping jacks. Botanists refer to these kinds of plant actions as turgor movements. They occur when the pressure in plant cells changes, causing the rise or fall of leaves or stems so that plants can maximize photosynthesis, protect their leaves from drying out, and reduce friction in high wind. Turgor movements occur in plants such as oxalis or lupine, whose leaves open and shut dramatically. For pearly everlasting, it is the tiny bracts that move to protect the seeds in rain and warm the flower-head in sun. In this way the flowers keep themselves warm for pollinators, who would rather visit a cozy hearth than a cold one. It is only when the seeds have all flown that the bracts open flat out—and for good.

The everlasting blossoms at my boots have yet to release their seeds. They are senescent—on the verge of dispersal. Although it has a moribund meaning for humans, senescence is a grand moment for the vegetable world—the moment before yellow leaves fall or ripe fruit drops. For pearly everlasting, a late-summer bloomer, it signifies the heart of autumn. Like goldenrod and other "short-day" plants, pearly everlasting blooms when nights are lengthening and days are shortening; they actually require a certain amount of darkness to induce them to flower. So while humans are counting sheep, pearly everlasting plants are also

*counting the night hours, ticking away the trail of the moon in
so many future blooms. It is no small matter: scientists who experi-
mented with short-day plants by shining light on them in the
middle of the night discovered that they had actually blocked
the flowers' ability to bloom.*

*Here, there is no shortage of lengthening nights—the rain
glistens on hundreds of dun-colored beads. The flowers look like
shadows of their summer selves—smaller, darker, edged with a
black mold. How different from late June, when the center seeds
didn't show and all that could be seen were the tiny white bracts;
or July, when the seeds' plumes protruded slightly, beaming a slight
chartreuse; or August, when the center plumes had deepened to
mustard and the bracts had dimmed to cream. Then, as autumn
seeped in, the plumes darkened to musty brown. And now mold
has blackened the crevices between bracts, so that they look like
wet crevasses in miniature, with black basalt in the cracks below.*

*From here in the Clearwater valley east of Spirit Lake, I spy
Loowit blooming between the trees with a fresh layer of snow.
For a moment the mountain shines white across the dark, wet
valley, then is lost in a luminous low fog. A peek-a-boo peak that
opens and closes like pearly everlasting in this autumn weather:
Here! Gone! Here again!*

Celeste rouses me with a question, What was that bird?! *A
flicker—no three, four, a whole family. They flash their white
rumps and flee as though we were hunters. But we have chosen
one of the few logging roads not marked today by four-wheel-drive
tread. It is our chance to see the snow-free forest floor before we
head up to Elk Pass at 4,000 feet elevation, where we expect snow.
Our destination is the backcountry, but an early autumn storm has
already foretold the weather that wants to close upon the land. We
swim through mist, anticipate showers, lose the treetops to clouds.*

*Family members think us hare-brained to travel to the moun-
tain today:* Wash-outs! Landslides! Ice! You won't see a thing, *they
say. But how can we not visit this place in the rain, when the Spirit
Lake we knew before the eruption was such a rainy place? Besides,*

*what we are deprived of in vistas we gain in the ground close up:
one cannot look up or out, so the view is down—at a damp earth
on fire. Trunks and twigs that were dusty and gray under the
summer sun are transformed to wet coal. On one black log, flabby
flames of witch's-butter fungi glow like bright-orange jelly. On a
grove of wet firs, Iceland-moss lichen bleaches the black bark
white. Across the clearcut in front of us, patches of huckleberry
burn a translucent burgundy. We stop in front of one leafless bush.
Shriveled berries hang from the branches, others lie scattered on
the ground, untouched by any bear, chipmunk or human. Celeste
plucks one berry and bites it in half. "Vinegarish," she scowls. But
the berries are one more bauble in a landscape of baubles. Everywhere are withered strings of stems, rags of different-colored
lichens, hemlock cones, toadstools, fertile peas wintering in each
lupine's long pod. The cloud-swaddled land has shrunk to the
size of a trinket. I pick up one such trinket the size of my thumb—
a pumice stone heavy with water.*

*So this is how the volcano marks its territory on cloudy days—in
miniature ways, the way a cougar marks its hunting grounds with
urine and scat. No mistaking who owns the forests and clearcuts
here, only a few miles from where Gary Rosenquist shot his famous
eruption photographs and then ran for his life. We are walking
through Loowit's backyard, where more than rain and snow falls
from the sky. The pumice stones scattered under my boots look like
so many pearly beads—how a volcano loves trinkets!*

Several Pacific coast tribes appreciated trinkets. In Chinook
jargon they were called hiaqua and included Pacific Coast shells
that were used as currency. According to early accounts, hiaqua
were highly prized. One legend, told to Theodore Winthrop, author
of Canoe and the Saddle, *tells of a young, greedy Indian who
wanted all the hiaqua on top of Mount Rainier for himself. He
climbed to the mountain's summit, where an enormous pile of
hiaqua lay, and ornamented himself with beads and shells. However, the mountain spirits became angered by his greed and punished him by casting him into a deep sleep from which he awoke*

an old man. Too weak to carry the hiaqua he had hoarded, he walked back to his village to find his faithful wife waiting for him. Hiaqua no longer mattered.

Pumice is not a gentle form of hiaqua. No tide-smooth shell soft to your palm, it is the product of frothy magma—molten, whirling rock—rupturing under extreme heat and high-pressure gas. Pumice is produced when magma boils to the surface of the earth and explodes to meet the open air. The concentrated gases rush out from the smelted rock as it cools, leaving traces of their escape routes behind in the hardening froth. That is why pumice floats: it traps air.

I once hoarded a piece of pumice from Spirit Lake. I had gathered the stone, about the size of a goose egg, several years before the eruption and had kept it next to some dried everlasting flowers on my bedroom bookshelf. When the mountain erupted, I turned the stone over in my hand to reassure myself that I still belonged in some way at Spirit Lake and that it still belonged to me. Then, in what seems like a bizarre incident to me now, I gave the stone away. Four years after the eruption, almost to the day, I handed it over to a famous French intellectual who had arrived from Paris to spend a few days at Portland State University, where I was finishing my undergraduate degree. I had driven to the Portland airport with my French professor and a small group of classmates to welcome the prestigious author. We each had a gift to welcome her. Because her name faintly resembled the mountain's, I had decided that my pumice stone was just the gift to impress her. So when she entered the terminal, towering above us in a white fur coat, I handed her the rock and stepped back, head down, mumbling clumsily in French that it was from the volcano. She appeared neither pleased nor displeased. The other gifts were then handed to her. Perhaps they were books? I no longer remember because from the moment the stone left my hand I wanted it back. But what could be worse, offering an old gray rock to a famous person as a gift—or asking for it back?

Now I no longer want it back. I see it for what it was: something I never owned. A few months later, I received a scholarship and left for France with a new suitcase and $500 I had saved from a job shelving library books. The dried everlasting was lost in the move.

Today I surrender the rain-soaked pumice in my hand to the weight of its water. It drops back to earth, and I move on, knowing it is best to travel light into the backcountry.

THE BACKCOUNTRY

Coldwater

The winds carry strange smells;
this is a day of change.

—Chinook Psalter

The first place Celeste and I wanted to visit in Spirit Lake's backcountry—the high country directly north of the lake—was a small, round lake named St. Helens Lake. The name was fixed on maps as early as 1912 but failed to describe the deep, cold body of water that peered like an aquamarine eye from out of its forested socket. At 4,567 feet elevation, St. Helens Lake sat less than two miles and more than 1,000 feet above Bear Cove. Its icy drainage tumbled down Spirit's steep northwestern ridge to form one of the tributaries of Bear Creek. As a common day-hike destination, the lake was our earliest memory of the Mount Margaret backcountry, a mysterious region we had only just begun to explore before the eruption. We had hiked to the lake frequently as children, and Celeste had camped on its shore under a full moon the summer before the eruption. She had photographed a mountain goat there in a meadow of paintbrush and lupine, and the picture was so dramatic it made the front, color pages of our high school yearbook. Ironically, the yearbook was issued the same month the volcano vaporized the backcountry's mountain goats and buried its wildflower meadows in ash. Since then, neither of us had seen the high mountain lake, perched like an entrance to the rugged, panoramic ridges that formed the backcountry.

The Mount Margaret backcountry was named around the turn of the century after its highest peak, Mount Margaret, which was itself named after an early settler's sweetheart. In 1979 the subalpine region had yet to be spoiled by rampant recreational use or logging and was on the verge of being designated a national wilderness area. Now, after the eruption, it seemed even more remote. Few trails had been reblazed into it, and except for the few hardy souls who returned to see what it looked like post-eruption, hardly anyone hiked there.

Before the eruption two trails accessed St. Helens Lake, but neither survived. Instead, two new trails had been completed when we began our hike in September 1994, not long after my trip with Laura. The Lakes Trail 211—originally on Spirit Lake's east side before the eruption—now hugs the western shore of Coldwater Lake and joins Trail 230, a long winding path that junctions with the Boundary Trail, to St. Helens Lake. It was a circuitous journey, roughly twenty miles over a period of two short days, and the trails were so new that there were no good topo maps plotting their exact location. In addition, the fall hunting season was about to start, and the trails crossed a popular elk- and deer-hunting area. Our parents solved the latter concern by surprising us with two neon-orange hunting caps. Ill-fitting and clownish, the wool caps nonetheless kept us from being mistaken for deer. A public school teacher, Celeste joked that we might be mistaken for gang members and shot at anyway.

We donned the caps along with our packs and started down the Elk Bench Trail from Coldwater Ridge, four miles west of Spirit Lake. A warm September sun illuminated the wind-chipped Coldwater Lake below us, making each wave twinkle. Pearly everlasting bordered the dusty path in cottony heaps, along with thistles and false-dandelion. We strode past smiling day hikers as we zigzagged down to the lake, then left them behind as the trail continued another five miles along Coldwater Lake's western shore. I hunted for signs of vegetation on the brown hillside, which had been clearcut before the eruption. Few forest species besides Oregon grape and bunchberry dogwood were thriving in the dry ground. Salmonberry vines, their fruit eaten or dried weeks earlier, trailed over rocks. After a while we entered a moist, shady stretch of twenty-foot-tall cottonwoods, their green leaves fluttering. There, ferns and mosses had sprung up in the shadows. As we emerged, the sun warmed the backs of our legs again, and our mouths tasted of trail dust. Everywhere grasses swung about in a fierce wind.

After two hours or so we reached Coldwater Creek, the stream for which the lake had been named. The iron-rich water threaded its way down the valley like orange yarn. Its rusty banks glowed from the oxidized mineral. I wondered if that was why one 1897 map had labeled the area Goldwater instead of Coldwater. It no longer mattered, since the water could be described as both cold *and* gold, and since 1912 the name Coldwater had become set in stone, so to speak, with the adjacent ridge also gathering the epithet, as well as Coldwater Peak, elevation 5,727 feet. The peak lay between us and St. Helens Lake like a craggy hurdle we would have to sidestep, although for the moment the only thing Celeste hurried to sidestep was a northwestern garter snake that had slithered underfoot. Its two yellow stripes disappeared in a tangle of horsetails.

Cattails crowded the lake's marshy northern shore, where the creek had deposited large mounds of ash from the surrounding slopes to create a mudflat. Celeste spotted her fourth tree frog while my eyes fell on a fiery vine maple. Flying grasshoppers clacked and fluttered around us, landing on prehistoric volcanic boulders that shone like oversized peaches in the late-afternoon light. The valley had once been part of a shield volcano hundreds of thousands of years ago. Volcanism had been shaping the area for millennia and continued during our lifetime with the lake itself; Coldwater Lake was a volcano-dammed valley, like Spirit. The lake was formed in 1980 when the exploding mountain roared over the Spillover into the valley's southern end, blocking Coldwater Creek's outlet into the Toutle River. Rainfall, creekwater, and snowmelt had accumulated quickly in the valley to create a lake that was now 186 feet deep— as deep as Spirit. Celeste noticed that Coldwater lacked Spirit's white-pumice beaches. Instead, its volcanic ash created a comfortable sandy shore.

As striking as the newly created lake was, I was dismayed by how quickly humans had altered it. Shortly after the eruption, the U.S. Army Corps of Engineers bulldozed an artificial drainage for both Coldwater Lake and Castle Lake, another post-eruption lake, because it appeared that the two lakes could breach their natural dams and flood the Toutle River valley. And like Coldwater Ridge, with its $10 million visitor center, the lake had been "improved" for recreation, with paved parking lots, a boat ramp, bathrooms, picnic tables, and walkways. Even the water itself had been altered when it had been stocked with rainbow trout, much to the disappointment of scientists studying its volcanic chemistry.

Twilight caught us far beyond the lake, at the valley's northern tip, where Trail 211 crossed Coldwater Creek to become Ttrail 230. Work crews had hewn a small crude bridge out of a blast-blown log to facilitate crossing the creek. We noticed that the wide valley had narrowed into a jagged canyon, and the sky had closed to a slit of pale blue. I stretched out both arms to fight off a vague cloud of claustrophobia. Despite the vistas afforded by the open country-side, the canyon's log-splattered walls seemed to trap us—as though we were walking inside a leviathan's fractured rib cage, with bones protruding every which way. On our left, the west wall terminated in erosion-knapped crags sharp as shark teeth. Around the crags, white snags soared upright like the remains of a massive skeleton.

"That must be Minnie Peak," I said to Celeste. Previously just a name on a map, now the 5,619-foot peak would glow in my memory as the dead leviathan's skull.

The trail climbed sharply on the canyon's other side, so we decided to camp near the bridge. Warm, desiccating winds hissed around us as we heated our dinner of instant soup and adjusted ourselves to the canyon's solitude. We had seen plenty of birds and insects along the trail, but once we set up camp, no ground squirrel, deer, or bat visited during the short evening. It was a severe kind of solitude I had experienced only in the blast zone—a feeling that the wildlife was not just elusive, it actually wasn't there. Above our heads, tattered cirrus clouds announced the edges of an eventual storm. With the wind roaring, we decided to pitch the tent. Even-tually, the thin clouds gave way to the Milky Way, and we crawled into the tent and bade each other good night.

Setting up the tent turned out to be a mistake. The warm winds failed to cool the night air, and with the wind flapping the tent's light fabric all night long, I found myself suffering through a hot, dry blizzard of sleeplessness. Scratched by the wind, my eyes ached.

I shut them only to find that my ears opened to the sound of the creek. *Whoosh.* Pause. *Whoosh* again. The wind funneled up the canyon, and the falling water echoed the drafts like an uproar, now close, now faraway. Then everything seemed to move. Was that scratching on my left a branch, chipmunk, or bear? Was the rainfly working its way loose? Even the creek seemed to shift positions with its crash and calm.

Whoosh, pause, *whoosh,* pause. David Douglas would not have thought twice about such winds. He probably wouldn't have even bothered to set up his oilcloth. Had he slept where we now lay, an upturned canoe or the stars themselves would have been his nocturnal ceiling. He would have heartened himself with a supper of tea and bread, noted the day's progress in writing, and collapsed under Douglas-firs whose tremendous bulk and height now flourished only in the pages of his journal.

I flipped from one shoulder to another in my sleeping bag. Curses on David Douglas!

Born in Scotland in 1799, David Douglas was already working outdoors at the age of eleven. By 1823 he had been sent by Britain's Royal Horticultural Society to the east coast of North America to collect seeds of fruit trees. This successful venture led to his next assignment, which began one day after his twenty-fifth birthday: the distant and exotic Pacific Northwest. He set sail from Gravesend in a Hudson's Bay Company ship bound for the Columbia River. It was the beginning of an exploration that would carry him thousands of miles, span several years, and result in the naming of more than thirty species of plants by a single naturalist.

Although he was haunted by the mountain range whose name arose from his own journal, Douglas never stood on the summit of any of the Cascades. He wanted to be the first European to climb Mount St. Helens, but no native guide would accompany him.

Instead, using rivers as his roadways, Douglas journeyed near the active volcano twice—in 1826 and in 1833. By his second journey he had grown accustomed to the salal-furry forests, with their sky-scraping conifers. Even so, in February of 1833 he found a grove of grand firs so astonishing he described it as "a spectacle too much for one man to see." Douglas introduced the grand fir to England, along with the tree that bears his name—the Douglas-fir.

The first Douglas-firs the Scottish naturalist saw soared above the Columbia River to "a magnitude exceeded by few if any trees in the world," he wrote. In fact, Douglas' use of superlatives was not mere nineteenth-century effusion. The forests he gazed upon were essentially the tallest in the world. The western slope of the Cascades still contains the most species of trees of any forest on Earth that reach 200 feet and higher. Douglas-firs alone can reach 330 feet high. At the time Douglas saw the mature *Pseudotsuga* groves they were also among the oldest living things, thriving on average for 700 years and surviving as long as 1,200. Like other gymnosperms—plants that have "naked seeds"—they were a species that had endured since the age of dinosaurs.

Born a century too late, I would never gaze upon the roadless forests Douglas walked nor drift down the wild rivers he canoed. Almost every river I knew was dammed, including the Toutle, and clearcuts had spread even to Spirit Lake, as evidenced by the clearcut we had hiked through that day on the Elk Bench Trail. Just the same, I was lying in a canyon that had once been as green and dark as any forest Douglas had tromped through. I had to remind myself of that, since the day's treelessness clung to me like a bleached-out dream. Coldwater still possessed its cold water, but its conifers were flung upon the canyon's cliffs like frozen bones, so close to the ground they seemed to own no shadows.

I eventually fell into a bad and brief sleep, then woke at dawn to the same dry gusts and pale timber. "All my dead friends," my brother Bernie would have said. *Whoosh* went the creek in the faint light. *Whoosh, whoosh.*

We ate a quick breakfast of bananas, cold water, and muffins, knowing we had a long day ahead. Not only did we need to reach St. Helens Lake, we also needed to return and hike out the last five miles along Coldwater Lake. That made the day's mileage at least twelve miles, maybe more. I stared at the map in my hand. It wasn't a topographic map, but it gave the trails' general location. I noticed that our proposed route looped around Coldwater Peak for what looked like miles. Why couldn't we just hike over the hill in front of us and reconnect with the loop on the other side?

Celeste had just recovered from the flu, so she hesitated when I pointed to the short but steep wall looming over us. The eastern sun poured over its ridgeline like daylight flooding a basement window. But the sunlight didn't brighten the fact that the rocky slopes lacked a trail and were smothered with logs.

"The trail to St. Helens Lake is just over that col. We can save ourselves five miles at least by hiking over it. In an hour we'll be standing over Spirit Lake with a view of the mountain."

"Are you sure?" she squinted, sniffing at my enthusiasm as though it were an ill wind.

"Absolutely."

We had no watches, so the hours spent clambering over the hundreds of logs that lined the three ridges—not one—between us and my hoped-for salvation were lost to an eternity of silent curses. We located an elk trail, which helped us skirt a few sheer cliffs, but by the time we stood in the last valley, surrounded on all sides by wild land and no recognizable landmark, Celeste's trust had evaporated with what little dew had fallen under the cliffs' ledges. Having stashed our packs at camp, we had scant water or food, no coats, a bad map, and hostile winds whispering change with every gust.

Face to face with the logs, however, I gained a sharper appreciation for the blast-flattened forests. Unlike the clearcut we had hiked through the day before, the pre-eruption trees encircling us had not been logged. As a result, they still clung together as a forest—a volcanic forest lying sideways. What had climbed the sky now swallowed the ground, so we hiked *over* the trunks, not between them. Some we used as walkways, following them up to their roots, then hopping off. Others we straddled or jumped over. Most were as wide as barrels and had lost their bark to decay, but the snapped-off branches were still sharp as sword tips. One scraped my arm; another punctured my left calf, drawing blood. Each time I stooped and swung around them, it seemed I was swimming through conifers, thrashing about like a jellyfish in a sea of barnacled whales.

That was when I realized that the decaying labyrinth of logs around me was still a wooded wilderness. The volcano had not so much deforested its foothills as rearranged the trees. It was an unconventional beauty compared to the lush, standing trees of Douglas' day, but a complex layering of life just the same.

Forest Service scientists Jerry Franklin, Frederick Swanson, and James Sedell discovered that complex layering of life when their helicopter touched down at Ryan Lake only a few weeks after the eruption. There, the three ecologists gaped at the scene before them—nothing but dead trees and sterile ash for miles. But their collective impression was just an illusion—a trick of the volcano—because within ten seconds of setting foot on the ground, Franklin saw the soft green stalk of a fireweed coming up through a crack in the ash. Astounded, he took a picture of it. But he soon realized that the more he looked around, the more fireweed he saw, along with other signs of life. Later that day the team touched down in the Clearwater valley. There, among the gray logs again, a white trillium bloomed. That was when Franklin realized that all life had not been destroyed. This discovery would lead to his theory of "biological legacy"—a simple but profound concept that would later lie at the heart of many arguments against clearcut logging.

Contrary to conventional models of ecological succession for Mount St. Helens—which projected that life would creep back into the blast zone from the outside edges—Franklin's concept of biological legacy emphasized that survivors inside the blast zone were as important if not more important than pioneers arriving from the outside. Life did not re-enter from the borders and move inward. Instead, the blast zone was made up of tiny islands, or "foci," of surviving plants and animals. The presence of these key survivors led to the recolonization of the blast zone by indigenous species— species that had lived near the volcano for centuries. Franklin believed that of all of the blast zone's pre-eruption plants, only noble firs and Douglas-firs had to seed in because they had been the former forest's oldest trees, leaving no young offspring in the understory to survive them. All other plants sprang back from survivors who lay hidden beneath the seemingly dead earth.

The focus of Franklin's research was the comparison of pre-eruption clearcuts and forests with those same areas after the eruption. Having studied Mount St. Helens' forests for decades before the eruption, Franklin was able to compare pre-eruption sites with their post-eruption conditions. He noticed soon after the eruption that the areas revegetating the quickest were the older clearcuts, where sun-loving pioneers such as pearly everlasting and fireweed grew. But now, more than a decade later, it was the unlogged areas—such as the fallen forest Celeste and I were clambering over—that were both the richest and best vegetated because they contained original forest species in addition to pioneer species. The lesson has been a sobering one. It was not eruptions but logging that removed life from Mount St. Helens.

Skeptical of generalizations, Franklin nonetheless concluded one other thing: that the complexity of old-growth forests was beyond current human knowledge. With knowledge gleaned from the blast zone, Franklin saw that nature was the best silviculturalist when it came to species diversity—the sign of a healthy forest. A year earlier, at the 1993 Timber Summit in Portland, the veteran forester had announced that "growing old-growth" was beyond human management, requiring "a great deal of humility." Franklin's colleague, James Sedell, learned the same lesson when it came to streamside areas. Traditional forestry techniques removed all downed timber around streams. But after watching how the blast zone's downed logs protected amphibians from intense sun, cooled the water, and created nesting habitat for fish, Sedell advocated leaving woody debris behind after logging. This strategy, along with many others, led the Forest Service scientists toward a philosophy of "New Forestry," where ecological values combined with economic ones to provide for healthier forests and sustainable harvests.

Franklin's concept of biological legacy clarified for me the difference between the volcano's destruction and the destruction caused by clearcutting. The blast was a form of *deposition*—it added things to the land. There was no clearer evidence of this than the logs I found so obstructive. In contrast, clearcutting was *removal*—a taking away. The first kind of destruction enriched the land, adding humus and pumice; the second impoverished it.

My thoughts about the fallen forests faded as I climbed to the last ridgetop. St. Helens Lake was nowhere in sight, and neither was Spirit, but at least there was a trail leading in the direction I had anticipated. It didn't look like a newly blazed one, but it was a trail just the same. Better yet, we had a view of the volcano right smack in front of us, so we could orient ourselves. We held onto our caps as we stared at the scene. The wind had stirred up so much ash the crater was nearly hidden by its own dust storm. Dirty clouds rolled en masse down the Toutle River valley like white, billowing smoke. But through the ash we could see that the crater walls were caulked with snow; autumn was advancing.

Although we had anticipated seeing the volcano, we were far from prepared for the sight immediately before us: as far as our eyes could see lay thousands of blown-down trees. They lined every curve of earth from our feet to the volcano. Some were lodged in ash, others were being buried slowly by shrubs. Some had been uprooted; most looked as though they had been snapped in half. Every last one of them was down—and pointed straight at us.

My eyes scanned the gray torsos for life. Nothing moved. No deer, elk, birds, or other mobile creatures could be seen. We were alone with the volcano, the wind, and thousands of pointing trees.

I couldn't help feeling that where I was standing a great flood had roared through. The logs lay combed like the braided debris of high-water marks on rivers. But as we stood on the ridgetop the wind continued to gust, as though to remind us of the power of air, not water. It shoved us against the slope and floured our faces with ash. Its direction was the same as the lateral blast's—outward from the volcano. Perhaps we were experiencing an echo of the May 18 explosion. Those who could tell me for certain were dead. One of them, geologist David Johnston, had been blown so far off the ridge on which he was stationed, only a few miles from where we now stood, his body was never found.

Loowit's lateral blast—the initial explosion heralding the volcano's nine-hour eruption—was described by geologists as a "stone-filled wind" traveling 650 miles per hour. Created by super-heated groundwater flashing to steam, the blast contained explosive gases, pulverized rocks, boulders, debris, and air. These ingredients seemed concrete enough, but most of the explosion's other characteristics haunted me. For instance, what did 650 miles per hour feel like? Did an explosion as fast as that mean that all of the trees in front of us—acres and acres—fell together? With an ash plume rocketing upward to 50,000 feet within minutes, when would darkness have fallen? And given that the winds were traveling at nearly the speed of sound, would it have been possible to observe a sequence of events or would everything have happened at once?

I thought of the plane ride I had taken that month, before my trip with Laura. The small commercial airliner had trundled down the runway of the San Francisco airport for take-off. Then its engines had thrust forward, gently pushing me against my seat. Was that impetus at all like the blast? While passengers disembarked, two pilots had smiled from the cockpit.

"Excuse me," I had asked, "how fast does this plane go at take-off?"

"Oh, pretty fast—about 140 miles an hour."

"And what's its maximum speed?"

"Oh, it gets up there—maybe 350 miles an hour."

Only half the speed of the blast! No wonder early philosophers believed that volcanoes were subterranean hurricanes—huge storms migrating underground to burst free in cracks. Yet even the average hurricane gusted at less than a quarter of the speed of the blast.

And what of the lateral blast's temperature of 700 degrees Fahrenheit—how hot was that? Experts had compared the explosion to twenty-seven atom bombs and ten-megaton bombs. What did that mean? Would our bodies have been vaporized if we had been standing on this ridge? I recalled the story of a party of climbers who had been enjoying the view from the summit of Mount Adams the moment Loowit erupted. For several minutes they endured a heat wave that raised the air temperature thirty to forty degrees—fifty miles away. Other eyewitnesses closer to the volcano described black clouds that bore down upon them. According to one, the clouds seemed to "jump" at ridgetops, rolling over four major ridges to span a 180-degree arc east and west. But the blast was not just a "cloud," according to geologist Dan Miller. It was something so powerful it churned up everything it rolled over and killed it immediately. Where we were standing, the blast winds had instantaneously seared and uprooted the thousands of trees lying before us. Lightning bolts shot out of the billowing clouds above the mountain, igniting forest fires. Most trees smoldered for weeks due to the foot-deep layer of sticky ash, which acted like a coat of asbestos.

As we took in the eerie scene in front of us, Celeste and I realized that we had run out of time for St. Helens Lake. Watch-less, we had only a vague idea of the hour, and without a topographic map we couldn't be sure whether we were on the right trail back. So we turned down the ridge as the wind followed us, swooping over hills, eager for our caps. Dry grasses and frothy waves of pearly everlasting shifted like ocean swells. Gusts ripped the elderberry leaves off branches and shredded them, then littered the ground with yellow-green confetti.

The confetti made me glance down. Tiny fragments of wood lay beside the shredded leaves as if they were further signposts to the blast. I bent down and touched them: whorls, arcs, blocks, arrows. Each piece of wood had confronted the blast in its own way. I picked up one piece that looked like half of a hand with two fingers extended. On one side, the cooked wood had cracked into tiny silver squares that chipped off easily in my palm. Where they fell away I could see the exact depth of the fire-baked layer: one millimeter. Beneath the blackish gray glowed the warm orange of softwood that had not burned. I put the hand back down. Not far from it lay a twisted ribbon of wood tempered into a wild S. The fire-bent cambium was paper thin and sinuous, curling back like a lashed whip.

I couldn't help but wonder what sound the trees had made as they fell, burning, to their deaths, but the only reference point I could muster was a distant memory from before the eruption. One summer day in 1978 I accompanied my brother Bernie on a snag-felling expedition. The Forest Service had identified a tall, decaying conifer near the Toutle River to be felled and removed for the fire-wood concession my brother operated. The day I helped him, we drove his old pick-up to the end of a gravel road and walked into the forest, looking for the ribboned tree. Chainsaw in hand, my brother walked up to the snag, about two feet in diameter, then paced around it. He sliced a wedge out of one side and told me to stand back, indicating with his gloved hand which way the tree was going to fall. Then my hands went to my ears and I jumped back as the ground at my feet flew up like a loose carpet. For a second the only thing that existed was a boom echoing off distant hills. And the tree—the tree was down, in the direction my brother had pre-dicted. It took all afternoon to cut it into rounds and load each one into the pick-up bed. My arms hurt so badly the following day I could barely lift a glass of water. If I multiplied the tremendous boom of that single tree by 100,000, perhaps I would have the noise of the crashing forests.

In 1980, Oregon resident Clara Fairfield conducted a survey to assess what people had heard the morning of the blast. Organized through the Oregon Museum of Science and Industry, the survey included more than 1,200 responses from residents all over the greater Pacific Northwest, from as far away as British Columbia, Montana, and the Oregon–California border. The loudest sounds—

strong enough to crack a garden wall in one location—had been heard along the coast, from Newport to Hood Canal and the San Juan Islands, while Portland residents and people within ten miles of the volcano had heard nothing. Perplexed by this seeming incongruity, Fairfield mapped all the areas where noises had been heard, their perceived volume, and if any shock waves or barometric pressure drops had occurred. Her sound map showed that the noise of the blast shot up 300 miles into the ionosphere, then bounced back down more than once across the region, creating "rings of sound" that mostly skirted the Willamette valley. Climbers on Mount Hood, Mount Adams, and Mount Rainier heard nothing, while people 400 miles away in Hamilton, Montana, thought they had heard heavy artillery fire. Barograms in Las Vegas and Helena, Montana, recorded pressure changes. Windows across the Northwest rattled, and many people thought that "someone in the family had fallen upstairs or down," or that "someone had driven into the side of their house." Doors opened and closed, light fixtures swayed, curtains were sucked out of windows. Residents near Puget Sound thought their houses had been hit with "giant, soft sledge hammers" or a "huge, padded wrecking ball."

In 1983 Seattle composer Alan Hovhaness composed a three-part "Mount St. Helens Symphony" to describe his aural impressions of the eruption. My mother had mailed me a tape of the symphony as a gift a few months before our Coldwater hike, and I had listened intently for the blast. Lyrical horns, flutes, and bells marked Spirit Lake's watery peace before the eruption. Then, in the third movement, drums exploded, and twenty instruments played at once to convey the cacophony ripping across the land.

On the trail back to Coldwater, it seemed that that cacophony was now traced only in the dead trees and wood fragments left behind. But as we wound down a grassy hillside bearing the stubble of clearcut stumps, I abandoned my study of the wood fragments for something else—something that suddenly answered my questions about the blast.

Only fifty yards down the trail, scraps of rusted metal curved above the tops of the swaying grasses like steelhead leaping upstream. Yet no splash marked their motion; these fish weren't going anywhere. They had sat on the ridge, frozen in place, for years. Sun, wind, and rain had etched their once-silver surfaces to sandpaper brown, but with tombstone perseverance they held their twisted positions against time and decay.

The metal shards had been flung from a one-ton bulldozer as it flipped and rolled downhill during the blast. At least, it looked like a bulldozer. For all that remained it could have been any number of tractorlike logging machines. The powerful earthmover had tumbled down the ridge like a helpless pebble seized by an outgoing tide. As if to commemorate the blast winds' indiscriminate force, the enormous vehicle had come to rest upside down, its heavy-chinked tractor treads soaring skyward like two impotent legs of a dead, belly-up crab.

We could not stop staring. The flipped-over, freakish wreck and its scattered shards sang the blast's heat, force, and speed so clearly that I suddenly saw the hot winds crown the ridge and descend upon me. I rose buoyant in the log-littered air, somersaulting with the rotating forest like a paper doll soaring on a coastal breeze.

Two black-tailed deer loitered beside the wreck as if they had some business to conduct there. They watched us approach, wary of our orange caps, then escaped through fields of pearly everlasting, sedges, and tufted grass. Leaping with ease over clearcut stumps, they disappeared south toward Johnston Ridge, leaving us alone with the rusted hulk. We paced around it, pulling down the visors of our caps to shut out the wind. I blinked hard to wet my burning eyes. The message was unambiguous: What was human industry to a volcano? A mangled monster, nose-down in the wind-bent sedges, with slabs of crumpled steel warmed by errant sunlight to embellish its ignoble repose.

Every moment we sat near the bulldozer it seemed that the volcano would erupt over our heads, so we abandoned the rusted mass to the deer who now owned it. Buffeted by steady gusts, we continued north down the trail, rounding bend after bend. Eventually we caught sight of Coldwater Lake below us and, finally, the creek. By the time we reached camp we were dirty, scratched, and exhausted. We hauled our packs out of hiding, drank the last of our water, then napped for a moment in the sun-warmed sand. But the wind had dehydrated us so thoroughly that within minutes we found ourselves propelled by a thirst that pushed back all fatigue. It seemed we had already hiked twenty miles, traveling to the land of the dead and back, but we hoisted our packs onto our backs anyway and began the long hike back. Too tired to talk, we hiked in silence, marching straight into the glare of the afternoon sun. As we reached the lake I listened to the gentle lapping of its waves— lapping reminiscent of Spirit Lake's murmur at the close of a sunny afternoon. The cottonwoods snowed down their pollen onto the lake's wave-wrinkled surface, just as other cottonwoods once did at Harmony Falls and Duck Bay. The lakeshore was even riddled with the same sort of beached logs found at Spirit. I inhaled the scent of the cottonwoods and closed my eyes. What a privilege to look upon Spirit Lake's geologic sibling—a lake born in my own lifetime—and understand the violent processes that had crafted its sleepy logs, shores, and water.

In a dream state born of exhaustion I recalled the lapping of water in a Northwest Indian story explaining the birth of the Cascade Range. In the story, recorded by Ella Clark, the Cowlitz-

Quinault-Chehalis storyteller uses the words *Ah tah lah tah la* to describe the noise of waves lapping. The story tells of Ocean and his sons and daughters, Clouds and Rain. In the beginning, Ocean sends his children to the dry country in eastern Washington to help plants grow. But the people there become greedy, refusing to let Clouds and Rain return to their father. So the Great Spirit scoops up a big mound of earth—the Cascade Mountains—to separate the dry country from the wet, so that Ocean might keep his children near him. The hole where the mountains are scooped out becomes known as Puget Sound. Although most of his children returned, years later Ocean still cries for the Clouds and Rain that never came back from the dry country. Come home, he says, *Ah tah lah tah la!*

With lifespans of several hundred years, the old firs that David Douglas had seen near the volcano had already lived through several of its eruptions. Some had no doubt sprouted even before the large eruption circa A.D. 1500. Yet here I was, in my own short lifetime, witnessing the birth of a lake and the lapping of its water. For all my fatigue, my envy of Douglas lifted from me like a swallow catching the wind. To think I had schemed of a shortcut across this tree-smothered land! The only thing I really needed was the strong-legged Scot's fortitude in walking twenty miles a day.

We climbed the Elk Bench Trail giddy with sunburn, windburn, hunger, and thirst. By the time we reached the car we were laughing like idiots. Everything seemed ridiculous: forgetting our coats; tipping our caps to deer; wandering elk trails over wind-pummeled land. What were we thinking hiking off-trail through the blast zone of all places? But even as we sang out our replies between fresh outbursts of laughter, neither of us mentioned the bulldozer lying nose-down in the windblown grass, or the thousands of dead trees whose tops did not lean skyward but toward us.

St. Helens Lake

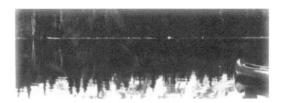

A cracked and fluent heaven, and a brown earth.
I had these, and my food and sleep—enough.

—Louise Bogan

As most backpackers know, there is an indigenous plant in the Northwest referred to as "Hiker's Nightmare." Its Latin name, *Oplopanax horridum*, means "bristly tool" or "horrible weapon." Its common name is no less reassuring: Who would want to bump into a bush called "devil's club"? At Spirit Lake it abounded in dark pockets of the pre-eruption forest and, to my child's eye, soared as tall and invincible as the trees.

The trail to St. Helens Lake was where I enjoyed my first brush with devil's club. In the sun-checkered understory of the closed-canopy forest, the gigantic maplelike leaves of the devil's club plant stretched flat as water. Its central club of bright-red berries rose like a solitary flame out of a leafy green sea. The six-foot-high shrub flooded creekbeds with its thorn-studded stems and branches. Both enthralled and repulsed, I stepped close to the red baton of berries, then touched the tip of a thorn. It pricked like a needle and stung like a bee. Had I pressed harder, an allergy-causing toxin would have seeped into my skin, and blood from my fingertip would have beaded as bright and round as one of the berries. *Horridum* indeed.

Before the eruption, the start of Trail 207 might well have served as a devil's club plantation—except that the shrub could hardly be considered a crop bound for market. Although some Washington tribes traditionally use the plant to cure colds, rheumatism, and tuberculosis, devil's club is not even considered edible. Instead, coastal tribes have relied on the plant as an emetic to induce vomiting, as a pigment for face paint, or as a fishing lure for bass. Its raw leaves are tasty only to elk, who rely on them for forage.

But the lush vegetation ignited my child's imagination more than any amusement park ride. Here was an attraction more threatening than any contraption of concrete, steel, or wire. The leaves were wider than my shoulders, their undersides furry with thorns. As the trail wound upward past creek after creek, the blades of water sliced the fir-needled path—only to disappear under huge green *Oplopanax* walls. Hoofing it uphill as a tired ten-year-old, I glanced downslope in delightful horror to ease my fatigue: *What if I fell down there?*

As one of the first trails I explored at Spirit Lake, Trail 207—or the Mount Margaret Trail—taught me the difference between a stroll and a hike. Unlike the flat portion of the Boundary Trail on the east side of Spirit Lake, Trail 207, on the west side, *climbed.* By adult standards the trail was of moderate difficulty—rising 1,500 feet over 3.3 miles—but for a ten-year-old the steady ascent from the Toutle River to St. Helens Lake was endless and steep. Each bend seemed as though it must be the last—St. Helens Lake would no doubt glimmer below the next corner, through gaps in the trees. But one switchback invariably led to another, and by the time I actually did reach the lake I was out of breath, starving, and ready to plunge into the icy shallows to cool off—all at once.

Like most Spirit Lake trails, Trail 207 was built during the Civilian Conservation Corps era, between 1938 and 1942. During that time, the Forest Service was steadily developing Spirit Lake as a recreation area, hewing picnic tables, blazing trails, and developing the main campground's water system and camp sites. At the program's zenith more than 200 workers—Depression-era laborers, unskilled youths, and other jobless men—were camped on the lake's south shore. The men built trails designed primarily for horses, and Trail 207 was no exception. It rose steadily through a dark forest, then traversed patches of old burns speckled with white snags and young firs. There, a hiker could feast on plentiful huckleberries without breaking stride. The clearings also offered views of Spirit Lake, whose flat blue waters were usually disturbed by the widening V of a ski boat's wake or the white triangle of a sail. Pearly everlasting and fireweed blanketed the burns, then grew sparse as the forest closed again. After three miles, the trail descended to encircle St. Helens Lake's east side, then continued north toward the Dome and Mount Margaret. Enchanted with lakes more than peaks, I often hiked to the lake but rarely beyond. For me, Trail 207 more or less ended at St. Helens Lake. There, a handful of picnic tables and tent sites were tucked among scraggly firs on the lake's eastern curve.

For my brother Michael, Trail 207 did not stop at the lake but led instead to one of his favorite haunts—the Dome. Along with Bernie, another avid mountaineer, Michael would dash up the trail I found so tiring to rappel off the Dome or continue to the summits of Coldwater Peak or Mount Margaret. Three years older than me and an experienced outdoorsman at eighteen, Michael started backpacking on his own when he was thirteen. For his first big trip he spent the night at St. Helens Lake with a seventh-grade friend, both of them shivering in cotton camping bags. By the time Loowit erupted, Michael was twenty-one and had scaled the volcano a dozen times. He had also camped at most of the backcountry's chain of lakes and had climbed Mount Hood, Mount Adams, and Mount Rainier. For him, Trail 207 was little more than a jogging path.

Having hiked with Michael on a few occasions I was intimidated by his maniacal speed, but considered him one of only a few people in the world who could recall the pre-eruption backcountry intimately, so I asked him to accompany me on my second attempt to reach St. Helens Lake. Michael had explored the backcountry only once after the eruption, in 1988, before any new trails had been blazed, and was eager to see the regrowth that had happened since then.

This time, we would take a different route from the one Celeste and I had attempted. Instead of starting from Coldwater on the lake's west side, we would start from Windy Ridge on the east, then head west and north up the new Trail 207, renamed the Truman Trail in honor of the dead innkeeper. The new trail was blazed differently from its old CCC predecessor but still zigzagged north up the lake's western ridge, now named Harry's Ridge, also to honor Truman.

With water containers sloshing in our packs, we hiked west around Windy Ridge on yet another warm September afternoon, traversing the Pumice Plain in front of the volcano and continuing west into the sun's glare. As we reached the edge of the plain, no other hikers passed us, coming or going. We knew we were entering little-explored territory.

As we hiked toward Harry's Ridge, Michael pointed out Spirit Lake's artificial tunnel, a gray square dotting the lake's western shoreline. Like me, he disliked the idea that the lake no longer found its way to the Toutle River naturally. We admitted to ourselves that the pre-eruption lake had been threatened by polluting motorboats and crowded with campers, but at least it had drained according to the folds of the land. Now it drained like a punctured radiator.

By the time we found ourselves on top of the debris avalanche, the lake had disappeared behind hummocks of gray rock. The trail began to ascend the Spillover, and we paused for a moment to guess where the family cabin had once lain. For the first time in fifteen years I scrutinized the place where I had once dreamed of living. But I might as well have been at Katmai, Pinatubo, or Krakatoa. As with Spirit Lake's south shore, nothing looked the same. There were hills where previously there had been none. The Toutle's North Fork had disappeared. And the pocket where the cabins had sat was replaced with the 600-foot-high lumps of the avalanched mountain. I had no idea where the cabin might have stood. Was it a quarter of a mile west, or a half-mile east, or was I standing right on top of it? And where was the small gorge where the unnamed creek had flowed? A trickle of water worked its way down one fold. Was that it? Was a new creek forming? We gazed upslope: miles of peach-gray volcanic rock crested gently like enormous, frozen waves of sand. We gazed at our feet: the same rock.

As the trail topped the Spillover, memories of devil's club and conifers along the old trail loomed as tall as the rising shadows on distant ridges. But although the new trail bore the same Forest Service number, it bore no resemblance to its pre-eruption path. Instead of devil's club, blond grasses rustled everywhere in the breeze. A few elderberry shrubs poked out of the grasses like solitary scarecrows. Michael wondered why so few clumps of bear-grass could be seen. The tall white lily, with its preference for high Cascade areas, had been conspicuous in the pre-eruption back-country. I found out later from Monument Scientist Peter Frenzen that the wildflower—so useful to Northwest Indians for their watertight baskets that it was called "basketgrass"—had not sur-vived the eruption as well as other plants. In fact, according to Frenzen, a mystery regarding beargrass had preceded the eruption. Before 1980, ecologists wondered why relatively little beargrass grew in the Mount Margaret backcountry compared with other high Cascade areas. But when the volcano showered the back-country with ash, the mystery was solved. Acting like glue, the wet, sticky ash pinned the plants' slender blades against the earth. Unable to grow and photosynthesize, the plants became dormant or died.

We wound our way over the bright, grassy hills. Winged grasshoppers rose up in clouds around us, clumsily hitting our legs. I had seen the same grasshoppers on my Coldwater hike with Celeste and was surprised to see such an abundance; before the eruption no such grasshopper was apparent. The air was filled with the clack-clacking of their courting calls. The wind tasted of grass. The sun dropped directly to eye level, burning an ache into my brain. Snags poking up like stalagmites lined the leeward side of the ridge north of Harry's Ridge. The blast had scrubbed the south side of the ridge to bedrock; nothing grew there at all.

As we wound over the ridge we stopped and cocked our heads to one side to hear a cry rising due north. It started high and faint like a distant whistle, descended into a plaintive neigh, then ended abruptly in a low snort. An elk bugling at Spirit Lake? It was some-thing we hadn't heard in years. Hunter-wary, the bull and his harem of seven galloped west to avoid us. We shielded our eyes to watch them, then picked our way up the heavily grazed ridge, pungent with the smell of bull elk urine. Apparently, the absence of devil's club had not deterred the elk from foraging along the new Trail 207. Pockets of trampled earth and matted grass marked spots where the bull had established his territory by pawing and rolling on his back. It was rutting season at Spirit Lake—and we were thick in the yelp and stink of it.

Before the eruption, Spirit Lake was home to several herds of Roosevelt elk. Each fall, the backcountry emptied of campers and filled with rutting elk, their barks and bugles resounding over the usually quiet peaks. The backcountry also came alive with territorial mountain goats who lived near the Dome and Mount Margaret. Transplanted from the Olympics, the goats were known to chase hikers who ventured too boldly onto their range, especially during the rut.

Spirit Lake's mountain goats were introduced, but no one is really sure where the lake's elk came from. A subspecies of Canadian elk, Roosevelt elk *(Cervus elaphus roosevelti)* are also called Olympic elk because they are indigenous to the Olympic Peninsula. Having once roamed from southern British Columbia to the San Francisco Bay, throughout both the Coast and Cascade mountains, the elk were slaughtered in most of their range by white settlers. Present-day herds are but a fraction of the ancient herds, and in many areas the elk have been extirpated.

Six subspecies of elk—or "wapiti," as they are called by biologists who recognize that they are different from the European elk—roamed North America before Europeans arrived. Of the six, four survived Euro-American settlement—Rocky Mountain, Manitoban, Tule, and Roosevelt elk. Of these four, Roosevelt elk are the largest, weighing as much as 1,000 pounds. In fact, they are the largest subspecies of elk in the world. They also have slightly shorter

antlers and are a shade darker than other elk. They were designated
a separate subspecies in 1897, when naturalist C. Hart Merriam
positively identified a specimen and named it after his friend,
Theodore Roosevelt. Four years later Roosevelt became president
and helped protect the elks' dwindling numbers by establishing a
preserve that later became Olympic National Park.

Some biologists believed that the elk at Spirit Lake were vestiges
of the aboriginal Roosevelt population, which had escaped being
hunted by remaining in the hard-to-reach backcountry. Others
believed they originated from herds of Rocky Mountain elk introduced to eastern Washington from Montana. In his 1955 book, *The
Roosevelt Elk*, William Graf quoted Washington state biologist Burton
Louckhart as being of the opinion that the lake's elk were "a remnant of the native Roosevelt variety." In 1943, Louckhart opti-
mistically estimated that the herd totaled 500 elk.

If the elk were indeed vestiges of the native herd, they would
have been the last remaining Roosevelt elk in Washington's Cascades. But regardless of their origin, there was no doubt that Spirit
Lake's herds had suffered in the same way as others had. At the turn
of the century, elk numbers at Spirit Lake plummeted as settlers
and hunters moved up the Toutle River. Then, according to Forest
Service records, the elk began to slowly increase due to a hunting
ban. In 1934, only 160 elk were estimated to exist in the entire
Columbia National Forest (soon to be renamed Gifford Pinchot),
but by 1938 the estimated total had reached 300. Hunting was
allowed again by the 1950s, and by 1979, "there were more elk
than ever," according to one ranger. In fact, many people in my
family had their own elk story to tell, whether it was of one or
several of the ungulates thundering past them on a trail or road.
Michael, for one, was acquainted with the herds, which scattered
each fall during the hunting season to high ground like the back-

country. One autumn Michael climbed the mountain and found elk droppings at the summit, on top of fresh snow.

But although the elk could outrun hunters, they could not outrun the volcano. Whatever elk survived the 1980 mudflows and blast winds were suffocated within hours by ash. One of the first stories I heard after the eruption was of catatonic elk standing immobile in volcanic debris up to their bellies. Within months of the blast, University of Washington researchers Richard Taber and Kenneth Raedeke collected roughly 100 dead elk. Two years later, the Washington Department of Fish and Wildlife estimated that 1,600 elk had died in the eruption. That number had been disputed, but what was indisputable was the death of hundreds of elk.

But here was powerful evidence that the elk had returned. As we stood next to a small fir whose top had been browsed clean, Michael and I took in the scene. Never before at the lake had we observed such obvious signs—nibbled shrubs, trampled meadows, well-worn trails. Even during his 1988 trek Michael had not seen such traces. How could it be that Spirit Lake's largest animal—a mammal requiring several pounds of vegetation a day to survive— had returned with such dominance?

Wildlife biologist Evelyn Merrill discovered one simple reason: elk are mobile opportunists. Along with Taber and Raedeke, Merrill studied the elk from 1982 to 1985 and documented their dramatic return to the North Fork of the Toutle as well as the Green River drainage, just north of St. Helens Lake. Merrill believed that elk cows living in areas adjacent to the blast zone wandered into the disturbed area soon after the eruption. These new elk were most likely a mixture of the original Roosevelt herd and the introduced Rocky Mountain subspecies from eastern Washington. Once inside the blast zone, they discovered tender new shoots springing up through the ash. They also discovered a huge area where few people traveled. They didn't even mind the intense blast zone sun. They coped with the lack of shade by sweating during windy afternoons, increasing their nocturnal foraging, or by bedding down in the ash, which drew heat away from their bodies. As a result, the population soared: in 1981 approximately 200 elk had re-established themselves west and north of St. Helens Lake.

Merrill began radio-collaring elk in 1982 to track their whereabouts and foraging patterns, then observed them for three years, sometimes around the clock. Conducted mostly on Weyerhaeuser Company's blast-blown timberlands, Merrill's research was partly funded by Weyerhaeuser because the company's silviculturalists were concerned about the elk feeding on newly planted seedlings. The foresters wanted to track the animals so that they knew where and when to plant trees with minimal impact from the elk. While loggers cleared Weyerhaeuser's plantation of downed trees, Merrill drove the gravel roads to observe the elk through high-powered scopes. She noticed that while the logging trucks—which peaked at 200 a day—at first affected the elk, they soon grew accustomed to them. What they didn't grow accustomed to were hunters who were allowed to shoot the expanding herd as early as 1982. During hunting season, some elk sought cover deep in the heart of the blast zone, in such areas as the Spirit Lake basin, where hunting was not allowed.

Even as she kept her ear to the radio for evacuation alerts and dusted ash from her face and hair, Merrill found that the elk were recovering much faster than anyone, including herself, might have predicted. The environment was so changed she thought it would take decades to recover. But by the spring of 1985, when her study ended, the elk numbered more than 600, an amount that approached pre-eruption estimates.

After her study, Merrill realized that it was in the nature of elk to recolonize the area. In the ecological web, elk are generalists—they exploit a wide variety of resources to inhabit different kinds of terrain. For instance, they will eat different things depending on what is available. In the blast zone, they munched on the first plants to erupt through the ash—willow, fireweed, cat's-ears, clover, horsetail, and pearly everlasting, their summer staple. They also traveled great distances to forage during the winter in low-elevation areas along the North Fork of the Toutle River and the Green River, then rounded out their diet with backcountry wildflowers in the summer and fall. And not only did they eat different plants, depending on where they traveled, they also ate different things depending on the plants' growth stages. They focused on easy-to-digest wildflowers during the summer, then switched to grasses and the leaves of shrubs like elderberry during the fall. This rich diet helped the herds to reproduce faster than some coastal herds inhabiting mature forests.

Such patterns of resiliency were "typical elk things," according to Merrill. Just the same, Michael and I were amazed at how thoroughly they had claimed the trail to St. Helens Lake. By the time we had crossed Harry's Ridge and were approaching the high wall west of the lake, we knew we were in an area visited hundreds of times more frequently by elk than by humans. Hardly a bootprint marked the ground, while hoof marks and droppings lay everywhere.

By the time we arrived at St. Helens Lake, shadows had claimed it. The log-lined ridges forming the lake bowl were capped with sunlight, but the deep, round pool sat dusk-dark. In the pocket where we stood, a few trees had been protected from the blast and remained standing as snags. But on the lake's northern ridge the combed, fallen torsos still recalled the blast winds' swirls and curves.

As I gazed down at the dark lake, my eyes instinctively scanned its surface for the silver flash of fish. According to biologist Bruce Crawford, St. Helens Lake—like the rest of the backcountry's dozen or so lakes—did not support indigenous fish, but the Washington Department of Fish and Wildlife had annually stocked most of the lakes from 1934 to 1979. St. Helens Lake had been stocked as early as 1914 with such species as lake trout, eastern brook trout, and cutthroat. Of the three, only the lake trout were found to have survived the eruption. The fish survived because they were protected under the lake's heavy layer of ice and snow, and then feasted on the blast zone's colonizing insect populations—in particular, mayflies. I watched for several minutes to see if anyone was planning on a late dinner, but no ripples disturbed the dark surface. Instead, floating logs clumped into tiny white islands. Like Spirit, St. Helens Lake possessed its own blast-blown log raft.

Michael noticed that the trail had been reblazed to snake around outcroppings high above the lake basin instead of following the old trail down to the lake. As with Spirit and other blast zone lakes, the Forest Service now prohibited lakeshore camping at St. Helens to protect its fragile shoreline and research areas from being trampled by hikers.

We continued up to the new trail's highest point, directly above the lake's southwest side, where it wound through a striking rock arch. Michael recalled how before the eruption he had seen a dark hole above the lake's forested basin and thought it was a cave. He had planned to climb the steep wall to explore it. Now he was doing exactly that. As we walked through the yarrow-lined arch, we gazed east to see Mount Adams rising out of a plain of blue foothills and west, behind us, to view the sun-honeyed Toutle River valley. The pre-eruption cave had windows.

We established camp above the lake, between Coldwater Peak and the Dome. As Michael boiled water for our dinner, I noticed that post-eruption grasses were interspersed around the lake's steep bowl with pre-eruption survivors such as sedges and partridgefoot, which had gone to seed in a tiny blaze of rust. Crimson huckleberry bushes, heavy with ripe berries, marked autumn's advance. The grasshopper clouds had subsided, at least for the night, along with the backcountry's bumblebees, who had done a brisk business that day with the late-summer wildflowers. As the sun dropped lower, Coldwater Peak threw its shadow upon the opposite ridge like a gauntlet challenging the fading day.

In the pink twilight I gazed down again upon St. Helens Lake and—1,500 feet below—Spirit. Here were the blue answers of two different volcanic questions. Spirit Lake was the product of the Toutle's dammed headwaters; St. Helens Lake was most likely a "maar" lake—an old volcanic vent now extinct. In the Cascade Range, water and fire knew no separation. Water followed fire, fire followed water, and gravity completed the geologic cycle.

The autumnal flora around us echoed this fire-water cycle: the glowing leaves of the sun-loving huckleberries would one day yield to an emerald gulf of shade-loving devil's club. As the forest matured and deep shade returned, even the meadows of pearly everlasting would subside like so many ephemeral white flames. In 150 years, perhaps the elk would weave through a forest of eighty-foot-tall firs at St. Helens Lake, and devil's club would re-establish itself along creekbeds to become as impenetrable as a hedge. Then, the elk would neglect the few scrubby stalks of everlasting lining the sunny trail and immerse themselves in the *horridum* wall again.

"I hope that when I'm seventy I'll still be able to hike up here," Michael said. "In another thirty to thirty-five years, who knows what will be growing in the backcountry?"

Whatever the vegetation, no doubt the adaptable elk would make a meal of it. A small herd of cows had strolled in among us to feast on the surrounding ridges' wildflowers and grasses. They walked slowly and horizontally along the sheer slopes, shifting their weight a hoof at a time as they grazed one tuft of grass, then another.

We had crossed the rock arch not knowing it was a door. But now we were guests once again at St. Helens Lake. The basin's curved walls sheltered us, its cool blue floor collected stars. Tomorrow we would stand on the tip of Mount Margaret, elevation 5,858 feet, and claim the wide, greening world of Spirit Lake with our eyes. At Norway Pass we would camp among snowing jungles of pink fireweed gone to seed. There, a single coyote would yip over the return of life to the backcountry—as if we needed to be told.

"There's Scorpio," Michael said, as he pointed to the volcano. The constellation was hugging the dark summit, defying the billions of miles stretching between mountain and stars. We sat down on logs smooth as driftwood and ate our dinner as the cows continued to graze, heads down, chomping.

Ghost Lake

The landscape imagines me.

—Jorge Guillén

Halfway through my blast zone journeys, I decided to hike alone for a day. Although I had often tromped by myself for miles through foreign cities, I had never ventured far out of earshot of another human being. As a woman I was repeatedly told not to. But early one morning in June 1995, I packed a lunch, borrowed my mother's car, and headed north out of Portland under rain clouds to see the blast zone in springtime, by myself.

As I crossed the Columbia River and entered Washington, I glanced down at the river, waiting for drops to freckle the water. News was circulating that the Columbia was one of the most radioactive rivers in the world. Images of its mutant fish swam before me, then disappeared as a male voice on the radio warned me that I'd better buy earthquake insurance soon. "Only 10 percent of Oregonians have earthquake insurance. Do you? Because it's not a question of *if* there will be another quake, it's a question of *when.*"

I smiled at the windshield. I was on my way to a volcano, after flying in from San Francisco, where during the 1989 Loma Prieta earthquake I had swung about in a four-story building like a toddler on a carousel. Some people were shaped by prairies, deserts, gentle sloping woodlands. In the Portland hospital where I was born, volcanoes stood on three points of the compass, and the Pacific lapped the west. I was a child of plate tectonics, that continual rubbing deep underground that manifested itself in both fault lines and lava. Earthquake insurance—*who me?*

The car buzzed by a loaded logging truck, and on a whim I decided to keep track of every truck I saw that day to gauge the status of southwest Washington's woods during the highly publicized Northwest timber crisis. This first truck carried matchsticks—pulpwood. By the time I reached Woodland it was 8:30 A.M., and I had counted four trucks, all with small logs. As I continued up Highway 503, past Chief Lelooska's longhouse, where as a child I had sat in the dark mesmerized by Kwakiutl ceremonial dances, I counted trucks five through eight. More small trees. I sped past clearcuts and second growth, past a church named Pleasant View, surrounded by anything but a pleasant view. I turned north onto Highway 25 and suddenly realized that the paved road I was winding up had been built for logging—not sightseeing. Access to Mount St. Helens, both pre- and post-eruptive, was first and foremost for resource extraction. No wonder I got angry every time I drove to the volcano. I was a wilderness seeker on multiple-use roads.

But when I parked the car in an empty lot at Bear Meadow and headed up the Boundary Trail, northeast of Spirit Lake, my anger receded. I had the woods to myself, and the cold air smelled of dew. Blue sky flowered out of the south. Thick, vigorous firs crowded the brown path in front of me. Overhead, huge cumulus clouds bumped each other in a soft *boom*. It was the gentle thunder of clearing weather.

I climbed a forested ridge—a forest uncannily missed by the lateral blast—and was dive-bombed by black biting flies and deerflies the size of hand grenades. Both were old acquaintances. No sunny day at pre-eruption Spirit Lake would have been complete without the small dipping head of a black fly as it bent toward your ankle, or a deerfly circling as it sought the right portion of shoulder. I had the pleasure of both, perhaps because I was the only mammal in sight.

Sprouting everlasting lined the trail, along with penstemon about to bloom, lupine, beargrass, and little waxy-leaved pyrola, a white woodland flower I had often spotted at Harmony Falls. Also known as wintergreen, the Northwest's five pyrolas are almost parasites because they possess only partial levels of chlorophyll, relying on a fungal partner for food in very dark canopies. But the leaves on these pyrolas seemed green enough to produce their own food, growing as they were, near the sunny path.

I wound up the ridge, chatting to myself about plants and the weather. I didn't quite want to admit it, but the immense quiet spooked me. There were no noisy streams, no wind in the trees, no squawking jays. The absence of noise gave rise to a furious phobic babble in my brain. Within seconds I envisioned a mother bear with cubs uptrail, a rabid coyote rambling during daylight, and a cougar twenty paces back. So I kept a little conversation going to distract my elated and terrified mind. It was sunny! Here was a trillium!

Over there, goatsbeard! How about a whiff of cedar? I had been raised on enough tales of solitary mountain men to feel ashamed. Hadn't Kit Carson fought off cougars and grizzlies? Apart from my brush with the baby otter at Bear Cove, my portfolio of wildlife thrills was painfully limited. It was my rule to avoid even rodents for fear of the plague. And like the victim of vertigo in love with the thrill of falling, I knew that as much as I feared cougars, I desperately wanted to see one. Of all the hikers I knew who had traveled the backcountry, only Chuck Tonn had seen a cougar. The ranger had fallen asleep on a sunny rock near Minnie Peak and had awakened in time to watch a mountain lion saunter by below him, upwind. The predators were elusive; until the 1940s, Loowit's cougars had walked the woods with a fifty-dollar bounty on their heads. In 1938 alone, eighteen bounties had been paid in Skamania County, along with bounties for sixty-eight bobcats, also now rare.

Just the same, I kept chattering to myself like an excited chickadee, inventorying my dearth of woodland-creature encounters: a few foxes, a brush with three bighorn sheep, several jackrabbits and coyotes, various birds, beavers, and otters, and the moo-ish grunt of an unseen grizzly.

Then, all at once, I stopped talking. Dead snags enveloped me. Sun struck my face. Views opened into valleys and distant ridges. I had entered the blast zone.

I was crossing what looked like an old burn. For the first time I was actually hiking into the scorch zone from an untouched forest. Also called the "singe zone," this outer zone marked the very edges of the blast, where trees were baked to death but not blown over. Although these "standing dead," as they were called, reminded me of forest-fire snags, very few were coal-blackened. A few even possessed bark. Most spread their downcast branches from weathered trunks smooth as granite. Why? Time had softened the fire's effect, no doubt, but perhaps it was also because many of the trunks had, in fact, not burned. According to scientists, when the blast swept through the area it seared the crowns—the trees' topmost branches—or stripped them of their lower branches. Severely injured, the old trees died slowly as ash and pumice rained down thick and sticky as wet snow. That day, a whole forest of them stood in front of me, still as winter. I took one step and felt conspicuously mobile, a shameful biped. Each tree was its own tombstone. I felt like a trespasser tromping over graves, a living thing on parade. I took another step, then another, and continued, step after awkward step, in silence.

It was already noon, but I seemed to be nowhere near my destination, a small backcountry lake called Ghost Lake. So I sat down on a sunny log and unpacked my water and lunch. A small black-and-white bird, probably a downy woodpecker, swooshed down the valley. It struck me that the blast zone rendered the most common forest animals exotic. Even a scampering chipmunk was a sight to behold among so many dead things. As I fought off a variety of winged insects eager for me and my bagel and cheese, I thought about the stories that had lured me to Ghost Lake.

Before the eruption, no trail traveled to Ghost Lake. To reach the remote lake, hikers started from Spirit Lake in the south or from Ryan Lake in the north. Knowledgeable hikers followed elk trails. It was rigorous travel, but the cross-country trip was worth the effort: Ghost Lake had some of the largest rainbow trout around. According to two habitués of Spirit Lake, brothers Don and Allen Cripe, Ghost Lake had some of the worst mosquitoes and best trout around. Charter members of the Longview Ski Club, the Cripe brothers first visited Spirit Lake in 1935. During that time, they became friends with Harry Truman at St. Helens Lodge and Jack Nelson at Harmony Falls. It was Nelson who told them about

Ghost Lake's "huge fish." One trout measured forty inches long. It had been hauled out by a mountain man named George Brunk.

As I washed my dry bagel down with a gulp of water in the fly-buzzing sunshine, it seemed to me that George Brunk himself stood nearby, chopping firewood, among the snags in the valley. According to the Cripe brothers, Brunk spent winters during the 1930s near Ghost Lake, holed up in an abandoned miner's cabin. Along with a cook named Curly Hill, Brunk brought in supplies and trapped all winter, catching otters, martens, and minks with lines he had all over the backcountry. There was no sign of the cabin now, but the trapper's presence stuck with me that day, if only because I knew how fierce those winters were. Before the eruption, Spirit Lake's annual snowfall was twenty-three feet. On a typical January day, temperatures never rose above freezing and snow was piled ten feet deep. Even Jim Lund, hardy as he was, once thought he was going to freeze to death on the lake's eastern shore, stuck like a popsicle in snow up to his waist. Wintering in Spirit Lake's back-country was like vacationing on polar ice floes. However, after the eruption the deep snows decreased because the trees that had helped create and retain them were gone.

The adventuresome Brunk was only one of many individuals seeking something from the Spirit Lake wilderness. Miners search-ing for gold, silver, and copper had burrowed into the Green River as early as 1897 and had set up camp all over the backcountry by 1910. More than a dozen mines were gnawed into the triangle of timbered ridges between Spirit Lake, Ghost Lake, and the Green River. They bore innocuous names like Minnie Lee, Polar Star, Chicago, Sweden, Norway, Black Prince, and Commonwealth. They represented the sweat of many workers and the investment of thousands of dollars. None of them panned out. Copper ore from 2,200-foot-long Sweden Mine resulted in a bronze statue of

Sacajawea in Portland's Washington Park and an unsmiling George Washington on the city's east side. But some prospectors persisted. As recently as 1976 the Sweden Mine, several hundred feet up Spirit Lake's north ridge, had been reopened by its owner. A battle was about to be waged over resource extraction and wilderness conservation when the volcano rendered the controversy mute.

Susan Saul was one of the conservationists who visited the mine. One afternoon in 1977 she watched yellowish ooze seep from the mine's settling pond into Coe Creek, the water source for the Portland YMCA camp. She and others wrote letters to local newspapers to press for closure of the mine, but the owner was operating under the 1872 mining law, which granted him the unbreakable right to mine. The only factor clouding the mine's future was the mediocre quality of the ore—the same ore that had discouraged miners several decades before.

As it turned out, the Sweden Mine was just the beginning of controversies for Saul. With a hardiness akin to George Brunk's wintry perseverance, she soon found herself battling another form of resource extraction—one that threatened such places as pre-eruption Ghost Lake.

A native of Eugene, Oregon, Saul first visited Spirit Lake after moving to Longview, Washington, in 1974. She joined the Mount St. Helens Hiking Club in 1975 and spent many a weekend trekking through the backcountry or sitting inside the club's lodge, tucked into Spirit Lake's eastern arm. In 1977 she joined the Mount St. Helens Protective Association, an eighty-member organization led by Kelso resident Noel McRae. McRae had formed the association in 1970 to stop the logging of the Green River's old-growth trees, known as the Valley of the Giants. His first battle was over a small sale of virgin timber at none other than Ghost Lake. In 1973 McRae stopped the Forest Service from selling

Ghost Lake's trees—the very trees that now formed the eerie scorch zone around me.

Saul worked with McRae to bolster the proposal of a national monument at Mount St. Helens. The association hoped to create a 90,000-acre preserve that would protect not only the Green River trees but the unique 1,900-year-old lava caves on the mountain's south side. In proposing the national park idea they were furthering a concept that had begun as early as the 1930s, proposed again in 1963 by caver William Halliday, then again in 1968 by University of Washington geographer Philip Pryde, and finally proposed a fourth time in 1975 by E. M. Sterling in his book, *The South Cascades*. Each time the idea was opposed by the timber-hungry Forest Service.

By February 1980, Saul was helping to organize a series of hikes to help publicize logging sales that threatened the backcountry and Green River valley. The veteran hiker was also riding her bike to work everyday to get in shape for an ascent of Mount St. Helens. Then the volcano erupted. Not only would Saul never touch the 9,677-foot summit, the trees she and McRae had fought so hard to keep alive near Ghost Lake would die standing up in a matter of days. The backcountry through which Brunk had wintered and Saul had hiked would freeze under a new kind of winter—where deciduous leaves crackled as though struck by ice, conifers bent their limbs as though weighted with snow, and the monochrome land lay blanched and still.

Despite so much natural change, both logging and mining interests persisted after the eruption as though a major geologic event had never occurred. The blown-down forests were a boon to Weyerhaeuser Company, which escalated its tree removal to six times above its pre-eruption levels. At the same time, an Arizona mining corporation expressed plans to level Goat Mountain, which formed the north wall of the Valley of the Giants. The company planned to take the entire mountain down, sift out the copper, and pile the leftover tailings in the Green River. But the world price for copper failed to make the idea economical.

During the spring of 1982, Saul hiked as far as she could into the blast zone to gather firsthand information for a trip to Washington, D.C. Along with University of Washington botanist A. B. Adams and eruption survivor Lu Moore, Saul planned to lobby Congress to set aside a larger area for the proposed monument—216,000 acres—an area that included most of the blast zone, including dramatic edges like the scorch zone at Ghost Lake. In contrast, the Forest Service proposed a preserve of 84,710 acres, and the state of Washington proposed an even smaller one of 84,030 acres.

In August 1982, President Reagan signed into law the Mount St. Helens National Volcanic Monument, preserving 109,900 acres. The decision represented a compromise, but at least part of the Green River had been saved, as well as some scorched, standing forests just north of Ghost Lake. When I considered the fact that Weyerhaeuser Company had refused to leave even a few snags on its blast zone land, the difference between 85,000 protected acres and 110,000 seemed no small achievement. More than eighty species of forest animals rely on snags for food and shelter.

As I finished my lunch among the dead trees, another woodpecker swooped past, landing on a snag. I shouldered my daypack and started down the trail, which switchbacked down the scorched ridge. At my feet I noticed that the little pyrolas and other shade-loving flowers had disappeared. Instead, non-native weeds, sedges, and huckleberries crowded the ground between snags. As I reached the valley floor, the air hummed with wings. Giant bumblebees

worked the early wildflowers; hummingbirds zipped overhead. The
"destroyed" land was noisier than the mature forest I had just left.

A third woodpecker flew past, ignoring the crowd of young firs
pushing up a new forest under the old burnt one. Yet another
downy—or was this a hairy woodpecker, similar in markings but
larger than the downy? I wasn't a skilled enough birder to say. Whatever it was, it wasn't the ghostly insectivore that had once haunted
Ghost Lake—the elusive black-backed woodpecker, one of the rarest
woodpeckers in the lower forty-eight states. Before the eruption,
Ghost Lake was home to several pairs of black-backed woodpeckers,
which have three toes, rather than the usual four. The rare species
has a bright-yellow cap, blackish wings striped with white, and a
solid black back. Although it is common in Canada and Alaska, the
black-backed is found only in parts of the Pacific Northwest and
the Rockies in the lower contiguous states. It is never abundant and
doesn't like to be seen. When present, its call is a soft *chik*, so bird
watchers must look instead for the handiwork the birds leave
behind—large patches of scaled bark on dead conifers.

Before the eruption, Audubon Society members came from all
over the country to see the chisel-billed birds at Ghost Lake. Chuck
Tonn escorted the birders to the lake so they could add the species
to their life list. Having traveled from distant states, the birders were
thrilled to spot the lake's two pairs nesting among its old-growth
trees. There, the adults fledged their young, feeding them larvae and
other bugs extracted from dead trees with their extremely long
and flexible tongues. The male's yellow cap darted like a tiny light
between the shadowy firs. But then the blast winds swept through
the dark valley.

Since the eruption, no black-backed woodpeckers have been
sighted at Ghost Lake. However, only a year after the eruption,
ecologist Charlie Crisafulli identified a pair nesting southeast of

Bear Meadow, in the deep-ashfall forest just outside the blast zone. Researchers called the area the "concrete forest" because it looked as though someone had laid down concrete everywhere. Only woody shrubs and large conifer saplings survived in the eight-inch-deep ash; all of the mosses and most of the wildflowers had perished. Nonetheless, Crisafulli had watched the black-backed woodpeckers fledge their young at least three times in the ash-paved woods, only a few miles from where I stood near Ghost Lake.

That day, as I continued on the trail, so much life accosted my senses I wouldn't have noticed a black-backed woodpecker if one had landed on my head. Alder saplings bunched into thickets. Young hemlock and fir trees blocked the sun. I was in a miniature forest—a valley of Christmas trees. I paused on a small wood bridge over what I guessed to be Ghost Creek and glanced down at the fast-flowing water. Filamentous algae waved in green flags. A twig-shaped shadow darted by. So there were fish in Ghost Creek! What next, a forty-inch cruiser?

In fact, as with the rare woodpeckers, at least one species of Ghost Lake's stocked fish had survived the eruption. Protected by snow and ice, the lake's cutthroat trout had escaped the searing winds and heavy ash unharmed. The resident population had even spread downstream to colonize the Clearwater valley. Though their numbers were still far lower than those in other Cascade lakes, these hardy specimens of native trout had persisted through ashfall, blown-down forests, and sun.

I followed the trail up the creek to the lake's pumice shore, where stems of young pearly everlasting plants and showy sedges shone in the sun. Other things, too, caught the afternoon glare—a soda can, aluminum foil, plastic fragments, and cigarette butts. I sat down next to the trash, crossed my legs, and took in Ghost Lake. It seemed so small and shallow it could almost be called a pond. How odd that large fish had once thrived here! The eruption had probably made the lake even shallower, filling its banks with ash. The willow-edged puddle, free of any log raft, contrasted sharply with Spirit, whose massive log-jammed expanse dominated its basin. Ghost Lake's shallowness made me realize that depth was to lakes what height was to mountains: the deeper the lake, the more mysterious. But perhaps the lake also seemed small for another reason: its banks were fenced in by its ghostly trees.

They were everywhere—and although I was busy watching them, I couldn't help feeling watched. They stood, silent and upright, of various heights and sizes, perfectly dead. The sun glinted from their pale trunks. Thousands of needle-less branches arched black against the cumulus-white sky. They had died abruptly, but death had not yet altered their hold on the land. They remained rooted, in the place they had first seeded in, and they were going to remain rooted there for a while. Their powerful profiles made me wonder whether human arrogance would be diminished if people also died standing up and remained standing for decades, arms outstretched. What if our species had to fare for itself by staying in one place forever? It seemed that although human beings had the strength to cut down trees they would never possess the strength of trees. Ghost Lake's ghosts were far beyond any time dimension a mobile biped might try to discern. Anyone who said they understood the pacing of trees—their slow growth and indefinite decay—was a liar or a mystic. I tried to root myself and imagine the pace of Ghost Lake, summer and winter, year after year, decade after decade, century upon century, day upon day. I tried to envision myself immobile, tapped on by woodpeckers, thwacked by a volcanic blast, unmoved by the moving sun and moon above me. It didn't work. No human with two feet and a desire to see the world could do it. I had to admit that as much as I was afraid of cougars and felt an affinity for trees, I could sooner imagine myself a four-footed predator than any herbaceous thing.

As I stared at the lake and its trees, I realized that I no longer needed to talk out loud or worry about what the weather would do. I didn't need to know what time it was, whether the toad crouched among the sedges was a *Bufo bufo borealis,* or what type of swallow looped above the lake. I had met no other hikers coming, and I knew that I would meet none going back. If a cougar was curled on a rock behind me, so much the better for the cougar.

I packed up the aluminum can, foil, plastic, and cigarette butts and turned away from the shore. The swallows continued to loop, the snags continued to stand. I looked back at the spot where I had sat for an hour. Except for the trash I had just removed, there was no sign of my passing. By the time I headed back up the scorched ridge—perhaps it was the position of the sun or the passing clouds—my slow-moving shape cast no shadow.

Meta Lake

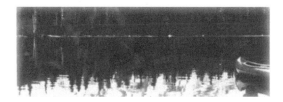

Nature is not benevolent;
Nature is just, gives pound
for pound, measure for measure . . .

—John Burroughs

After my journey to Ghost Lake, there remained one final place I longed to visit in the backcountry. Nestled a few miles north of Spirit Lake amid the backcountry's rugged peaks, Grizzly Lake was the first in a chain of alpine lakes that seemed to stretch north forever. I had camped on Grizzly's shore with my sister Terese when I was sixteen. At that time, I looked upon the lake as the first of a chain I would visit, summer upon summer, for the rest of my life. I hardly thought that Grizzly would mark a terminus rather than a stepping-stone for my relationship with the pre-eruption backcountry.

Like most of the backcountry, Grizzly Lake lay in the direct path of the lateral blast. Nearly every conifer surrounding the lake was hurled into its small basin. Ash buried its shore. What little was known about Grizzly Lake after the eruption was gleaned by flying over it; all of the backcountry's trails had been obliterated. It would require fifteen years for a trail to be blazed down into the steep basin shaded by Mount Margaret's north face. In fact, crews were still completing the new Lakes Trail 211 at the time Celeste and I planned to hike it. We weren't sure whether we would be allowed in.

But our concern over the trail was nothing compared to our battle against the weather the afternoon in late June 1995 when we piled our packs into a rented car and headed for the mountain. The sunshine of my recent Ghost Lake hike seemed centuries away. We knew that the storm bearing down on us would either be awful or worse. Blue sky was out of the question.

We camped at Iron Creek and woke in the middle of the night to the storm hammering the tent's rainfly and a military jet screaming so loudly overhead we were certain the little red tent was its target. Fortunately, the dawn brought a break in the rain and the darting black hoods of hungry Steller's jays. We made tea and munched on poppyseed muffins while the Cispus River whispered its name over and over. The stretch of river where we were camped was an ancient site for the Taitnapam, or Upper Cowlitz, who fished the Cispus in the 1800s before a railroad was constructed to haul out the valley's 200-foot-tall trees. The campground contained the few ancient trees that had escaped harvest, their crowns still dripping from the previous night's rain.

As the forest brightened, we rolled up the wet tent and headed for the blast zone. We planned to hike 1,500 feet up to Norway Pass via Independence Pass, then continue another mile or so over Bear Pass. There, weather permitting, we would see Grizzly Lake.

Little did we know that we had other obstacles to face besides rain. With wet gear stashed in our backpacks, we started up toward Independence Pass only to discover that a landslide had removed a significant portion of the trail near Tephras Pinnacle, a conspicuous outcropping of columnar basalt on Spirit Lake's east side. We tried to hike around the slide, but it ran a smooth course straight to the lake, several hundred feet down.

"Foiled again," I said, turning back toward the trailhead. Irked by our sloppy planning at Coldwater, I was anxious to see Grizzly Lake no matter what the circumstances.

"It's interesting to see how nature alters things so quickly around here," Celeste said, trying to consider our predicament in a positive light. "All it takes is one winter for a road or trail to go. The first onslaught is leaves, then downed trees, then slides. Obviously, this part of the lake wasn't going to tolerate a trail."

Celeste's observation made me realize that I had become obsessed with one type of disturbance—a volcanic eruption. Here was an ordinary landslide, something that happened frequently in mountainous terrain like that which surrounded Spirit Lake. Last year there had been a trail here, this year, a smooth gully of gravel. Land was a fluid concept in the Cascades; eruptions were only the starting point.

On our way down we stopped at an outcropping Celeste nicknamed Contemplation Peak because we were able to contemplate Spirit Lake from several hundred feet above the water. We watched the log raft swirl and disperse far below as winds pecked at it. A hoary marmot strolled a blast-blown log near us that jutted out over the cliff like a deadly high diving board. The log pointed away from the volcano, its twisted-off top ending abruptly in the moist air encircling the peak. The muscular mammal didn't seem to mind the vertigo-inducing height. The blond tips of his fur shimmered as he promenaded back and forth, sizing up his visitors. For a good fifteen minutes we watched the marmot as the marmot watched us. Then we hiked down the trail as the afternoon wind rose and a fresh rainstorm began. By the time we reached the car I felt grateful for any shelter—even an automobile. We threw our soaked gear in the back and changed into dry clothes as the windows fogged up.

"What now?" I asked in despair.

"Well, how about some soup?"

By the time we passed Cascade Peaks viewpoint, the storm had blocked out what little daylight was left. Lacking a plan, we continued down the road until we reached the Meta Lake parking lot, the last place to stop before we turned south or north out of the monument. There, with the wind buffeting the car and the rain splattering the windows like BB pellets, Celeste cooked instant minestrone soup on the passenger-side floor while we considered returning to Iron Creek. By the time we had eaten the grainy mush, inertia had claimed us.

"Why don't we just day hike tomorrow?" Celeste proposed. "We can still make it to Grizzly Lake and back, and by that time maybe the storm will have passed through and we'll be able to see more than fifty yards in front of us."

I resisted any thought that the storm might continue for days, despite vivid memories of entire weeks soaked in rain at my family's cabin and Harmony Falls Lodge.

We passed the night in the waterproof car, wriggling in our sleeping bags like astronauts shuttling through space. Celeste had the luxury of the passenger seat; I had to negotiate the steering wheel. I was somewhere around my thirtieth position, with my feet propped between the side window and dash, when Celeste started talking in her sleep in Spanish. I squished my feet into damp boots and threw on my wet jacket. With toilet paper and garbage bag in hand, I jumped out of the car and watched my urine dissolve in a runnel of rainwater. Things were so perfectly miserable they were wonderful. I felt like flipping off the volcano, shouting at the top of my lungs, standing on the pavement until every inch of skin had been claimed by the wind and rain.

Then dawn arrived. As the darkness eased, thunderheads scudded by without rain. The winds had subsided a bit, and the air smelled like forgiveness—sweet, unexpected, an offering out of nowhere.

We slipped into our boots and walked quietly to Meta Lake.

Neither Celeste nor I had seen Meta Lake before the eruption. At that time Meta had been considered a backcountry lake—accessible mainly to those on horseback or loggers slicing their way up the 100 Road. In contrast, after the eruption it was difficult to avoid, lying so close to Highway 99 that cars could be heard from its shore. But as we walked the paved trail in a light rain, the only noises we heard were water dripping off the firs and an occasional bird.

We were strolling through a forest of green miracles, young trees so tall they were already several feet above our heads. In fact, these youthful-looking Pacific silver firs were already fifty years old, according to Monument Scientist Peter Frenzen. They looked young because they had spent many slow-growing years in the dark understory of Meta Lake's pre-eruption forest. It was only when the huge Douglas-firs and hemlocks composing the forest's overstory were killed by the eruption that the little silver firs had their own chance to grow. After adjusting to the burst of new sunlight and ash on their needles, they started to soar.

This small pocket of survivors told a curious story at Meta Lake—a story of luck and life. The little firs had endured not only because they were hardy but because they were protected from the blast by Meta Lake's southern ridge. Because it faced north, away from the volcano, the leeward side of the ridge protected its trees and shrubs from the searing winds. More fortuitous still, the north-facing ridge possessed a layer of slowly thawing snow, which insulated the plants from the blast's heat. As it melted, the snow further helped the plants by forcing cracks in the foot-deep layer of ash, which hardened like concrete after rain. Frenzen and other scientists determined that where the snowbank lay that May morning was where plants survived.

Because of the ridge and its snow, Frenzen has watched two different forests grow back at Meta Lake: the snow-blessed survivors and the lake's opposite ridge, where south-facing slopes possessed neither the topography nor snow to protect plants from the crackling winds. Even as Celeste and I walked the wet path, the difference between the two slopes was strong enough for the casual observer to detect. Cool, shaded, and moist, the north-facing slope supported three times the amount of plants the sunny south-facing slope did, including devil's club, salmonberry, and many species of wildflowers. In contrast, the south-facing slope contained mostly pioneer species, such as fireweed, pearly everlasting, willow, and alder. According to Frenzen, it would be decades before the two hillsides looked similar again.

Frenzen began studying Meta Lake in August 1980, when he arrived as a member of Jerry Franklin's research team. As a graduate student in forest ecology, Frenzen was dumbfounded at the scale of the disturbance—not just at Meta Lake but everywhere. The young ecologist felt that he was in some sort of prehistoric land, and even dreamed of dinosaurs as he camped outside. All the while, even in the middle of the night, he waited for the volcano to erupt again. Sometimes it did, and the crew would wake to discover that ash had fallen on them while they slept. By the time he was hired by the

Forest Service in 1987, Frenzen had tracked hundreds of research plots and had begun to understand how the blast zone's living things had responded to the eruption's different levels of disturbance. As with his study sites at Meta Lake, each of Frenzen's research plots had its own story to tell, at its own pace, and with its own protagonists. With so much contrasting life to keep track of, Frenzen had come to understand his role as just one life-form among thousands, and where the volcano stood in relation to them all.

It was easy to understand Frenzen's humility after a brief walk through the forest at Meta. But for the weather and steep land—two factors I had cursed only the day before—the trees around us would be dead.

We sat on a wet log and gazed out over the lake. Even fish had survived in Meta's waters. Only two months after the eruption, Jerry Franklin and two of his colleagues spent the day examining Meta's ash-covered plants while the helicopter pilot and his foreman waited at the lake. When the researchers returned to the helicopter they asked the two pilots how they had spent their time. "Oh, we caught some fish," the pilot said. "Yeah, sure!" the scientists laughed. But it was true: the two fishermen had caught several brook trout that had been stocked before the eruption and had survived under the ice and snow.

Now, fifteen years later, Meta Lake was providing the Clearwater valley with proliferating brook trout. Celeste and I watched the water for splashes, but only wind and occasional raindrops rippled the lake. Instead we glimpsed black tadpoles squiggling at our feet, and a bobbing head with two round eyes in the distance. The head floated toward us like a peaceful aquatic Buddha. It was so large we almost mistook it for a baby beaver's. But then we noticed that it was attached to a dark body about the size of a human hand. The Buddha floated a little closer and I recognized it as a western toad.

The eyes glanced over us then looked away—and still the creature floated toward us. Like the marmot we had seen the day before, the *Bufo* seemed as curious about us as we were about it.

According to ecologist Charlie Crisafulli, Meta Lake is an important breeding ground for the prolific toad. Each spring, while patches of snow still hug the ground, hundreds of western toads converge at the lake for what Crisafulli calls a "three-day orgy," which results in millions of eggs. Such abundance belies the species' perplexing status worldwide. Like many other toads and frogs, the western toad is believed to be on the decline. Even as we watched the warty bather, scientists around the globe were trying to piece together why the world's amphibians have been dropping like canaries in so many coal mines. Even in undeveloped areas like national parks, some species have declined to the point of extinction. Herpetologists speculate that such things as acid rain, climate changes, and disease are killing the sensitive animals. Some believe that the western toad is disappearing due to the combination of ultraviolet radiation and a fungus. With its immune system damaged by increased solar radiation due to ozone depletion in the upper atmosphere, the toad has trouble fighting the fungus, which attacks its eggs, killing them before they can become tadpoles.

The global declines intrigued Crisafulli, whose blast zone research told a different story. Since 1980 Crisafulli had studied how a wide range of organisms—including birds, small mammals, and plants—fared in the wake of the blast. Having loved frogs and salamanders since he was a child, Crisafulli kept an eye out for pockets of surviving amphibians. At Meta Lake he found hundreds of them. The same snow that had protected the Pacific silver firs also insulated the lake's northwestern salamanders, Cascades frogs, and Pacific tree frogs.

In 1994 Crisafulli began an intensive amphibian survey and found that the blast zone's frogs and salamanders were anything but declining. In areas like Meta Lake and the debris avalanche the populations were actually skyrocketing. For the toad, a pond-breeder, this news contradicted the plummeting numbers found elsewhere in its range, which runs from northern California to Alaska.

With his research still in the early stages, Crisafulli could only speculate as to why the blast zone's amphibians were thriving. He believed that although in many cases the eruption destroyed habitats, in other cases it actually *developed* habitats, particularly for frogs. He tracked one frog that spent an entire month holed up under the north side of a boulder on the Pumice Plain, one of the blast zone's most severely impacted areas. He would hear it croaking daily, out in the middle of nowhere, where there was no water in sight and surface temperatures reached 122 degrees Fahrenheit. He believed it survived by waiting for nighttime temperatures to reach dew point before foraging for insects.

Celeste and I played stare-down with the toad until he finally tired of us and swam toward the lake's outlet. A small wake emanated from his brown-bubbled rump. For a brief time we had entered the amphibian's universe. The slow-motion moment reminded me of one other time I had penetrated that damp, cool world—as a child, immersed up to my waist in Spirit Lake. With toes digging into the bottom of the lake's south shore, I had captured rough-skinned newts as they swam underwater like schools of fish. The moment I touched one of the sepia-skinned torsos it froze, feigning lifelessness, and descended, knobby limbs outstretched, to the lake bottom. Fascinated by their bright-orange bellies, I turned some of the newts upside down as they sank. Little did I know that the bumpy skin secreted toxins that made the troll-like animal the most poisonous newt west of the Rockies. Today, I knew enough to leave the embattled newts alone. As a forest species, the rough-skinned newt was not among the blast zone's list of hardy pioneers. Crisafulli had located only a few individuals throughout the entire blast zone. Not surprisingly, one pair lived at Meta Lake.

The toad had disappeared and daybreak was over, but Celeste and I lingered one moment more. We had walked the paved path in silence in the hope of spotting another aquatic creature. But we were too late or too early or too noisy. Meta Lake's beavers were nowhere to be seen.

I had spotted one of Meta Lake's beavers only once before. The shy family was a far cry from the beavers that had paddled the Toutle River before the eruption. Having set up shop so close to the highway—one of their two dams lay within a few feet of the pavement—Meta's beavers avoided all contact with humans. It seemed a little ironic to me; according to Crisafulli, it was probably due to human-planted cottonwoods and willows that the pioneering beavers were able to reach Meta Lake. After the eruption, the Forest Service planted the deciduous trees along Clearwater Creek, downstream from Meta. By 1987 the beavers had stumbled upon the delectable stands. They munched up all the trees, then continued upstream to Meta. Now, eight years later, Crisafulli's research crews had happened upon gnawed twigs and trees at nearly every body of water in the blast zone except Spirit.

My mouth had fallen open the day Crisafulli had told me where the beavers were the most plentiful. My wringing of hands over their disappearance on the Toutle River had all been for nothing. It seemed that now, not even two decades after the eruption, the beavers were feasting and breeding on none other than the debris avalanche—the very place I thought it would require centuries for them to reinhabit. The enterprising mammals had built four dams on Maratta Pond near Coldwater Ridge—only a few miles from where I had watched the North Fork residents swim years ago.

We rose to go. I knew we would see no beavers that day. The resourceful animals had long ago outsmarted us. For all the walking and driving Celeste and I had done thus far in the blast zone, it was nothing compared to the rodents' quick journeys up the Clearwater and Toutle River valleys. The only mourning to be done now was over the fact that Celeste and I could not keep up with the beavers' pace.

We turned onto the highway as the windshield blurred increasingly with raindrops. Another front was moving through. My spirits rolled downhill as we drove a mile north to the Norway Pass trailhead. There, an outhouse awaited us, as well as a water pump for fixing our breakfast, and the trail to Grizzly Lake—if we wanted to brave yet another downpour.

Grizzly Lake

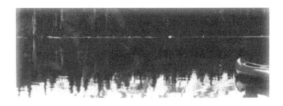

Every natural fact is an emanation,
and that from which it emanates is an emanation also,
and from every emanation is a new emanation.

—Ralph Waldo Emerson

Here," Celeste said, as she handed me a cup of peppermint tea. We had set up the cookstove in the roofed entryway of the outhouse at the Norway Pass trailhead while the downpour worked its way overhead. Rain bathed the car while occasional fumes from the toilets swirled past. I tried to remain optimistic, but my hopes began to fade as I watched the trail to Norway Pass and Grizzly Lake disappear in a solid white bank. Celeste's knee was sore and her boots leaked. How could we hike 2,000 feet up a winding trail in a storm, then back down again?

I turned around to take the cup and caught my breath. It was from the same pottery as my little sugar bowl from Harmony Falls Lodge. A devoted explorer of rummage sales and antique shops, Celeste had happened upon two cups of the old pattern. A maroon leaf marked the handle. Inside each small white bowl steeped the pale mint tea, its steam swirling in the cool mountain air.

The cups were the most recent addition to a small stash of china Celeste had unearthed at various estate sales in Portland. On several of our trips she had presented each piece as a surprise, so that I now possessed six dinner plates, eight saucers, a pair of salt and pepper shakers, a creamer, and the original sugar bowl.

The weather was awful, the outhouse stalls odoriferous, yet I sipped my tea with a smile. It wasn't that Harmony Falls was suddenly going to reappear, or the cabin, or the lake's forested shores. The hand-painted cup warming my hands alone sufficed. I had seen enough shattered fragments—the log raft at Spirit Lake, the volcanic crater, the clearcut woods—to accept those fragments not just as echoes of once beautiful things but as concrete things themselves. Two years earlier I had returned to Spirit Lake to piece those fragments back together. But now I understood that it wasn't a matter of making something shattered whole again. All one could do was try to make sense of the fragments as they were. For there is a beauty to fragments when fragments are all one has.

It was only an hour past dawn, so we lingered over our oatmeal and tea. As a bold chipmunk slinked around our makeshift camp, we contemplated the weather from under the outhouse's eaves. Was that thunder? Was the horizon lightening just a bit? After a while we dashed across the rain-slick parking lot to pump water from the well at the trailhead. After washing dishes and filling water containers we set off for Grizzly Lake in the rain.

To my relief I found that the winds had died down. As we climbed the two miles to Norway Pass, I discovered that we weren't getting half as wet as we had the day before. There was only the dripping fireweed and alder to brush out of our way. Water worked its way under the cuffs of my rain jacket, but otherwise I felt I could hike for miles through the damp, delicious air. However, Celeste's boots—the same boots she had worn on her backcountry hikes as a teenager—were taking on water faster than a sinking schooner. We stopped so that she could change into dry socks, unwrap our lunch from two plastic bags, and place them over her feet. With the bags sticking out of her boots, she found that her feet stayed dry and the hazard of blisters was prevented. We soon reached Norway Pass and discovered that we had the view of the lake to ourselves, although thunderheads concealed the crater. A young osprey circled over the devastated basin, uninhabited and vast.

"Devastation" was one of the words most heard at Mount St. Helens. In fact, "devastated area" was considered synonymous with the "blast zone." The name had been used to describe the area affected by Lassen Peak's 1914–21 eruptions in California, and was adopted soon after the 1980 eruption at Mount St. Helens to designate the area affected by Loowit's blast. But many scientists now avoided the term, seeing the fifteen-year-old eruption as merely part of a cycle, not bad or destructive. Frenzen, for one, looked at the eruption as a "shuffling of the deck"—where everything was still present, just rearranged. Humans tended to focus on what was taken away after the eruption, but in most instances, the plants were still there, although with the majority being dead they played a new role. Even the ash—which many people considered harmful—was just soil for the next system.

Having survived a shattering of things at Mount St. Helens, I wasn't sure I agreed entirely with the scientists. I found their preferred terms—such as "re-establishment" of ecosystems or the eruption's "disturbance"—as euphemistic as "devastation" was value-laden. Like the blast zone's survivors, my own life was marked with a transient violence whose effects lingered like thin growth rings inside a thick-barked tree. It seemed to me that science itself still lacked appropriate words for describing things like eruptions. If the eruption at Mount St. Helens was a "disturbance," did that mean that things here were still "disturbed"? And if so, wasn't "disturbed" as value-laden as "destroyed"? The question, it seemed, was whether humans had the right to call volcanic destruction "bad." In my own life, the destruction had certainly been painful, but not necessarily bad.

"I love to close my eyes when I'm away from here and think of this huge silence," Celeste said. "I carry it around like a great calm."

That silence was something I had first found troubling in the blast zone. The "destroyed" land's complete calm—the lack of wind in the trees, the absence of birdsong, the missing crunch of a deer's hoof on leaves—was so overwhelming at first I had found it unnerving. Now I relished the immense noiselessness. It was no longer an absence so much as a quality. But ironically, like the eruption's "destruction," the blast zone's silence was ephemeral. Over the last few years the quiet of the ash-covered land had been eroding along with the ash; nature was now sloshing, cawing, and hooting. What had begun as a single buzz had become a splash, then a croak, then a full chorus of coyotes. The entire volcanic wilderness was like one giant winter melting into spring. As we continued up the trail toward Bear Pass, the dripping masses of fireweed alone combined in a loud collection of whispers. And among them, junco, junco, junco. And at our feet, the sudden rustle of a gopher departing underground.

"Did you see that?" Celeste shouted at the sight of the speeding rump.

We laughed. Gophers were considered nocturnal—did we actually see one? We stepped over what looked like gopher cores—little mounds of pumice snaking across the path like erosion-control dikes. The gophers created these heaps of unwanted soil as they abandoned snow tunnels during springtime melting. We had seen the same cores on the Independence Pass Trail and had kept an eye out for the burrowers. But like their larger cousins the beavers, these nonhibernating rodents showed no interest in humans and foraged mostly at night. Also like the beavers, their residing in the blast zone seemed hard to believe. Like Meta Lake's trout and trees, the little mammals were survivors, not colonizers.

On that May day in 1980, while deer died standing up and birds dropped lifeless from the sky, Mount St. Helens' northern pocket gophers munched on caches of food stashed along the damp, dark walls of their burrows. Something like winter was raging aboveground, but the gophers were safe and sound, at least for a while. But by the next day they had to figure out how to get by without a reliable supply of plants—just at the time of year when their winter caches were emptying. Although many gophers probably died in the ash, a significant number lived long enough to reproduce. Among these, some probably even completed their short three-year life spans, reproducing many offspring. These tough burrowers were the blast zone's early cultivators, pushing up buried humus so that it mixed with the nutrient-poor ash, and creating depressions in which seeds could take root.

Of the six species of gophers native to the Northwest, the northern pocket gopher (Thomomys talpoides) is the most common, adapting its diet to a wide variety of plants. With its complex network of tunnels, the rodent works its way to roots, eats them, or hauls them off in its fur-lined cheeks to store in a cache. Its powerful forelimbs, poor eyesight, and long claws all bespeak its subterranean lifestyle. Despised by gardeners, golfers, and farmers, the rodent is recognized by naturalists as an important erosion-controller and rototiller, keeping mountain meadows tilled and healthy. The pocket gophers were the subjects of Charlie Crisafulli's first study. With his research mentor James MacMahon, Crisafulli trekked around the blast zone in 1980 with live traps and a bait of peanut butter and rolled oats to entice the hungry rodents. The two ecologists hiked for miles across the ashy, sun-seared terrain, catching deer mice, squirrels, beetles, and whatever else strayed into their traps. The work was grueling, but having studied desert animals at Utah State University, Crisafulli and MacMahon were familiar with dry, windswept land. That year, they documented thirteen other small mammal species besides the gophers. These survivors formed islands of life that then multiplied throughout the blast zone. By 1987, Crisafulli and MacMahon had documented the presence of twenty-five different species of small mammals in the ashfall zone and the blast zone. The list, which included shrews, voles, mice, chipmunks, moles, pikas, gophers, squirrels, mountain beavers, marmots, weasels, minks, and hares, represented more than three-fourths of the thirty-two species of small mammals believed to have inhabited the area before the eruption. Crisafulli and MacMahon failed to locate pine martens, otters, and fishers.

That the gophers were one of Loowit's star players seemed funny to me, given that the analogy between burrowing rodent and volcano had been made centuries ago by one of the world's first volcanologists, Déodat de Gratet de Dolomieu (1750–1801). Dolomieu, commemorated in the naming of the Dolomites, in the Italian Alps, likened volcanoes to moles because both push up soil from "just below the surface." Naturalist Eugene Kozloff also observed a likeness between molehills and volcanoes. Kozloff believed that a molehill was usually more like a volcano than a gopher mound because the mole's dirt is "pushed straight up," rather than to one side, like a gopher's. But Kozloff wasn't thinking of directed blasts, like Loowit's, where the dirt was indeed thrown sideways like a gopher's mound. Unlike a vertical, symmetrical molehill, the 1980 eruption was one giant gopher mound; "fan-like" was an adjective used for both the lateral eruption and the pocket gopher's handiwork.

Now, fifteen years later, the gophers were still working the soil, although "beneficial" was not a word Crisafulli used with abandon to describe the ubiquitous rodent's activities. In some places the gophers were selectively dining on such flowers as lupines, or inhibiting overall revegetation. However, given that predators such as hawks and coyotes were now plentiful, it wasn't clear that the gophers would dominate. And as the forest returned the meadow-loving gophers would perhaps diminish, while such forest-dwellers as the northern flying squirrel or Douglas squirrel increased.

Stepping over more gopher cores beyond Norway Pass, we continued uphill toward Bear Pass. After less than a mile we reached the turn-off for Grizzly Lake as the clouds fractured into pieces of blue sky. Amid thickets of mountain ash we marched down the freshly blazed trail and smiled at the moist, green earth. Celeste's yellow rain slicker beamed brightly among the brilliant-green huckleberry bushes, mountain azaleas, and young noble firs. We were on the leeward side of the ridge, where the tall, rain-glazed snags were being replaced by a young forest. Ten-foot-tall cedars dripped rain from their tips. I walked with the same joy I had experienced at St. Helens Lake with Michael. The backcountry was back. The lush slopes blazed with rain-fed life. And to think I had cursed the storm.

We followed the trail as it zigzagged down the back side of the ridge. The view north of the blown-down trees and replanted forests ended in clouds. Directly below, Grizzly Lake reflected a dark jade. Logs congregated in clumps along its shores. Others poked out of the rain-freckled surface as snags. As we reached the basin I ransacked my memory, trying to remember the hike I had taken to the lake in 1978 with Terese. Didn't a trail go around the shore? Wasn't the campground on the left? Hadn't the topography been gentler? That summer, we had camped at the lake's south-western corner amid other backpackers' tents and campfires. Expecting bird chirps for an alarm clock, we lay paralyzed as a giant rockslide careered down the back side of Mount Margaret, terminating in a tinkle of gravel only a hundred yards away. If that rockslide had happened at the current lake, we would be under it. Or, more precisely, we would be under water. It appeared that the lake had risen, and the camping area between water and cliff was gone.

Grizzly Lake had no doubt endured a similar fate as Spirit, swelling upon receiving a heavy dose of ash and logs. The ridge Celeste and I had just descended was lush partly because its ash had ended up in Grizzly. At the lake's west end, a waterfall tumbled in an ash-gray valley down to the lake. We were looking at what the blast zone biologists called "lakeshore burial." Most of the back-country lakes had experienced it—tons of ash inundating their basins to raise their bottoms and bury shoreline plants.

The longer I looked at the lake, the clearer it became that Grizzly Lake was no longer suitable for camping. Not only did it lack its former shoreline—complete with trail and old 1930s picnic tables—but the earth around it was covered with logs. It was just as well. Like St. Helens Lake, Grizzly was now off-limits for campers because its shores were protected as one of the monument's research sites. We scrutinized the jumble of barkless trunks that had accumulated around the lake's outlet. Most were driftwood gray; but some shone orange, as though recently cracked by the storm. Pools of rainwater collected in depressions near their root wads. Somewhere among them lay the shattered remnants of the old campground's picnic tables. Backcountry ranger Hans Castren had told me about the hewn slabs tossed amid the pile of decaying logs.

Two pikas scampered to and fro over the log maze. Like Loowit's other small mammals—the beavers, gophers, and chipmunks—these subalpine lagomorphs had made a quick comeback in the decade following the eruption. Celeste and I had happened upon the squeaky haymakers in several areas besides Grizzly Lake, including highway scarps on the way to the mountain. Preferring rocky terrain, pikas harvest wildflowers and grasses and dry them in piles before storing them under rocks for winter. The puny, big-eared foragers had taken up residence at Grizzly Lake, eeking and darting among the logs, which seemed to mimic broken boulders. No doubt the lake's narrow basin and returning plants offered the perfect refuge from hawks flying overhead. The pika's other enemies, weasels and martens, were an uncommon sight before the eruption and were now even more rare, making things easier for the pika.

The rain was easing up, so Celeste and I broke out some water and bagels, and I soaked up the new, post-eruption image of the lake. What I was seeing would forever alter my memory of the old, pre-eruption Grizzly. But I let the old vision go. The dim, dreamy lake of my past was the reason I had waited out the storm to hike that morning, but suddenly it seemed like a faded still life compared to this strange new lake flooding my senses with its sweet wet odors, leaping pikas, and spliced logs.

As we stood next to one log, the old picnic tables emerged at our feet. They had been right in front of us all the time—thick, gray, rough-hewn planks. One slab lay cracked in half, with enormous rusted nails poking out of it. I bent down to run my fingers across the damp wood. The weathered fibers had been sanded down like the rest of the wood in the blast zone. Perhaps, seventeen years ago, I had sat on this very slab. Now, sedges and pearly everlasting were claiming it.

Instead of exploring the lake further we decided to stay on the trail, rather than disturb the lake's neotenic salamanders. An odd combination of larva and grown-up, Grizzly Lake's neotenes were one of ecologist Charlie Crisafulli's current objects of study. Instead of metamorphosing slowly from larva to adult as most salamanders do, Grizzly's salamanders develop sexual organs while still in the larval stage, and stay underwater instead of exploring moist ground.

According to Crisafulli, neoteny may have been a survival mechanism for the backcountry's salamanders after the eruption—a sort of sexual contingency plan in the blast zone's harsh environment. Or it may have been that the backcountry lakes were full of neotenic salamanders before the eruption. Or, even more likely, the eruption may have favored the neotenes which, like the backcountry fish, survived underwater. Without pre-eruption data, Crisafulli had no way of knowing. Just the same, he had no doubt that overwintering larvae woke to challenging conditions after the eruption. Just being alive on the morning of May 19, 1980, wasn't enough; the trick was how to stay that way in a foot of desiccating ash. Crisafulli believed that both the ensatina salamander and western red-backed salamander were extirpated from the blast zone due to such severe conditions, but he remained curious to see at what point the salamanders would return to the volcano's north side.

Having hiked to Grizzly for the sake of the past, I now found myself fixed on its future. When would the ensatinas and western red-backeds return? When would martens creep up to hunt the pikas? When would beargrass regain its former abundance throughout the backcountry? Would the mountain goats return? If so, when, and how many? At what point would the silver firs and cedars overtake the snags and shade return? At what point would we not be able to see Spirit Lake from Norway Pass, except through a canopy of conifers, as I had the first time I came to Grizzly?

And so it was with the rest of the blast zone's fluctuating land. In a decade alone, Harmony Creek had metamorphosed from a rusty-red thread to a bushy green snake. Spirit Lake somehow already had trout in its clear waters. So when would the otters return to feast on the trout? And the great blue herons? And noble firs at Bear Cove? Which changes to the land would be temporary—like the beavers' brief absence from the upper North Fork of the Toutle—and which would prove permanent? Which would I live long enough to see, and which would require decades long past my death?

We returned up the ridge as the clouds held back their rain. The air smelled of another deluge, but somehow I knew that tomorrow would be a dry day in the blast zone. I also knew that as the sun returned, the white clusters of pearly everlasting that now shone like snowdrifts against the dark damp slopes would fade in the sunny light, in the same way they would melt eventually under the growing conifers in the blast zone's inescapable spring.

I thought of what Frenzen had told me when he spoke of the "disappearing" blast zone. A few weeks before our hike to Grizzly, he had mentioned that he and Crisafulli were already mourning the end of the blast zone. The time of the ash and logs was over; it was a whole new place now. He had said it with a certain melancholy, as though I might understand.

Everlasting: Winter

As it does in the deep forests, ice-crusted deserts, and brittle-grass plains, snow falls without sound in the blast zone. It falls in silence and silences the land. If I close my eyes as it descends, I hear nothing. But I know it is there, because snow has a taste and a touch and a fragrance. It coats my cheeks and eyelids for a moment, then melts. Gravity takes the watery drops down even as another light flake lands.

Weightless as these dry flakes seem, they land heavier than Loowit's ash. On a cool June night in 1980 I was sitting on the banks of the Willamette River when the volcano erupted with its first major ash plume since May 18. I thought I was being enveloped by a warm mist—the start of a common June rain. Then I licked my lips. Grit. The Earth, not the sky, was raining. I covered my face with my sweater and hurried home while the windshield wipers streaked gray across the glass. That fall I took a Greyhound bus one weekend to visit Laura at the coast and sat beside a woman with asthma. She had lived her entire life in the Pacific Northwest but was going to leave, she said. Couldn't live near an active volcano. According to newspaper reports she'd read, Mount St. Helens' ash sliced lungs faster than cut glass.

But here today, on the volcano's foothills, there is only snow—snow that tastes and smells like the mountain when it is not erupting, like the memory of Spirit Lake flat and white as a winter desert. Snow that covers my boots in minutes, that buries stumps and young trees the way the volcano buries them in mud and pumice. Upon its bright surface is one black spider. Or, a few yards farther, hundreds of soft brown fir seeds released in a warm December wind.

Nowhere do I see even one everlasting. The white wildflower is now buried in white. What few strong stems were standing only days ago are now flat against the earth, freezing along a horizontal plane the way Spirit Lake used to freeze when it was shaded by a tall forest. Celeste's ski poles make a sound like someone digging. We have shed our coats, sweating our way uphill with each pole-stab and slide. We are celebrating our birthday today: the winter

solstice, the day of least sunlight in the northern hemisphere, when
the sun reaches one of its solis stationes—its greatest distance
from the celestial equator. Now, all over the northern hemisphere,
pearly everlasting has finished one cycle of its life.

Perhaps I am treading on dead everlastings even as I ski. Who
would know? We live on one layer of earth at a time. On the
winter solstice of our birth, doctors failed to hear the heartbeat
of the second twin after the first was born. Seventeen minutes
passed, and then I slipped into the world like a dormant everlasting—alive after all. Today that one layer of earth is blinding:
white snow, white sky, white volcano. No wonder the snowshoe
hares around here change their coats accordingly. If not for a
small hare's black-marble eye I wouldn't have seen its snowy
haunches, hidden behind an old fir a hundred yards back. Shall
I, too, disguise myself in white and drift into this land? The past is
a heavy coat. I am steeped in an older vision, continually shocked
by the present mountain, the present lake, the present river. But
snow has now tucked inside it. Even the winter solstice spells
summer on the lower half of the globe. Shall I shake off an old
landscape the way the mountain did?

Pearly everlasting wears its own white coat. It is tomentose—a
botanical term for furry. Each everlasting leaf is swathed in white
hairs from tip to base. The hairs deflect harsh sunlight during hot
days. They also retain moisture, insulate the leaf during freezing
nights, and protect the plant from wind. When the leaf is wet,
some of its hairs remain white, looking as though the leaf still
bore a touch of ice or the last of a fast-melting snowfall.

Pearly everlasting belongs to a whole genus of furry plants.
Even the genus name Anaphalis, though obscure, may have a furry
etymology. Botanist Lewis Clark claimed that Anaphalis may have
been invented by Linnaeus as an anagram of Gnaphalium, from
the Greek knaphalon, or tuft of wool.

Some species of everlasting outgrow their wool. I have seen
adult everlasting plants whose large lower leaves were shedding
their hairs, bursting out of their fur as though it were too small

*or ragged, while the smaller leaves at the stalk's tip were still com-
pletely woolly. Why should the lower leaves lose their wool? Perhaps they endured less wind. Or perhaps they were reaching the
end of their photosynthetic life and no longer needed their wool to
protect them. Or perhaps they were simply adapting to a slightly
warmer habitat in the same way a horse disposes of its winter coat.*

*Today the mountain, too, wears a white coat. Before 1980 it
kept its coat longer in the winter and gained it faster in the fall.
Now, 1,300 feet shorter, it, too, darkens and whitens from solstice
to solstice like a snowshoe hare. It is a stratovolcano—a volcano
of many layers. Also known as composite cones, stratovolcanoes
coat themselves with a fresh layer of rock each time they erupt.
These coats eventually form a steep-sided cone. Andesite, dacite,
cinder, pumice, basalt: Loowit is an ancient composite of its hundreds of eruptions, a constant reminder that the Earth exists in
thousands of layers, not one, and that these layers shift, undulate,
and expand for hundreds of miles. I think of the mountain as a
protrusion upon the land. But its roots sink deeper than those of
any fir. Its magma chamber lies eight miles below my skis. Meanwhile, I am blinded by a single layer of snow, unsure of the location of dormant everlasting flowers only inches down!*

*A composite volcano before me; a composite flower below. The
composite cone sends its ash plumes miles high; the latter, its
plumed seeds miles wide. So this is how composing goes—layer
upon layer, seed upon acre, plume upon plume, not always seen
by human eyes though we might measure and surmise. Roots,
rhizomes, aquifers, magma. A burrowing gopher senses more of
the earth than any house-dwelling human. We glimpse the world
mostly by its tips, anthropomorphize it in domestic metaphors:
blankets of snow, moss-draped firs, towering trees. We live first
through our own constructions, always a little blind to the wild
world. All it takes is one snowfall for us to forget the vegetable
kingdom for a while, to think that plants are dead instead of
sleeping. Or one dormant volcano for us to build and scurry
on old mudflows. See how the volcano lies white and tranquil*

today—as though it were as easy to love as the sweet steam of valleys, the soft slurp of tidepools, the rivers and trees.

"Were you ever angry at the mountain?" I ask Celeste while we pause to catch our breath. Unsnapping our skis, we sit for a moment in the snow, our coats spread beneath us to keep us dry.

"Yes, but then I climbed it a while back. It was all snow, so we step-kicked the whole way. That meant that I got to kick the mountain—again and again. I mean, I literally kicked it."

Around the globe stratovolcanoes often appear white and tranquil. They are tall, conical mountains topped with glaciers and snow. Japan's Fujiyama, Ecuador's Cotopaxi, New Zealand's Mount Egmont, Italy's Vesuvius—all stratovolcanoes whose snowy coats belie their cyclic violence. Unlike shield volcanoes—gently-sloped mountains that erupt mostly with fluid lava—stratovolcanoes explode with pasty lava, pumice, and ash. When they erupt, their picturesque glaciers melt in torrents, creating mudflows that gush ten times faster than any downstream resident can run. In 1985, more than 23,000 people died when Colombia's Nevado del Ruiz sent a massive mudflow through the town of Armero. Disaster, destruction, devastation, danger, death: these are the D words humans associate with stratovolcanoes—in particular, stratovolcanoes under snow.

We pick ourselves up and snap on our skis. I have already fallen twice and powdered my knees in the last hour, but I think of how grateful I am for one layer of snow—for all of the back-country's frozen lakes and meadows, for its small mammals and wintering fish, for its seedpods and roots. When the lateral blast swept through, it flashed against snow. When the ash rained down, it rained onto snow. One layer of white for incipient life.

We are one-layer creatures, dependent on air, ready for solid earth only as a grave. But I have tasted the planet from the inside out on a soft spring night. I have watched a river go 600 feet under. I have felt the earth ripple like a wave, have heard the silence of miles of ash, have dreamed dreams of a mountain whose insides have circled the globe. And I know what one layer of snow means when the volcano goes. What layer do I live on now?

The last time I set eyes on Spirit Lake before the eruption it was completely white. A cold December had transformed the lake's sur-face to ice, and several inches of snow had fallen. On a cold clear day, I abandoned a snapping fire at my family's cabin to visit the winter caretakers at Harmony Falls Lodge. I ventured out over the frozen water, plowing the snow with my boots. For more than an hour I carved a line from the campground to the lodge, where I paused to sip coffee with the caretakers before the short day ended. As I returned across the ice, not once did I think of crashing through.

A stupid bliss, I think now, plunging my pole in the snow. It was not the calculated risk of someone familiar with ice-covered pools. It was the gesture of one enamored with the appearance of things and not the things themselves. Enthralled by ice I had forgotten water. I lived the poverty of perceiving one layer alone.

THE VOLCANO

The False Summit

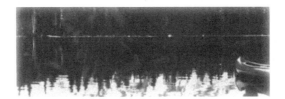

Only the hand that erases can write the true thing.

—Meister Eckhart

A false summit is a summit that tricks climbers into thinking they've reached the top of the mountain. It is an optical illusion that occurs for those who are too close to the mountain's flanks to see its true dimensions. Climbers have found false summits on many mountains. Before the eruption, Mount St. Helens was no exception. Some of the first climbers to scale the mountain were also the first to be tricked into thinking they had reached its top.

One such climber, it seems, was an anonymous author who described his ascent in 1860 with a group of prospectors whose interests turned to mountain climbing when they failed to find gold along the Lewis River. Guided as far as timberline by a Native American, the party of five white men ascended the south side. To record their ascent, the author took the mountain's Indian name, Loo-wit-Lat-kla, as his nom de plume. Of his position on the summit he wrote, "We looked upward, at an angle of about sixty degrees, and there, only a short distance from us, stood the little peak, which forms the summit of Loo-wit-Lat-kla."

The little peak was the false summit.

On March 27, 1980, a loud boom was heard at Mount St. Helens. For the first time in 123 years the volcano was erupting, venting ash into low clouds that hugged its cone. The ash came from a crater 250 feet across. Located on the mountain's northeastern tip, the crater gaped on the north side—at the base of the false summit.

Then, from March 27 until May 18, Loowit's two summits wandered slowly apart. As the mountain inflated itself with gas and magma, the false summit migrated nearly a quarter of a mile north and cascaded down hundreds of feet while the true summit remained more or less in place. By the dawn of May 18, Mount St. Helens' false summit was no longer false. Cracked by fault lines and yanked north by the volcano's bulge, it was no longer capable of fooling any observer into thinking it was anywhere near the top of the mountain. In fact, it wasn't a summit at all: it had become part of the volcano's 2,000-foot-long crater. In this way, the false summit foretold in miniature the profile of the volcano to come.

Since the eruption, Mount St. Helens' false summit, like its true summit, has been a summit of air. It is the dotted line inked onto photographs, the elevation that hovers above the crater like a ghost, the outline that begs completion.

False summits are false because climbers want something from the mountain: they want to touch its highest tip. Since the eruption,

Loowit's false summit still floats on top of the mountain because observers want something from the volcano. They want to see it whole again. One of the most frequently asked questions at Mount St. Helens is: "Will the dome grow as high as the mountain once was?" Loowit is a mountain of absence, a hole people want to see filled.

But the volcano announces, again and again, that destruction is only a form of instruction; there are no false summits, only climbers who err.

The Pumice Plain

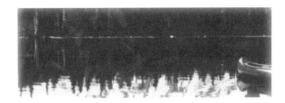

They are alive and well everywhere,
The smallest sprout shows there is really no death,
And if ever there was it led forward life . . .

—Walt Whitman

On the worst of days there is a flowering of lupines inside me. Even while I am stuttering in conversations, tripping on curbs, cursing the built-over world with its perpendicular edges, there is a flowering of lupines so fierce and broad their scent rises in my rib cage like incense. It is the smoke of the Pumice Plain, the smoke of pyroclastic flows once they have cooled, the smoke of petals smoldering from the spark of a wildflower poised upon fertilization. *Today!* the smoke curls inside me: *What are the lupines doing today?*

Celeste and I gazed upon them one July day after our Grizzly Lake hike as inland Amish might gaze upon a first-glimpsed ocean:

silent, grateful. On our left, the volcano steamed white. On our right, Spirit Lake shuffled its log raft like a deck of tattered cards. In the distance, the debris avalanche climbed the saddle between Johnston and Harry's Ridges like a giant peach staircase. Above, thunderheads knocked against the backcountry, their shadows darkening the ridges to charcoal, while all around us the silver-green lupines burned their riotous purplish petals. We stood alone in the fragrant cloud, smiling at each other and the flowers.

How could it be? It was just another day on the Pumice Plain. We had hiked here before. But on this particular day the wind was slightly calmer, the air slightly warmer, and the flowers in full bloom. Or perhaps it was as so many other travelers had scribbled in notebooks: the change was in us. Whatever the cause, I felt compelled to touch one lupine leaf in a shaking of hands. I lacked leaves, the lupine lacked hands, but a simple how-do-you-do seemed fitting. Not only did I feel grateful to this flower, I wasn't really acquainted with it.

Unlike pearly everlasting, *Lupinus lepidus* variation *lobbii* was to me a new, post-eruption flower. No doubt it had bloomed near my boots as I plowed through the pumice below Dog's Head or wandered the volcano's slopes at sunset, but I had failed to notice it. At that time, lupines were all the same to me, and I never thought to pay much attention to the flora at timberline. The peak overhead and pumice between my toes demanded my attention—not the flowers.

I wasn't alone. Before the eruption, Mount St. Helens was hardly studied for its flora. Only three botanists had bothered to inventory its timberline species. In 1898 Frederick Colville collected specimens for the Smithsonian on the southwestern slope, and in 1925 Harold St. John documented 315 species on the north and south slopes, including Spirit Lake. Finally, in July 1979, less than a year before the May 18 eruption, Arthur Kruckeberg visited the volcano and compiled its most extensive survey. At timberline he found not only lupines, but an abundance of partridgefoot and Cardwell's penstemon, along with pearly everlasting, arnica, buckwheat, wild strawberry, Newberry's knotweed, and Cascades mountain ash, among others. But the ecologist also noticed that Mount St. Helens was flora-poor. Having erupted so frequently and recently, the volcano lacked "endemic" species—species unique to it. Most other Cascade volcanoes possessed their own species or subspecies of alpine wildflowers, but not Loowit.

A lack of wildflowers at Mount St. Helens! It seemed funny now, considering the fields before us. I shook one lupine leaf whose slender flat blades stretched like fingers from an outspread hand. Unlike everlasting's "linear" leaves, the lupine's were "palmately compound": each of the little leaflets radiated from a central point, like a clock with seven green hands. I wanted to shake the leaves of each plant to congratulate it for growing on one of the roughest, most sterile, least secure places in the world. But how does one begin to shake hands with hundreds of thousands of lupines?

Unlike those pre-eruption days at timberline, today I knew that *lepidus* was not just any kind of lupine. Known commonly as alpine or prairie lupine, *lepidus* was a rugged inhabitant of high, dry places. With its silvery, low-growing leaves, the mat-forming wildflower hugged the windblown land like a barnacle clutching a surf-slathered reef. Here was a flower that preferred bare pumice over damp forest duff. According to Kruckeberg, *lepidus* bloomed on every Cascade volcano from Lassen Peak to Mount Rainier. It was "xerophilous"—a lover of "xeric" or dry places where life must start from zero—which was exactly what life had to do after the eruption in the area where we now stood.

The Pumice Plain was brand-new earth on May 18, 1980. We were standing on rocks that fifteen years ago had existed as magma deep underground. As in the native legend, Loowit became young again here in an instant, flinging lava hundreds of feet high, which solidified into pebbles and boulders even as it fell to earth. Like the Hawaiian Islands birthing themselves straight from the sea floor, the Pumice Plain was a new frontier in a matter of hours and in the most violent way. One of the most deadly volcanic processes had created the ground here. Geologists call the process a pyroclastic flow—from the Greek words *pyro* (fire) and *klastos* (fragmented). Also known by its French name, *nuée ardente*, or "hot, glowing cloud," a pyroclastic flow is a tumbling furnace of gases, ash, and rock that pulverizes the land it rolls over, incinerating all living things. It races across hillsides like an itinerant explosion, its lower half churning with boulders and pumice, its upper half swirling with gas and ash. Loowit's pyroclastic flows ripped out of the volcano at 100 miles per hour, fanning across the north slopes with temperatures of 1,100 degrees Fahrenheit. Geologists estimated that most of the flows began around noon on the day of the eruption, as the eruption plume shifted from dark, older rock to white—the fresh magma. The pyroclastic flows continued on and off for at least six hours, leaving behind a seventy-foot layer of rock that was still 780 degrees Fahrenheit two weeks after the eruption. The fresh pumice was so new, so huge, and so plentiful the ground where it lay would be given a new name: the Pumice Plain.

Over the last fifteen years, however, gravity had worked the pumice into the landscape, pushing it down streams, rolling it into canyons, burying it under mudflows. Many stones had also become less conspicuous, darkening from chalk-white to tan. Still, as we walked the Truman Trail we noticed some bright-white stones the size of pumpkins. One lay on the ground, cracked. Water had seeped into its porous pockets and frozen, snapping the stone's brittle latticework. But the pumpkin maintained its round shape, like a hard-boiled egg whose shell was cracked but not scattered. The cracking had been a gentle relenting along fissures instead of the violent explosion that had first formed the stone. The pieces reminded me of a jigsaw puzzle or the shards of a plate: things that begged to be pieced back together. But like the planet's plates—the continental fragments that 180 million years ago were joined as the ancestral supercontinent Pangaea—these stones would not be pieced back together. Like the Earth's plates, the pumice fragments would drift apart or rub together indefinitely, depending on whatever forces played upon them.

Although physical processes had removed some pumice, plants like *lepidus* were finishing off the job, obscuring the stones with stems and leaves. We were witnessing the gentle tyranny of green things—the gradual but inescapable working of surfaces, the way tree roots slough off sidewalks, fences bulge from trunks, or walls grow furry with moss. This was ecological succession—ponds filling marshes; fires burning meadows; meadows closing to forests; forests changing from one tree species to another until they reach a climax stage. Then a disturbance like fire is necessary to start the cycle again. Here, on the Pumice Plain, ecological succession meant that at this seral or early stage in the cycle, lupines ruled. But it had not always been so, nor would it always be so. We were here for a moment with the purplish-blue petals. Like the pumice upon which they now burned, the lupines were also vulnerable to the ebb and flow of the plain.

That the lupines were blooming everywhere was a twist in conventional ideas of succession. No one would have predicted that the little wildflower would conquer the plain to such a degree. According to David Wood, one of the dozen scientists now tracking the volcano's flora, prolific seed-dispersers like pearly ever-lasting and fireweed were the plain's presumed champions. A botanist at Chico State University, Wood began studying the blast zone in 1984, when he teamed up with University of Washington ecologist Roger del Moral, who had walked the volcano's slopes as early as July 1980 to observe "ad hoc" islands of life, like a ladybug turned herbivore in the absence of aphids, or a busy anthill in the middle of a mudflow. In 1986 the two ecologists established 2,200 plots on the plain. At that time, the solar-baked, windblown slopes were nearly plant-free. Even fireweed and pearly everlasting had dif-ficulty surviving in the nitrogen-poor pumice; for every pearly ever-lasting that seeded in and lived, roughly eight died. Such slender odds were nonetheless the highest survival rate the scientists found, and in 1988 they predicted that pearly everlasting would be the plain's most widespread plant, if only because it produced thou-sands of seeds to overcome the obstacles of survival.

But something soon happened. Around 1990, Wood and del Moral saw their plots filling up. Many more plants were seeding in—and the seedlings weren't just everlasting and fireweed. Other plants had arrived, and among them, the lupines.

The little pea plants caught the scientists off guard. According to the textbooks, *Lupinus lepidus* was not a traditional pioneer. For one thing, it didn't disperse its seeds by wind. Its peas were far heavier than either fireweed's or pearly everlasting's, which could be blown for miles. Nor did the little lupine produce as many off-spring per plant as the two larger, bushier species.

Nonetheless, the first plant found on the Pumice Plain was none other than a lupine. On a hot summer day in 1982, Charlie Crisa-fulli and James MacMahon stumbled upon a lone lupine in the center of the plain. After marking the area with white-plastic piping, Crisafulli tracked the single lupine year after year as it escaped mudflows, high winds, ashfall, and gully-carving rains. By the time of our July hike, Crisafulli had counted more than 100,000 plants in the area of the first lupine, as well as thirty other species that had seeded in.

Celeste and I located Crisafulli's original plot, now marked with a Forest Service interpretive sign. Along with Wood's and del Moral's plots, the intensively monitored research site seemed a far cry from the scarce plant surveys of the volcano's pre-eruption days. I had trouble seeing how Crisafulli could keep track of so many wildflowers. To a nonscientist, it was difficult to discern where one lupine ended and another began. How had they been so successful?

According to Wood, lupine's round, green peas have more energy reserves than either fireweed's or pearly everlasting's paper-thin seeds. The fat little peas supply crucial energy for the lupine seedlings during their first few critical weeks. The alpine wildflower also possesses a deep taproot that allows it to collect subsurface moisture, of which there is plenty on the plain. And, according to ecologist John Bishop, who began studying the lupine in 1990 for his doctoral research at the University of Washington, the wild-flower can self-pollinate in the absence of pollinators. But most importantly, the wildflower travels with its own portable fertilizer. As a member of the legume or pea family, *lepidus* fixes nitrogen— converting it from the air into organic ammonium, which enriches the soil. The wildflowers accomplish this by relying on *Rhizobium* bacteria on their roots. Found in symbiotic relationships on other plants besides lupines, these bacteria convert more atmospheric nitrogen than any other organism in the world. With such nitrogen-fixers, the *lepidus* plants are capable of thriving in soil that other plants would find uninhabitable. At the same time, the pioneering wildflowers improve the soil for other plants that can't fix nitrogen. So even while Celeste and I were enjoying the sight and fragrance of the lupines, the small legumes were chemically changing the plain, taking it from a volcanic wasteland to life-sustaining soil.

Strangely enough, the lupines weren't the first to ameliorate the plain. They weren't even the Pumice Plain's first complex life-form. Something less conspicuous had arrived before Crisafulli found the first lupine. Its appearance turned ecological theories upside down. Textbooks around the globe had to be rewritten after what researchers found trundling amongst the pumice: beetles.

No one had heard of an ecosystem starting with beetles. Most people thought that ecosystems began with primary producers like plants, then herbivores and carnivores followed, feeding on the primary producers. Stranger yet—the beetles were carnivorous. What could they possibly feed on? Fortunately, zoologist John Edwards happened to be fascinated by insects that inhabited harsh, mountain environments. A native of New Zealand, Edwards had grown up with the same sort of stratovolcanoes that make up the Cascades, and by the time he moved to the Pacific Northwest in 1967 to teach at the University of Washington, the avid climber had scaled several mountains. On each Northwest peak he climbed, the neurobiologist would notice the most unlikely thing: insects at 9,000 feet, or 11,000 feet, or even 18,000 feet, as on Denali. These observations led him to pursue studies in alpine entomology. He was soon counting ice worms on Mount Rainier—tiny worms that live only at the freezing point in glacier-ice columns.

On Mount Rainier, Edwards found an answer to why some insects could survive at altitudes as high as 18,000 feet, where no food source was apparent. The high-mountain dwellers were actually scavengers that fed on dead insect bodies falling out of the sky or blowing up from the valleys below. With help from his colleagues, Edwards estimated that each summer ten to twelve tons of dead insects and spiders were blown onto Rainier's glaciers, which acted like giant refrigerators for the tiny carcasses. This "arthropod fallout" provided hearty feasting for such rare creatures as the earwig-sized grylloblattid, a shy nocturnal cave-dweller, and such common ones as the daddy longlegs spider, Rainier's highest permanent resident.

Having explored Mount St. Helens before it erupted, Edwards was eager to track what sort of insects would take up residence in the blast zone. Like Mount Rainier's glaciers, the blast zone was an extreme environment. And one of its most extreme areas was, of course, the Pumice Plain, which had been cooked to temperatures higher than any known life-form could survive. Edwards visited the plain by helicopter in July 1980. In a landscape so void of color the scientist thought he had lost his color vision, Edwards began to monitor what sort of bugs would arrive and, more importantly, remain.

With help from his students, including doctoral candidate Patrick Sugg, Edwards first tested the volcanic ash to find out how lethal it was. The scientists subjected laboratory cockroaches to a vial and found that the insects lost water six times faster than cockroaches left untouched. The ash abraded the cockroaches' waxy, waterproof carapace like sandpaper, causing the insects to dehydrate. Within twenty-five hours, every cockroach encountering the ash was dead. This experiment confirmed the scientists' hunch that wherever ash fell heavily in 1980—anywhere from Loowit's summit to eastern Washington—insects such as cockroaches and grasshoppers that had already emerged from their winter hibernation were obliterated. They also concluded that the Pumice Plain was a particularly tough place for an insect if only because the ash was everywhere—in the wind, on the ground, erupting anew from the volcano.

After their ash experiment, the entomologists set about collecting specimens from the plain. After building various traps with mixed results, they finally developed a sampling system that would reflect the plain's pumiceous surface: used golf balls from the University of Washington's driving range. They placed the balls in a wood frame with a nylon mesh on the bottom that trapped anything that blew in—pollen, lichen, seeds, mosquito carcasses, fly wings. After placing and replacing hundreds of golf balls, Sugg and Edwards logged 2,000 different species of insects that blew onto the plain during the decade following the eruption.

It was this massive arthropod fallout that was missing in conventional ecological theory. The carnivorous beetles didn't need plants at all; their food rained out of the sky. With 2,000 kinds of dinner to choose from, the beetles decided to stay, ash or no. Belonging to the genus *Bembidion*, these carabids or ground beetles—not so different from common backyard beetles—prefer barren river bars, glaciers, and other desolate sites that most other organisms avoid. Roughly sixty-five different species of such beetles flew onto the Pumice Plain or were blown in on the wind. Then, within a year and a half of the eruption, fifteen of those species took up residence on the plain, feeding on the dead-bug debris.

While the beetles were munching away and having families, another carnivore rained out of the sky. It fell to earth with its own silken balloon, having traveled into the blast zone from far away. Unlike the beetles, this predator caught its food in a web spun across the pumice. Two years after the eruption, just as the first lupine was blooming, the cooled pyroclastic flows were crawling with spiders—ballooning spiders.

That ballooning spiders had parachuted in to such a remote place as the six-mile-wide plain was no surprise to Edwards, who knew that the eight-legged migrants could travel hundreds of miles, flying into such isolated places as the Hawaiian Islands. To launch themselves, the pioneering spiders crawl up to the top of a tree or promontory, then start to release threads. The forest canopy in autumn is full of such strands. Once the spiders let go of their perch, the wind carries them aloft for miles. Then they land and begin a new life.

With the help of Northwest spider expert Rod Crawford, Edwards and Sugg identified so many ballooning spiders in the blast zone they were able to contribute to the world's list of known spiders that travel by balloon. But of the 150 species they found, only four were able to reproduce successfully on the plain.

With his hefty collection of specimens, Edwards realized that it was the insects who were building a foundation for the plants—not the other way around. The real story of succession at Mount St. Helens was upside down: the predators and scavengers arrived first, helping the primary producers to become established. Edwards conducted yet another experiment to prove his point. After collecting hundreds of dead, unwanted fruit flies from his colleagues' labs, he dried the corpses and set them in a plot on the volcano. Within weeks the phosphorus and nitrogen content in the fly carcasses leached into the ground. These results echoed a soil test done by geologists: in 1980 the mountain's ash contained little phosphorus and practically no nitrogen, but five years later it contained higher quantities of both. Edwards concluded that while some of the nitrogen and phosphorus were produced by bacteria on the volcano, the rest was contributed by tons of windblown insect carcasses. The plants took root in a bed of insect compost.

Now that the lupines had seeded in and the entire ecosystem had exploded, Edwards was limiting his monitoring to every five years. His 1995 sampling—taken in tandem with John Bishop's lupine research—reflected the complexity of life now interacting on the plain. An evolutionary ecologist, Bishop had tracked the genetic makeup of sixty lupine populations since 1990, which now totaled 10,000 individuals, and had observed three species of caterpillars that had eaten so much lupine that some of his colonies were extinct. But Bishop and Edwards also noticed yet another player: a parasitic blowfly that used the caterpillars as living nests for its eggs. How the blowflies would affect the caterpillar populations—and the caterpillars affect the lupines—had yet to be seen.

Other things remained to be determined as well. Crisafulli wondered whether native grasses would overtake the lupines one day, and Bishop speculated that pearly everlasting might soon re-establish itself as the plain's most abundant wildflower. Edwards, too, remained puzzled by one thing: why the pioneering beetles disappeared soon after the plants arrived. Edwards and his colleagues hoped to sort out the mystery as they continued observing the plain. But the beetles' mysterious appearance and disappearance taught Edwards one lesson: Loowit's inhabitants had seen it all before. Their comings and goings were based on cycles established thousands of years ago. For these plants and animals, the lateral blast was just another day.

As Celeste and I turned away from Crisafulli's plot, I thought of the first time I had seen the Pumice Plain. At that time, I had assumed nothing grew there. The sight of the terrible gray expanse convinced me that Spirit Lake was a dead place—and would remain a dead place in my lifetime. And yet even at that time the lupine, fireweed, and everlasting had seeded in. Even then the flying spiders' threads were entwined among the broken boulders, and the beetles, bored or bothered by so much life, had taken leave.

We hiked back from the Pumice Plain in a brief, windless downpour. The lupines and pearly everlasting flowers balanced raindrops on their leaves as we climbed back up the old 100 Road to return to the Windy Ridge parking lot. A few minutes before we reached the gate, we were accosted by another fragrant cloud, this time unseen. The showers had stopped, and a crisp rainbow arched below us, over Clearwater Creek's wide valley. Just as Celeste was remarking on how strange it was to be *above* a rainbow, we rounded the bend, and there they were, fresh-leaved young alders pushing out new catkins. Like the lupines, the nitrogen-fixing alders were also improving the soil for other plants.

"We should name this Alder Bend," I found myself saying. "And the Pumice Plain should now be Lupine Meadows." It seemed to me that names in the blast zone should come and go like the weather. For here was a place where forests disappeared in the blink of an eye, where rocks flew up like flocks of swallows, where ash-banked canyons cracked open overnight like fungi, where beetles evaporated like dew. Did not mountains fall away in this area like so many leaves, and leaves smother mountains? Would one name alone suffice for an earth so fugitive?

The Crater Rim

Never measure the height of a mountain until you have reached
the top. Then you will see how low it was.

—Dag Hammarskjöld

During the first year of our return to Spirit Lake,
Celeste and I entertained the notion that by climbing Mount St. Helens we would somehow conquer
the volcano. Having never climbed a mountain before, let alone
Loowit, I could think of nothing more satisfying than gazing down
upon Spirit Lake from atop the crater rim. Thus it was that on a wet
July morning early in our journeys I found myself lacing up my
boots at the volcano's south base as rain-soaked fir boughs pelted
me in the pre-dawn dark.

It was 5 A.M. The rain had stopped, but there was no sign that it
wouldn't begin again. The storm hadn't broken since our arrival the

previous evening. The fog, cold as sleet, refused to lift. The forest around Climber's Bivouac, where we were camped, sang in a slow-tempo drip. I leaned back against an old-growth stump to watch for a break in the clouds along Monitor Ridge and to listen to the territorial chatter of birds. As Celeste abandoned the wet tent like a shipwreck survivor seeking dry land, I resolved for the third time in the last twenty-four hours to scale the mountain.

Having climbed the volcano in a whiteout in 1989, Celeste found such resolutions naive in inclement weather. She had also slept all night with her knees to her chest to avoid an inch-deep puddle at her feet, and was ready to head home for a hot bath and dry clothes.

"It'll clear in an hour or so," I announced in as confident a voice as I could muster. How many times had I read of climbers reaching a mountaintop as sunlight broke over the land? I had even read of one such ascent of Mount St. Helens—the 1860 climb recorded by the anonymous author "Loo-wit-Lat-kla." As with our sopping adventure, the party of prospectors had suffered through wet woods and fog on the mountain's south side. But as they approached the summit, "a propitious gale" erased the clouds, compelling the nineteenth-century gold seeker to utter a breathless riff of superlatives:

We felt that nothing could transcend the grandeur of the scene or surpass in interest and incident the magnificent panorama then present to an enraptured vision . . . the placid lakes and meandering rivers; dense forests and lovely plains; beautiful cascades and purling rills; the glistening glacier of the mountain and the dark brown volcanic scoria of the valley; all combined their peculiar features to form the most gorgeous, the most sublimely grand, picturesque and wonderfully attractive spectacle upon which the eye of man ever feasted.

As we breakfasted on muffins and tea, I felt certain that we would enjoy at least half of such superlatives. So we packed our wet gear in the car and started out in the pea-soup darkness. For two miles the trail wound up through a drip-dropping forest of huckleberry, thimbleberry, and Pacific silver fir. Loowit's southern slopes had hardly been affected by the eruption, so we found ourselves in the middle of woods that resembled pre-eruption Spirit Lake. Stalks of blooming beargrass and the fluted leaves of false-hellebore brightened the forest floor. Rain-soaked logs, their bark rotted away, resembled tanned torsos lounging in the mist. Wild columbine and pink bleedingheart poked out amongst the logs, as well as pinesap uncurling new fronds. Suddenly, out of the fog-frozen lull, a solitary bird started to trill, and all at once I found myself immensely happy, surrounded by the living rhythms of a Cascade forest.

We continued past a snow-banked creek bed that cradled a patch of avalanche lilies. The fog lifted to form a low ceiling just above our heads. Then, as dawn suffused the dark understory, the puffy beargrass gave way to bushes of pink mountain heather, and small subalpine firs glowed in slender, green triangles. Timberline.

I had crossed Loowit's timberline only once before—in 1977, when I had hiked to Dog's Head, a well-known lava dome poking out of the volcano's northeast side. First named "Black Butte" at the turn of the century, Dog's Head earned its permanent name due to its resemblance to the smiling face of a St. Bernard. The August day I climbed to the old dome with my sisters, I suffered up slopes of pumice a foot deep that buried my shoes with each step. But the view of Spirit Lake that day had been worth every pumice blister.

As Celeste and I hiked among the subalpine firs I suddenly remembered that the eruption had shaved Dog's Head clean. If we were hiking there today, we'd already be on the summit—the crater's north rim.

My brother Michael was probably one of the last climbers to stand on Dog's Head before its top was blown off. Michael climbed to Dog's Head in March 1980, a week before the volcano broke its 123-year dormancy. Two years later, while the volcano remained off-limits due to dome-building eruptions, Michael hiked again to Dog's Head and camped the night with a friend on its new top. With the fiery aura of the crater's incandescent dome glowing beneath their perch, neither one got much sleep. In the morning they walked the volcano's new summit, the crater rim, and tried in vain to orient themselves to the surrounding blast zone topography, while the growing dome steamed beneath their feet.

The pointed firs disappeared as we climbed onto the volcano's haunches. Black, dun, and burnt-red igneous rocks replaced the soft fir-needle humus of the lower trail. Suddenly there was pumice, too, everywhere. We stopped for a gulp of water and a handful of gorp, but it was mostly hope—as the fog dissolved into patches of bright blue sky—that fueled and propelled us upward.

I felt a certain ambivalence about climbing any higher. The Cascade volcanoes are considered sacred by Northwest tribes; to travel above timberline is disrespectful. In contrast, when Euro-American explorers arrived on the West Coast, they were tempted by the peaks and immediately assigned place names to their features. Loowit was scaled as early as 1853 by Thomas Dryer, founder of *The Weekly Oregonian,* and one of its glaciers was soon named after him. Another glacier was named after the first Native American to climb the mountain, Leschi, who guided a group up the north side in 1893 and lived in shame among his fellow Klickitats for having trodden upon the summit. One of the volcano's largest glaciers was named after mountaineer Charles Forsyth, who in 1908 led a group of

Mazamas over the mountain to rescue an injured logger. The first woman to climb Mount St. Helens did so in 1883, but no glacier was named after her. The other glaciers bore the names of rivers or canyons they headed (Swift, Toutle, Ape) or arbitrary names like Wishbone, Talus (for rocks collected on it during summer), and Shoestring, the mountain's lowest glacier.

But a century of historic ascents and glacier naming meant little to the volcano. On May 17, 1980, geologist Dan Miller flew over Mount St. Helens in a helicopter to record physical changes to its slopes. As the helicopter swept over the north face, the USGS scientist glanced down at the glacier named after Charles Forsyth. The 1.5-mile-long mass of ice spanned most of the area between Dog's Head and Goat Rocks, where the ominous bulge protruded. To Miller's astonishment, torrents of melted ice cascaded like spring rivers below the glacier. Having trouble locating any white snow unsullied by ash with his bare eyes, Miller scanned the broad plain with a thermal monitor. His equipment told him that large areas of hot rock lay beneath him. Forsyth Glacier was mostly gone.

Forsyth wasn't the only glacier to melt. Weeks before May 18, earthquakes and steepening had cracked portions of Loowit, Leschi, Wishbone, Nelson, Shoestring, and Toutle. Crevasses groaned wide as the mountain mushroomed inside. Then, on May 18, three-fourths of Loowit's glaciers exploded. Survivors at the edge of the blast were pelted by pieces of ice falling from the sky. Glacial blocks the size of houses were heaved down the Toutle valley where they remained intact, under rock, for more than two months. Melting ice caused mudflows not only on both forks of the Toutle, but on Swift Creek, Pine Creek, and the Muddy River as well.

By October 1980, it became clear to geologists just how few glaciers had survived. Most—such as the Shoestring, Swift, Dryer,

Nelson, and Ape—had been "beheaded." Forsyth was reduced to a small chunk of ice on the east side of the Sugar Bowl. Wishbone, Leschi, and Loowit were gone entirely.

As Celeste and I continued onto Monitor Ridge, I looked for the beheaded remnants of Swift and Dryer Glaciers, which still hugged the southern slope we were climbing. I noticed sun-hardened ice on both sides of the ridge, but the white fields terminated in clouds; whatever glaciers remained were obscured by fog. But at least I could discern something white; in 1980 geologists could hardly detect what little ice was left due to foot-deep layers of dark ash. Most casual observers thought the volcano had lost its ice entirely.

In addition to the May 18 plume, five other ash plumes obscured the glaciers for most of 1980. The plumes—called Plinian columns (after the philosopher Pliny, who first described the characteristic cauliflower clouds)—sealed the glaciers under an opaque mantle. When USGS glaciologist Carolyn Driedger studied the mantle, she discovered that although thin layers of ash (about one-tenth of an inch) caused glacial ice to melt faster due to their heat-absorbing color, thick layers (approximately one inch) actually blocked the sun's rays. The thick ash slowed "ablation," or snow and ice loss, by keeping out solar radiation. Loowit's new dark coat protected portions of its old white one—at least temporarily. As I saw during my climb, the thick ash was now eroded, leaving the glaciers exposed to the sun. According to Driedger, the prognosis for Loowit's fragmented glaciers was not good. Eventually the volcano would lose most if not all of its old, beheaded glaciers, whose ice volumes lay mostly at snowline but not above.

The glaciers struck me as symbols of Loowit's gentler days, and I found their disappearance sobering. But like everything else in the volcano's equilibrium, their vanishing was but half of the story. As I found out later, the mountain had not abandoned its ice entirely.

In a heat-defying twist it had rearranged some closer to its 1,600-degree-Fahrenheit core.

In 1982, glacial speleologist Charles Anderson visited the volcano to explore its glaciers. Having mapped and studied eight and one-half miles of ice caves on Mount Rainier, Anderson was familiar with the way fumaroles and steam passageways carve tunnels in glaciers, offering the researcher the chance to look inside. There, he followed the caves to their terminus and documented inhabitants such as ice worms and grylloblattids. This form of speleology was new to glacier research. Most scientists had only studied the masses from above, not inside.

By the time it erupted, Anderson had already climbed Mount St. Helens five times, finding caves in Swift and Dryer Glaciers. In 1982 he flew into the crater to see whether any ice or snow had collected in the steep bowl. None had. But each successive summer the wiry alpinist trekked up to the steaming dome, optimistic that ice would appear somewhere. His hunch was correct. From 1983 on, Anderson documented the formation not only of ice caves but of a new glacier inside the crater.

Forming near the base of the crater walls behind the lava dome, the incipient glacier is being created by avalanches of snow from the rim and walls. Unlike most Cascade glaciers, which begin forming at 9,000 feet and move downward, the new glacier is forming below 8,000 feet due to shade created by the dome and steep walls. Little sunlight hits the area where the firn snow is packing into ice. The heat melting the ice is mostly from geothermal activity rather than from solar radiation.

Anderson deduced that in certain areas the ice had already reached glacial density. In other areas crevasses had formed, confirming that the ice was in fact moving and therefore a young glacier. By hiking into the crater more than a hundred times,

Anderson also mapped 8,000 feet of ice caves behind the dome as well as on its sides. Taking into account the ice caves as well as the new glacier, USGS geologists estimated that the crater's total ice mass had doubled from 1988 to 1995, but this post-eruption mass was still only one-third of the volcano's pre-eruption ice.

With little experience in alpinism and no crampons, Celeste and I opted to avoid the glistening glaciers, where the sun skipped by. The ascent might have been easier—no boulders, just ice. But we were afraid of getting lost in the fog, so we continued like mules, plodding from blue-flagged post to blue-flagged post. We could remember when Mount St. Helens was known as "Death Mountain," for all the climbers it had claimed. Neither one of us wanted to risk breaking a leg.

Long before it killed fifty-seven people in a single morning, Loowit lured many climbers to their death. By the hundredth anniversary of Dryer's 1853 climb, a special rescue unit had been designated for the 9,677-foot peak. Headed by brothers Val and Rob Quoidbach of the St. Helens Ski Club, the unit was kept busy from 1948 to 1953 retrieving the bodies of ten dead climbers and several injured ones. By the 1970s, the mountain was recognized as having an exceptionally high number of deaths for its height and difficulty. Eleven people alone died there from 1975 to 1977. Rescue experts theorized that the mountain's very smoothness attracted beginners who underestimated the challenges posed by crevasses, ice walls, and avalanches. Since the eruption, the number of climbers has skyrocketed, with a hundred people a day ascending the volcano from May to October. Not only is the ascent 1,300 feet shorter, the new summit promises a knee-weakening view of the crater walls and dome. Even on that foggy day we spotted climbers above and below us.

We heaved ourselves up and over black, fog-slick boulders to approach the volcano's upper reaches. The alpine vegetation—an occasional snow willow with puffy mustard blooms—disappeared completely. But the altitude was still not too high for a chipmunk, who, dashing back and forth, seemed unnaturally aware that we were carrying nuts and dried fruit. We abandoned him for an immense scree slope and a distant snowfield—the last leg of the climb.

When you scale a mountain, you make an appointment with nature: you obtain a permit, arrange to take a couple of days off from work, pack a load of supplies, drive a winding road with a slippery steel bridge that spins your car out of control, endure a cold night of drumming rain. For what? The mountain has made no reciprocal engagement. It's just a volcano, and when you reach the summit, you understand this. It gets hammered into you, actually, because when you reach the summit after four hours of scrambling through rock and snow, you can't see a damn thing.

Celeste tried for a celebratory gesture, brandishing chocolate bars from her daypack, but it didn't help. From the grand delusions of expecting to see Spirit Lake, the backcountry, Mount Adams, Mount Rainier, Mount Hood, and maybe the Pacific Ocean all in one 360-degree panorama, we were brought down to the patch of wet pumice at our feet. We couldn't even see the rest of the crater rim, the sheer walls, or the steaming dome. All we could do was listen, fog-blinded, for an occasional boom as rock and snow crashed down the crater walls. I was standing on the clipped edge of Loowit's exploded summit, jagged as a cracked bowl and dangerous. But I might as well have been strolling the Oregon coast for all I could distinguish.

"Maybe it will clear in another hour," I found myself mumbling. So we plopped ourselves down in the snow and waited.

Once again I was brought down to zero by a simple act of nature. In 1980 it was the predicted cataclysm of the collision of the Juan de Fuca and North American plates. Today it was a routine storm swallowing a mountaintop in July. But it was this moment of humility that made me want to abstain forever from waxing nostalgic about nature. Thoreau, the man I wanted so badly to emulate at seventeen by living in the shadow of the volcano, was wrong. "Every little pine needle expanded and swelled with sympathy and befriended me," he once wrote. Romantic hogwash. We might imagine pine needles befriending us, but ultimately we have to build a wall and roof to sleep through a winter night. Even Thoreau walked back to the comforts of Concord after two years.

A mosquito buzzed my kneecaps, but I lacked the energy to swat it. Instead I stared blankly into the fog as the hour crawled past. We had planned for an alpine epiphany, but the only brilliant insight I could entertain was that a volcano was nothing other than a volcano, subject to subduction from below and clouds from above.

The wind came up. We rose to our feet and marched down the snowfield, letting gravity take us down and down. Again I heard the singing of a solitary bird—there, at the summit. It swept down in front of us, unafraid. I memorized its markings by repeating the colors to myself as I walked—gray crown, rust breast, red-gray wings. Back at the car I consulted my field guide: it was a gray-crowned rosy finch, lover of alpine summits, a friendly bird that feasted on insects, seeds, and snow. Like pearly everlasting, it had relatives in Asia and was common to mountain ranges from the Rockies to Alaska. This one had made Loowit its home.

As we raced down the snowfields, I began to realize that the summit had given me a new bird to remember, a mysterious mountain bird whose trill outlasted any fog. I thought about how Spirit Lake was where I first learned the name *queencup bead lily*. Where an amazing bird circled like a giant boomerang overhead, and only later did I hear the word *osprey*. Without volcanism we would have no Cascade mountains, no alpine wildflowers, no windy sights.

"I've climbed this mountain twice now with no view," Celeste shouted as we galloped farther down the snowfields. "Next time I'm not climbing it unless it's *per-fect-ly* clear."

"Right," I shouted back. *And we'll take the snowfields,* I thought. *Next time we'll stay on the snow.*

The Crater

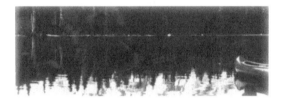

On my volcano grows the Grass
A meditative spot—
An acre for a Bird to choose
Would be the General thought—

How red the Fire rocks below—
How insecure the sod
Did I disclose
Would populate with awe my solitude.

—Emily Dickinson

Despite our fog-ambushed view from the summit, I prided myself for weeks afterwards on my ascent. Little did I know that ascending a volcano was not quite the same thing as ascending a nonvolcanic mountain. Every mountain has a summit, but only mountains that have blown themselves apart have something more: an exposed heart. Two years after that July ascent, I had yet to learn that there would be no conquest of a volcano; there would be no compensation for a buried creek or a drowned waterfall; there would be no revenge held against a chunk of earth. There was only the crater, and the long journey toward it.

When I told my brother Bernie I had received permission to hike into the crater, he asked me if I had a death wish. I couldn't really answer him. I had climbed the mountain, hiked the backcountry, and visited the lake; why, indeed, enter such a place? I had no memories compelling me there. None of my Spirit Lake dreams took place in the crater. It was uncharted territory—vaporous, stony, lifeless. Even the word sounded ominous.

It was Aristotle who first used the word crater to describe the cuplike depression at the top of a volcano. The carved-out shape reminded him of a *krater*, a wide-rimmed bowl in which the ancient Greeks mixed water and wine for dinner guests. Many volcanic craters do in fact cup water in their basins. However, Loowit cups something else: its new lava dome. In the same way that pearly everlasting cups its seeds, Loowit cups its future. Consequently, what was a frequent ritual for the ancient Greeks—the placing of something into a bowl from which it would spill out—is also a frequent cycle for a Northwest volcano, and an annual cycle for the wildflowers at its base.

It was only after I had hiked into the crater in July 1995 that I learned the etymology of the word. By that time, any notion of defeating the mountain had been discarded like a pair of worn-out boots. I felt the need for conquest—along with a host of other assumptions about the mountain—teeter then crash as I hiked into its heart.

My first assumption was that the hike would be impossible. "Torturous death march" had been used to describe the day-long ordeal. On the eve of the trip, when I chatted with the other hikers —a group of twenty-year-old Forest Service naturalists who looked like they ran marathons in their spare time—I had hoped that there might be some charitable soul among them who would hang back when I lagged behind. But although the hike was indeed a day-long trek, I found that I could keep pace with most of the others, even Don Swanson, when he slowed a bit.

Don Swanson—who saw pumice for the first time when he was a child visiting Loowit—was accustomed to covering a lot of ground. Not only had the geologist climbed Mounts St. Helens, Adams, and Hood by the time he finished graduate school, but by the time I met him he had also canvassed vast tracts of Washington, Oregon, California, and Hawaii as an employee with the U.S. Geological Survey. As we began our hike at 8 A.M. on that clear July morning, Swanson led the group of twenty booted hikers down the Truman Trail with the unobtrusive stride of someone intimate with his surroundings. I noticed that while most of us wore T-shirts and shorts, the red-headed scientist wore patched jeans and a long-sleeved shirt to protect against excessive sun and rockfall. He also wore a waterproof watch and glasses attached to an expandable cord around his neck. Like most of the geologists I had met, he had a beard. For a good part of the journey his pick never left his hand.

Swanson began working with the USGS in 1965, when he created a geologic map detailing the age and location of every rock, river, and nook for part of eastern Oregon. From 1968 to 1971 he studied shield volcanoes in Hawaii, then moved to the Survey's Menlo Park office in California, where he remained until Mount St. Helens began venting in March 1980. He then began monitoring the mountain with a team headed by geologists Dwight Crandell and Donal Mullineaux. The small group included Rick Hoblitt, Dan Miller, Bob Christianson, Jim Moore, Peter Lipman, and a new recruit named David Johnston. Swanson's life-risking forays would begin in April with a hovering-helicopter ride over the summit to scoop up a rock sample with a large soup ladle. They would peak on May 17, when he and pilot Lon Stickney would rest the helicopter, engine off, on the volcano's summit. It was only some time after 8:30 A.M. on May 18—after David Johnston had radioed in his 6:45 A.M. report saying everything was normal—that Swanson realized that "but for a fluke" he would have perished along with his colleague. Being in charge of the electronic monitoring effort, Swanson was standing in the observation room in Vancouver, Washington, that morning when the seismograph's needle started to swing. He watched for a few seconds, then ran upstairs to call Johnston, who was positioned at the Coldwater II observation post. But the radio wasn't working. It had been catapulted, along with Rick Hoblitt's camper and the thirty-year-old Johnston, into the canyon of South Coldwater Creek. Bits of the camper would be uncovered but not the geologist's body.

Fifteen years after the eruption, Johnston's death still haunted the team that worked at Mount St. Helens, including Swanson. Johnston was the first USGS volcanologist to die on the job. More importantly, he was a respected scholar and an affable young man. After finishing his Ph.D. at the University of Washington, he was expected to become a pioneer in the study of magma and the mechanics of eruptions. He had already conducted research at Katmai in Alaska by the time he arrived at Mount St. Helens. After the eruption, an annual scholarship award was established in his name at the university. Oddly enough, Swanson taught and conducted research at the same campus where Johnston's reputation lingered.

On that warm breezy day of our trek, the events of May 1980 seemed far away. Hikers chatted with each other as the morning sun struck the ridgetops and bees buzzed overhead. We worked our way across the Pumice Plain like a slow, multicolored caterpillar, then abandoned the Truman Trail for the Breach—the long, arduous entrance to the crater. Noise from construction crews on the ridge named for Johnston beeped and grumbled like distant insects. The

Forest Service was constructing an observatory atop the spot where the geologist had died. Although the observatory was to be named after Johnston, its construction seemed disrespectful, like paving over a grave. But as we hiked farther the noise was swallowed by a steep canyon of boulders. Wary of rockfall, we picked our way in silence up the eroded wash, each hiker's eyes searching the ground to avoid a debilitating sprain.

Small green willows lined the dry wash. Blue sky arched overhead. On our right and left, enormous gray boulders hemmed us in. The crater was nowhere to be seen. But as we worked our way up to the head of the canyon, a snow-spotted rock emerged from behind the pumice wall in front of us. Was it the rim or the dome? Then suddenly we topped the canyon and found ourselves on the west side of Step Creek Falls. Behind us, to the north, lay the Spillover's rumpled mass. Far below, to the east, lay Spirit Lake. The blast-scraped ridges that formed the lake basin revealed their stratigraphy like scrubbed bones. The steep slopes jutted upward from the lake on a diagonal. That was when I realized that the once-forested ridges were not simply hills but folds in the Earth's crust, heaved up by powerful forces. From our viewpoint it was clear that nothing in the area had formed peacefully.

Not far from Step Creek Falls lay an ancient forest that had itself suffered a violent action roughly 2,500 years ago. Swanson told us how the buried trees—upright stumps and prostrate logs—had been discovered by geologist Brian Hausback only a few years earlier. Swanson had collaborated with Hausback to determine just what had happened to the well-preserved copse, whose trees still possessed their bark. He believed that one of Loowit's "hydrothermally altered domes"—domes cooked into clay by water moving through them—sloughed downslope in a massive landslide. The avalanche crashed into Spirit Lake, causing a temporary dam that soon failed, releasing mudflows down the North Fork of the Toutle. The trees were either buried in place or carried downslope with the slide. Their fate reminded me of the south shore's firs and hemlocks; they, too, had been swallowed by the shifting volcano.

While Swanson began to recount Loowit's past we gathered near where he stood on a sheer cliff above Step Creek Falls. My fear of heights kept me from the edge, which yielded to a 250-foot drop. Nowhere had I seen erosion so spectacular. Most canyons required centuries to form; this one had been carved in a matter of years. The falls were one of the fastest-eroding in the state of Washington, etching backward and downward several feet a year. The milky water was like liquid sandpaper, Swanson said. Flowing gray instead of clear, the jet had etched away more than fifty feet of the pumiceous cliff. And not only was the top of the falls dropping, its basin was being raised as sediment piled up below. Too heavy for the stream's power, the mountain's silt lay at the bottom of the gorge, along with boulders that had avalanched to reach their angle of repose. If left undisturbed, the waterfall would soon carve itself into nonexistence.

Swanson was one of a group of USGS geologists who had named Step Creek Falls. As with the Spillover, the Pumice Plain, Harry's Ridge, and Johnston Ridge, the falls were named in 1983 by the Washington State Board of Geographical Names, to which the scientists had made recommendations. The falls took their name from a series of "steps" into the crater—mountains of rock forming the Breach. Finding "Steps" too generic, the board added "Sasquatch" before them to honor the mountain's elusive giants. The Sasquatch Steps would be our path to the dome.

We continued up and over broken rocks to our lunch stop, where each hiker found a boulder or pumice bank to sit on. It was here, at a spot Swanson called the "Volcano in a Volcano," that I had to let go of another assumption. As I brushed a curious hover fly from my apple, I stared at the red rock marking an ancient cinder cone that had been buried deep inside the volcano. The 1980 eruption had unearthed the cone, now visible as a distinct layer of rusty-red cinders. Despite my knowledge of composite cones, I had somehow thought of the mountain as a whole—a solid mass of rock that had emerged within the last 2,000 years in a perfectly symmetrical fashion. I knew that this 2,000-year-old rock stood on an ancestral Mount St. Helens, which dated back 40,000 years. But it was only in front of the cinder cone that I understood how stratovolcanoes were actually chaotic piles of smaller domes and cones that emerged willy-nilly around the central core and were glued together with black magmatic dikes. Like Spirit Lake's log raft, Loowit was a fractured rabble.

The sun peaked overhead, darting in and out of huge cumuli, as we continued our final leg. An occasional helicopter circled while the crater enclosed us in its immense stone cage. Dirty patches of snow and ice clung to the sheer crater walls. Boulders tripped down the walls like gravel, booming out their collision with the crater floor.

We crossed a mile-long stretch of pumice to reach the dome, where wisps of steam swirled. I found myself trusting fate as I walked toward the incipient mountain, black as obsidian and arched like a tortoise shell. From all signs, Loowit was cooling off; the dome's internal temperature had dropped in the last few years from 1,742 degrees Fahrenheit to a little less than 1,600 degrees. According to Swanson the dome would probably continue to cool because the magma trapped below was literally "running out of gas"—the sort of high-pressure gas that causes magma to rise. Nonetheless I felt a light-headed abandonment of control as I walked toward the cracked, snow-flocked hump.

The dome had stopped growing in 1986, and Swanson doubted whether it would ever fill the crater and reach the mountain's former height. However, despite its cooling, the volcano had not stopped erupting. Twenty-eight explosions of steam, gas, and tephra—but no fresh magma—had occurred intermittently from August 1989 to June 1991. Produced mostly by shallow earthquakes below the dome, some of the more powerful explosions had destroyed several monitoring stations. In November 1990, a pyroclastic flow ripped out of the dome at sixty miles an hour, stripping an antenna on a monitor and littering the crater floor with boulders six feet wide. A month later, a new crack opened on the dome's eastern flank, sending up an ash plume 10,000 feet high and causing one airline in Portland to cancel its flights. And on February 5, 1991, both new vents erupted with a pyroclastic flow, ballistic boulders, and an ash plume that rose 6,000 feet and sprinkled ash south of Mount Adams.

Geologists weren't sure what caused the 1989–1991 eruptions, although most occurred soon after a rainstorm. In 1993 Larry Mastin, one of Swanson's colleagues, proposed that storms had sent rainwater down inside the dome, opening up cracks for magmatic gas to be released suddenly and explosively. But Mastin stopped short of concluding what the eruptions meant for Mount St. Helens' future. Either gas was building up again inside the dome and new eruptions would occur, or the cracks created from 1989 to 1991 were now allowing the slow release of gas—in which case future storm-triggered eruptions would be unlikely. Even more perplexing was whether the eruptions were only shallow events related to the dome's cooling, or whether the volcano's deep magma chambers were releasing gas upward.

The boulders ejected during those recent eruptions now lay around us. But as we approached the dome, my eyes were drawn upward to the cliffs encircling us—the crater walls. Within my life-time their sheer faces had been revealed like the insides of a broken thunder egg. I had assumed they would be black. Instead, I stared in disbelief at the black dikes intersecting huge swaths of vibrant pas-tels—peach, cream, even magenta. Sweeping shadows illuminated a rust-red patch, then lavender, then minty-green. A volcano of many colors?

"If you could peer inside almost any volcano, my guess is that you would see a lot of colors because that's where hot water perco-lates through the mountain and causes chemical changes," Swanson explained.

If anyone understood the volcano's shifting colors, it was Swanson. The geologist had witnessed almost all of Loowit's erup-tions since 1980, and after the May 18 eruption he began focusing immediately on the crater, measuring cracks on the new dome with pieces of rebar and a steel measuring tape. Within a short time his knowledge of the volcano became so profound that from 1981 to 1986 he and his colleagues predicted virtually every one of its dome-building events. Two to three weeks in advance, the team would issue a time window in which they thought the dome would grow. Then they'd narrow the window to within a day or two, as the magmatic eruption approached. Never before had volcanologists been able to foretell events with such accuracy.

As a geophysicist, Swanson studied how the volcano cracked, inflated, and tilted as magma seeped upward into its dome. This kind of monitoring enabled him to observe something perplexing as the dome grew. Around 1985 he and his colleagues noted the timing of the eruptions relative to lunar tides and found that there was a true correlation—that dome growth tended to occur three to five days after tidal maxima and minima. Although the exact physics of such tidal triggering of eruptions was up for debate,

Swanson believed that what could be happening was that "as the moon pulled across the earth, it increased pressure slightly on the magma inside the mountain, causing it to rise."

A volcano affected by the moon? It seemed plausible etymologically, given that the word Helen was, after all, Greek for moon.

The group congregated at the base of the dome to take in the view. Rockfall distracted most of the hikers from listening to what Swanson had to say. I asked him if all the groups he escorted into the crater were as easily distracted. "Actually, it used to be worse," he said patiently. "The avalanches used to be so loud and frequent I had trouble getting people to listen at all."

After nine years of leading hikes into the crater, Swanson remained impressed not so much with the dome as with the crumbling crater walls. Still unstable after fifteen years, the walls were avalanching boulder by boulder onto the crater floor. He doubted that the crater would fill completely with its own refuse, but it was definitely piling up. In 1989 the volume of collapsed material was as great as the dome, and now it was even larger. Given that the dome measured a nearly a mile across and 1,150 feet high, the rockslides had amounted to the size of a small metropolis. According to Swanson, the dome could be cruising toward an inglorious end, much like a city getting buried in its own garbage.

We sat down on boulders as the dome loomed above. Some of the hikers tossed a Frisbee. Others lit cigarettes. Swanson's colleague, equipment specialist Andy Lockhart, inspected the USGS monitors. While Swanson explained how rainwater and melting snow were leaking into the dome and cooling it in a process called "convective cooling," I lost track of what he was saying. Crawling right next to my left boot was a ladybug.

And I had fancied the crater a lifeless place! In fact, Swanson had seen birds, insects, and tree frogs in the crater. Ravens gargled over-

290 Return to Spirit Lake

head; hummingbirds dive-bombed him. During the early years, while the dome was still growing, hungry mice had begged for a snack. The most hostile of places possessed its own menagerie.

Before we rose to go I asked Swanson whether he thought of the volcano as an it, a male, or a female. I had asked others and was surprised by their answers. Laura considered the mountain feminine, as did Celeste, who heard the Spanish feminine noun *montaña* echo in her bilingual brain. Roy Wilson of the Cowlitz Tribe was careful to distinguish the *mountain* from the *volcano*. "When we talk of Lawe-latla we talk about many things," he had told me. "The mountain includes the volcano, but the volcano does not include the mountain. The mountain gave us good berry patches and sacred places to which we could go for vision quests. The mountain gave us many sacred basket trees like the cedar. Thus, the mountain is more to us than a volcano."

Swanson's reply was given with the detached smile of a scientist. "I don't really think of it as anything, so I guess I'd say the mountain is an it." He disdained human-valued words like "devastation" and viewed the crater and its blast zone as part of a cycle to which human judgments should not be applied. In contrast, over the last fifteen years, rampant anthropomorphism had been released on the volcano. Human-centric words such as *monarch, lady, empress, sentinel, queen, witch, raiment of evil,* and *belching behemoth* had circulated in newsprint to describe the rock upon which we now stood. Each time I had read one of those epithets I had grimaced. But I also understood why humans needed such references. Metaphors make the inconceivable conceivable. Should the mountain be called a magmatic expression of plate tectonics?

The afternoon was gaining on us, so Swanson led the group out of the crater. Taking a different route from the one by which we had entered, we tromped down a gully carved by the headwaters of

Loowit Creek, a stream that emanated from the volcano itself. Winding its way down a deep, narrow gorge, the creek cascaded directly out of the crater in a 150-foot waterfall with a plume so tall it could be seen from the backcountry. On cool days, clouds of steam rose from the lip of the waterfall, evidence that the creek was fed by hot springs deep inside the volcano. In the early years after the eruption, Loowit Creek gurgled at boiling point. Now, it had cooled somewhat, although some seeps were still too hot to touch. As we walked down the gorge, I bent down to touch one of the sulfurous, steaming trickles. My hand sprang back. Luckily I was able to dunk my stinging fingers in an icy sliver of snowmelt that drained right beside the scalding seep. Mats of filamentous blue-green algae glowed chartreuse against the creek's gray pebbles where seep and snowmelt collided.

We were stepping over one of the most crucial organisms in the history of life on Earth. The blue-green algae were actually strings of cyanobacteria. These photosynthetic bacteria belong to a group of microorganisms thought to have originated 3 billion years ago. Scientists believe that cyanobacteria, which photosynthesize the same way as plants, were responsible for contributing enough oxygen to the planet's atmosphere for aerobic organisms to evolve. The bacteria's oxygen output also helped create the Earth's ozone layer, which blocks out harmful ultraviolet rays. Because some cyanobacteria can fix nitrogen in addition to photosynthesizing, they are considered one of the most independent life-forms known. It is not uncharacteristic of them to grow in a hot volcanic stream; extreme environments are often where they fare best.

The cyanobacteria were discovered in August 1980 by freshwater ecologist Cliff Dahm and microbiologist John Baross. According to Dahm and Baross, a similar species also inhabits thermal springs in Yellowstone National Park. Dahm and Baross also found other life-forms basking in the hot temperatures of Loowit Creek and in fumaroles on the north slope. In 1981 they identified two kinds of Archaebacteria, a large group of single-celled organisms whose cellular structures are so different from those of other bacteria that most scientists consider the group a separate kingdom. Believed to be among the most ancient of life-forms known on the planet, many Archaebacteria don't need oxygen to survive. Instead they produce methane from carbon dioxide and hydrogen or metabolize sulfur. As a result, they proliferate in places such as swamps and sewage treatment plants. Some Archaebacteria thrive in volcanic vents on the sea floor off the coast of Oregon and Washington. At Mount St. Helens, one of the Archaebacteria Dahm and Baross found enjoyed temperatures as high as 200 degrees Fahrenheit and fed on little more than hydrogen and sulfur.

The sulfurous vapors rising from the creek seemed a humble if not pungent announcement of the planet's living origins. As we walked in and out of the steamy puffs I breathed a little uneasily. A few years back, *Legionella* had also been identified in Loowit Creek.

As we descended into the gorge, we lost sight of the dome. The trek was far from over, but it was then that I felt a door close. Or perhaps another one had opened. Somewhere I heard the words "So long, Loowit!" It was what my mother had written in the cabin journal a month before the March earthquakes. "We'll shovel the snow next time!" she had penned confidently in her elegant hand.

As we topped the waterfall and continued out of the crater, one final assumption began to course down Loowit Creek like so much sediment loosed from the mountain's heart. I asked Swanson if he felt he knew the mountain intimately. It seemed to me that his fifteen-year examination of the volcano was as much as anyone could ask for. "No," he said matter-of-factly. "I don't know it at all. I don't think anybody does."

So volcanoes were a blemish on human arrogance. Volcanoes would not be negotiated, administered, or postponed. Humans could not trim them into poodles and elephants, could not corral them into corners, could not trick them into erupting on parade. The crater, respiring with its ancient bacteria, was a last frontier, a void at the edges of human comprehension, a wild ride there was no getting off.

We dropped down onto the Pumice Plain, walking across what seemed in my fatigue to be an endless monotony of boulders. Dusk drenched the plain in peach light and tipped Spirit Lake's waves with fire. In the approaching twilight I held the image of the crater walls in my mind's eye like a stone I would never lose. It was not so much the new dome that had astounded me as those ancient walls. Curved like the sides of a clay bowl, they had been fired at a hundred different temperatures, a hundred different ways. The colors had leapt out of the dark mountain like iridescent wings unfurled from a beetle's black shell. Pale viridian, dark sienna, ochre yellow, smoky-blue: old Loowit was a rainbow—a luminous, moon-influenced rock rainbow, arcing toward the sky.

Loowit Falls

Mountain is mountain, water is water.

—Zen Saying

Who can say with any certainty what is liquid and what is solid, what burns and what drowns, what is straight and what curves, what is past and what is future? People once thought the planet flat. Even water carves a straight line as it falls to earth, belying its cycle from land to sea to air. "The fate of every waterfall," Don Swanson told me after our hike, "is to erode itself back to where there is no more resistance." Waterfalls, then, are their own nonexistence. But what isn't its own nonexistence? "You have seen everything created running toward its death," wrote the poet Petrarch. At the moment the blast zone was created, it was moving toward becoming something other than a blast zone.

On our final trip, one month after my crater hike, Celeste and I talked of many things as we drove to the mountain. We discussed the migration of people into the Northwest, the deterioration of schools such as the one where she taught, and whether we were fraternal or identical twins.

I had expressed doubts about settling the last matter without genetic testing. But my sister had made up her mind. It didn't matter whether we took a test, she said. She knew we were identical because she possessed her own lived experience as fact. Her data were compiled from birth: we had spoken our own secret language as infants, were constantly mistaken for each other even in college, exhibited similar handwriting, and so forth. Most importantly, she recalled her first few years of grade school: she had always searched for me at recess by looking at her own dress. If it was a green one, then she knew to look for the same green dress out on the playground. She only knew herself through another, and only knew that other through herself.

Listening to her evidence I felt persuaded but not convinced. Perhaps we were half-identicals, or very similar fraternals. Or maybe it would be best not to know. Nonetheless, I had to admit that my journeys to the mountain had revealed to me more similarities than dissimilarities among the Earth's diverse things. Even the difference between the pre-eruption lake and the post-eruption blast zone was no longer stark and discrete.

Oddly enough, on that day we discovered another strange sibling phenomenon. As we hiked in and out of morning clouds on our way to Loowit Falls, Celeste confessed that for as much as she had tried to recall the events of that Sunday in May 1980, she couldn't remember a single thing. She couldn't remember where she had spent the day, whether she was working, what the weather was like, or who had informed her that the mountain had erupted. "It's strange," she said, "Usually when something traumatic occurs, people remember exactly what they were doing."

I had been haunted by the same problem. The day of the eruption was one of the most intensively chronicled in the history of the Pacific Northwest. Reports, computer data, and broadcasts all logged the day minute by minute as the eruption developed. And yet the only memory I had was of talking to Laura on the phone that evening. The rest of the day was gone.

We crunched along the old 100 Road's pumice assembling memories out loud. No other hikers were braving the unstable August weather. The morning sun peeped out of the ridge-swallowing clouds. I wanted Celeste to see Loowit Creek's 150-foot waterfall up close, as I had seen it weeks before, but we would have to hurry if we wanted to see the falls in anything less than a downpour.

As we reached the junction of the Truman Trail and the trail to the falls, we were caught in the fleeting shadows of two ravens speeding overhead. They squawked as they flew, then disappeared east. In the distance, the volcano was still consumed by clouds. A black rock poked out every now and then, then sank back into its white sea. In contrast, the flowers at our feet blended into a brilliant kaleidoscope. Cardwell's penstemon was going to seed, but many of the small green mats still bore purple flowers. Lupine and fireweed shared the same purple-pink tones as the penstemon, while pearly everlasting sprinkled the tan slopes white. Tiny, yellow-needled conifers fought the sun and poor soil. Their presence reminded me of something Peter Frenzen had said—that no plant was truly extirpated in the blast zone. As far as ecologists knew, there wasn't a single species that hadn't returned in some way. To Frenzen, such diversity was proof that disturbance was what created the complex palette on which Earth's organisms thrived. As destructive as it was, the eruption was only one point in a long cycle.

It seemed odd that after so many journeys into the blast zone, Celeste and I were just now talking about the day of the eruption. Great distances had been crossed to reach such a basic event in our lives. But I wondered whether that event was meaningful now, stripped of its reverberations.

Several months earlier, on the fifteenth anniversary of the eruption, Celeste had given me an old mayonnaise jar full of ash. She had bought the jar for five cents at a garage sale in Portland. I laughed out loud when I opened the box. Sealed since July 31, 1980, the jar was heavy with the past, weighing at least two pounds. Its yellow cap was taped shut, hermetically sealed. "Mount St. Helens Volcano Ash, 2nd Fallout, June 13, 1980" read the penciled handwriting on the yellowed masking tape label. It was the same ashfall I had tasted on my lips that June night I had sat beside the Willamette River. I considered what to do: Open it and taste that same ash again? Crack it on the sidewalk? Toss it into the Pacific? Bury it in the yard? I turned it around in both hands. The ash tilted inside like hourglass sand going nowhere. I decided to keep it, maybe because it was a glimpse of what volcanologists must feel when they have just risked life and limb to grab a sample from an incandescent dome: here was a bit of the mountain in my palm. A chunk of the god of the rocks to ponder for five cents.

Perhaps that was why we hadn't dwelled much on the eruption itself: it was an old mayonnaise jar, a roadside attraction, a souvenir ashtray. A mountain only known because of its eruption is a piece of earth fenced in by a date. On one of our earlier hikes Celeste and I had stopped to chat with a man from Tacoma who was hiking with his nine-year-old son. I asked the man if he had ever visited Spirit Lake before 1980. He laughed. "Whoever heard of Mount

St. Helens before the eruption?!" Another man I had spoken to had likened the volcano to the assassination of John F. Kennedy. Mount St. Helens was an event—not just a place but a place locked in time. Unlike other wilderness areas, there were no timeless photographs of the mountain or Spirit Lake, only photographs forever dated "Before 1980" or "After 1980."

But Loowit defied time. As much as the eruption had been chronicled to the second, it exploded conventional notions of chronology. For geologists, who watched processes they thought required hundreds of years occur overnight, the mountain collapsed time. For microbiologists, who found relicts of unicellular life from the early stages of evolution, it reversed time. For forest ecologists, it swung ecosystems back and forth between seral and climax stages like a wild pendulum. For Celeste and me, it erased an entire day. Where were those twelve hours of our lives now?

And like time itself, which slinked through hourglasses and scrawled itself on seismographs, Loowit *moved.* Loowit was not only a mountain to visit but a volcano that visited itself upon people. How many stories had I heard of an ambling volcano?—of ash destroying crops in eastern Washington, ash filling four Washington State landfills, ash dusting the hoods of cars in Reno, ash raining like soot in Missoula, ash flying around the globe like a crazy plane, tipping the pollution index in Japan, circling, falling everywhere, in microscopic flakes. Who could say where Loowit wasn't?

Our talk of the eruption ended as we came upon the deafening crash of water. Without our realizing it, the trail had taken us to what was unofficially known as Willow Springs. I had heard the Pumice Plain scientists refer to the spring, but that hadn't prepared me for the sound or sight of it. The mountain water exploded from a cave of black and red boulders. Cool air swirled up. Ferns grew at the spring's mouth. Moss greened up its boulders. Fireweed clung to its banks, which ran all the way to the lake, more than a mile away. I crouched beside the steady tumble and cupped a handful. A dull ache infused both hands up to my wrists. Not even Bear Creek was this cold. We sat down in silence for a while to hear the creek sing.

Such a watery place! It was my brother Michael who pointed out to me that before the eruption, no creeks drained from the mountain into Spirit Lake. He had always thought this strange—that a lake at the base of a mountain was not fed by the mountain itself. But other pre-eruption residents had different theories. Retlaw Haynes believed that underground springs ran all the way from the mountain to the lake. Haynes noticed that the earth where his family camped was saturated with spring water. His family created their own refrigerator by digging a hole in the cold, soaked ground.

It was the eruption that unearthed the watery relationship between Loowit and the lake. Since the eruption, several streams now flowed directly into Spirit—the one we sat beside, as well as Loowit Creek and Step Creek. The eruption had reinforced the topographical relationship between volcano and lake, making the subterranean link plain.

We left the creek and followed the trail as it curved around the mountain's northern flanks. We were nearing the vegetation line; hardly any plants grew on the bare volcanic rocks. Then we rounded one final bend and found ourselves at the base of the falls. Pearly everlasting seemed to be the only plant growing in the canyon. As we reached the falls it made its presence known in flecks of white and green.

Although the sky refused to clear, it was warm enough for us to shed our coats. We sat down to eat our lunch, and I looked at the falls. Cumuli obscured everything uphill from the narrow strip of water. The clouds were the same white as the crashing stream; it looked as though the sky was cascading into the mountain, draining itself in a sliver of white before it disappeared into the canyon below.

As we lunched on bagels and fresh tomatoes, we took in the rapidly deteriorating view. The moist atmosphere was gaining on our vision, but we managed to see the debris avalanche marching up the Spillover. The backcountry was cloud-dark, with the Dome and Mount Margaret disappearing fast. Down at the lake level, the log raft bunched up on the northeast arm. As the clouds closed in, I felt no apprehension at losing the view. Now that we had seen the falls, we could let the weather claim us along with the land. We could move with the clouds or sit still for a while longer with the rocks and everlasting flowers at our feet.

Mist ballooned off the top of the waterfall. The creek was making its brief journey from crater to lake. Which did the water belong to—lake or volcano? If I considered its origins, it belonged to the mountain—hence the name Loowit Creek. But its completion was Spirit. Still, given that the volcano had slumped into the lake, and the lake had gushed over that slumped earth, at what point did the mountain really end and the lake begin?

"You know, I understand now how the loss I feel over this place is minuscule compared to the victory for the mountain," Celeste said. "For the most part, the eruption was a triumph over logging, roads, and people. As much as Spirit Lake seemed like a wilderness to me before the eruption, it's even wilder now."

I thought about the ancestors of the Cowlitz and Klickitat peoples, who had learned to leave Spirit Lake alone hundreds of years ago. Unlike other mountainous areas in the West that Europeans had termed "wilderness" but that were in fact inhabited by Native Americans for thousands of years, Spirit Lake had indeed been abandoned. Until the late nineteenth century it had in fact remained uninhabitable—a true wilderness, if "wilderness" meant a place where people weren't. My brief habitation at the lake had been an aberration in the region's history, not the norm. The loss Celeste and I had found so painful was but a balancing of the land. I remembered again what Frenzen had said: no species of vegetation has actually disappeared from the blast zone. In making the land inhospitable, the volcano had protected its flowers, shrubs, and trees from a different sort of eruption—an eruption of human activity. When it avalanched into Spirit Lake, the mountain was simply gathering the water to itself. The eruption was an embrace, a claiming of kin.

The imminent rain bloomed around us. I could taste it on my lips, smell it, feel it like a shawl enclosing us. We sat at the base of the volcano waiting for an event—the silent onset of rain.

We were wedged between the mountain and the lake, listening to Loowit Creek negotiate the world between. From all appearances, we were sitting between two opposing things: solid and liquid, high and low, hot and cold. One was large, the other small. One ascended while the other plummeted. One cradled scorching magma, the other icy water. During my lifetime the mountain had lost elevation while the lake had gained it. But I had realized long ago, somewhere along our journey, that seen from above both lake and volcano were U-shaped bodies facing north. Loowit's new dome was just another way of announcing that both mountain and lake were depressions: the lake was a small surface depression, while the volcano was a massive depression in the continental crust that gushed at times like a spring.

Because of their U shape, people called the lake a "horseshoe" and the volcano an "amphitheater." But those two nouns—metaphors of human-made objects—failed to reflect proper proportion or causal relationship. An amphitheater does not forge a horseshoe. But the volcano created Spirit Lake. "People often think of fire when they think of eruptions," Dan Miller once told me. "But water is a dangerous factor, too. Eruptions in the Cascade Range are as much about water as they are about fire." The fact that Spirit Lake mirrors Loowit on its surface is not only an aesthetically pleasing coincidence, it is testimony to the fact that the volcanically dammed lake belongs to the mountain.

So where does solid earth end and water begin? According to Don Swanson, volcanoes have "rotten hearts and feet of clay." Swanson confirmed this when he discovered Loowit's rotten heart. A few years ago the geologist tossed his pick into portions of rock upstream from Loowit Falls. The rock crumbled like sandstone. It was then that Swanson realized why the north face had bulged and blown apart rather than the mountain's summit or its south side. He discovered that the mountain's north side was full of old dacite domes that had been cooked by boiling water percolating through their cracks. These weakened domes became easy conduits for rising magma. Instead of flowing up the central conduit to the top of the mountain, the magma pushed out the north side, creating the famous bulge above Goat Rocks. Mount St. Helens could only crash and tumble in one direction—its path of least resistance. And now that the volcano had breached its north side completely, Swanson believed it would always erupt north, toward Spirit Lake.

If Swanson was right, and it was water that weakened the mountain, then there was little distinction between creator and created, destroyer and destroyed. If the mountain crashed into the lake, it was only because water had first seeped into the mountain.

What if the lake and the mountain bore the same name? Perhaps I would have understood sooner that it was ridiculous to be in love with a lake and angry at a mountain. Spirit Lake would not exist without Loowit. The volcano would not exist without water. For as much as they were different, mountain and lake were the same.

Everlasting: Spring

Damp ash smells like manure. Old snow feels like wet gravel. Salal and wild strawberry have survived the winter unscathed and green. But wait, what is this? One, two, three, four, five trilliums—all pink-edged. And here, at my feet, is a crowd of pearly everlasting sprouts rising from a stringy mat of dirty, snow-flattened stems. I am taking an inventory as I hike to the site of a buried creek. It is a spring inventory of stems, leaves, and petals.

The miles are counted in syllables of water. Up ahead, Loowit Creek roars. I am deep in the season when water is heard before it is seen. Before the eruption, Loowit Creek did not exist. Today, it announces itself uptrail as loud as the ocean. Here is a volcanic inventory: one spring for another, one waterfall for another, one cove for another, a smaller mountain and a bigger lake. The ledger is balanced, the landscape clean.

Inventories tell us what we'd rather keep than lose. We make them to assess our situation, to tell us what we have. Ask any Spirit Lake survivor what he or she lost in the eruption: a 1957 map, a set of antique wicker chairs, a rifle, a drift boat, a trunk full of scuba-diving gear, a pair of Irish hiking boots, a house, a canoe, twenty kerosene lamps, a blue bikini, a lodge, a loved one. It is an inventory the survivor no longer uses, but keeps just the same.

"It's better that all that stuff went down with the eruption," cabin owner Sam White told me. "It was a part of the place. It belonged there."

Stripped like a blast-blown tree bereft of bark, I keep an inventory of what I own here. It is an inventory of lessons, not things, taken from a flower whose family dates back 25 million years:

1. Roots: Sink early and deep. Resist winds. Defy rock.

2. Stem: Go tall as fast as possible. If you can't go tall, shoot sideways.

3. Leaf: Know the economy of place. Be neither too wide nor too delicate.

4. Flower: If you're going to trouble yourself to bloom, bloom severally.

5. *Seed: Travel light. Go far by wind. Be ready to call unlikely places home—including a volcano.*

I hum to myself a hum of creek water as I walk, two worn maps in my pocket. I am hiking to the site of the unnamed creek. If I don't get there due to washouts, or can't find it due to land-slides, I won't worry anymore. My obsession is my comfort. Wher-ever I walk in the wide world, I can think of a lake and walk its shores, and begin to get my bearings.

Here on the Pumice Plain, the wrens forget me. The lupines will bloom in a while. Steam rises off the dome, dirty with ash-dusted snow. And the bees, they think me a flower. They circle and cruise, circle and cruise. A slap of water, a slip of wind, a volcano dumb as the distant sun. How many times has this place tricked me? But today I am tricking its bees.

Once, in late spring, I walked the mile and a half from my family's cabin to Spirit Lake after a few hours of hard rain. It was early afternoon, and the sun had burst through heavy clouds as I strolled alone beside the road's northern bank, glancing at the green earth overtaking the previous summer's gray stalks. In one sunny area I happened upon a pearly everlasting about to bloom. It had closed its flowerheads but was not quite drooping, as some do in the rain. On one rain-tightened cluster slept a bumblebee. Or was it dead? At fifteen I was ignorant of the cold-blooded habits of the order Hymenoptera, genus Bombus.

I had no idea that, like everlastings, bumblebees inhabit most of the northern hemisphere and come in many different species. Also like everlastings, all Bombus species wear a woolly coat, thereby retaining more heat than the average European honeybee. They are a furry bee for a furry wildflower.

And I had no idea that bumblebees are renowned for regulating their own body heat. Although they require a higher body tempera-ture than most insects, bumblebees are capable of generating heat by three different activities. They keep their thorax warm (and there-fore their flight muscles operable) by flying, but they also stay warm by producing an energy-releasing enzyme, and by "shivering," or contracting their flight muscles. Using these techniques and their warm coats, bumblebees are important pollinators of alpine wildflowers, which bloom at colder temperatures than low-elevation plants. Many species of bumblebees are also out early and back late to the hive, if they don't in fact stay out all night, dozing on a particularly pollen-heavy flower.

The cold rains had been too much for this bee, I was certain. It must have drowned. In bright sunlight and entomological darkness I continued on to the lake, wondering whether it was dead or alive. If dead, why had it not fallen to the ground? Could a bee die clutching a flower? If alive, what was it doing?

The possibilities now seem many. Perhaps it was a tired queen who had overwintered and just begun her search for a new nest for her colony. Or maybe it was an early worker foraging for her queen, trying hard to come by whatever pollen she could find. Or maybe it wasn't of the Bombus genus at all, but a cuckoo bumblebee, Psithyrus, who after napping on the everlasting would invade a true bumblebee colony, kill the queen, and enlist her workers to labor for her. Cuckoo bumblebees are sometimes drowsier than true Bombus bees. Perhaps that was it: it was a cuckoo queen, ready to awaken and raid a true bee's nest. She would lie near the nest, quietly spreading her scent. Then she would either murder the real queen or subject her to the same slave labor as the colony's unsuspecting workers, who would grow familiar with the false queen's scent.

But on that rainy day, what did I know of what Aldo Leopold called the chitchat of the woods? I had much to learn about the rebirth of flowers, forests, volcanoes, bees. Today I am no longer surprised to recall my discovery that sun-washed afternoon: by the time I returned along the same stretch of road, dusk was falling—and the bee was gone.

Geologic Chronology

Ape Canyon Eruptive Stage   at least 40,000 to 35,000 years ago

This period marks the birth of the modern Mount St. Helens volcano. Enormous eruptions of tephra (labeled layer "C" by geologists) characterize this period. Recent investigations suggest that even earlier episodes of volcanism may mark the creation of Mount St. Helens.

Cougar Eruptive Stage   20,000 to 18,000 years ago

A 15,000-year-long dormancy separates this stage from the earlier Ape Canyon stage. The volcano then erupts for 2,000 years, mostly south, west, and southeast, with mudflows and pyroclastic flows, then collapses southward to form a debris avalanche.

Swift Creek Eruptive Stage   13,000 to 8,000 years ago

A 5,000-year-long dormancy separates the beginning of this stage from the end of the Cougar stage. The volcano then erupts intermittently for 5,000 years with pyroclastic flows and tephra (layers "S" and "J"). Mudflows occur along Pine Creek, Swift Creek, the Lewis River, and the South Fork of the Toutle. Some dome building occurs.

Spirit Lake Eruptive Stage   4,500 years ago to present

4,500 years ago   **Beginning of Spirit Lake Eruptive Stage.** A 5,000-year-long dormancy separates this stage from earlier Swift Creek stage.

2050 to 1350 B.C.   **Smith Creek Eruptive Period.** The largest known eruption in the volcano's history (roughly 3,500 years ago) results in Yn pumice deposits ("Y" for "yellow," "n" for "north") that extend into Canada. Pyroclastic flows and mudflows occur mostly to the north and east. An ancestral Spirit Lake perhaps forms at this time.

1000 to 550 B.C.   **Pine Creek Eruptive Period.** Pyroclastic flows occur on the volcano's south side. A layer of dacitic tephra ("P" for "Pine Creek") is deposited. Silver Lake is created when mudflows dam its outlet.

250 B.C. to A.D. 350   **Castle Creek Eruptive Period.** The volcano's lava composition mysteriously changes from mostly dacite to basalt, andesite, and dacite. One basalt flow c. A.D. 50 creates Ape Cave. A dacite eruption results in the Dog's Head dome on the northeast flank. Scoria of this period labeled "B" for "brown."

c. A.D. 700   The Sugar Bowl lava dome is formed on the north slope.

A.D. 1480 to 1700s	**Kalama Eruptive Period.** An eruption in 1480 marks an explosive period of heavy pumice deposits (layer "W" for "white") and ash—some six times larger than the 1980 deposits. Another eruption deposits a layer of andesitic tephra ("X"). One flow dams the Toutle River valley and raises Spirit Lake's level by 60 feet. The volcano's pre-1980 summit is formed, as well as the Worm Flows on its south slopes.
A.D. 1800 to 1857	**Goat Rocks Eruptive Period.** Goat Rocks' dacite dome is formed, as well as the Floating Island Lava Flow (both destroyed by 1980 eruption). Volcano deposits pumice (called layer "T" for "timberline") on northeast slopes and emits ash that falls as far away as Canada.
A.D. 1857 to March 1980	Steam explosions are observed but no eruptions; volcano considered dormant.
A.D. May 18, 1980	Collapse of north flank and summit initiates major lateral blast with ensuing mud-flows, pyroclastic flows, and widespread ashfall.
A.D. 1980 to 1986	A new lava dome grows inside the crater in eruptive spurts.
A.D. 1989 to 1991	Phreatic explosions and pyroclastic flows occur sporadically near the crater dome.

Sources: U.S. Geological Survey (Crandell and Mullineaux); Pringle 1993; Shane 1985

Human Chronology at Spirit Lake

c. 12,000 years ago until present   The Cowlitz people reside north, south, east, and west of the mountain, which they call Lawelatla. The Klickitat reside mostly east of the mountain.

1792   British Captain George Vancouver sights the volcano on May 19, then names it on October 20.

1805   U.S. Captain William Clark (part of the Lewis and Clark expedition) notes in his journal on November 4 that he sees "Mount Helien," and that "it is perhaps the highest pinical in America" and "rises Something in the form of a Sugar lofe." Historians believe Clark confused the mountain with Mount Adams.

1826   Scottish explorer David Douglas travels the Columbia River and botanizes near the mountain.

1829–1830   More than 80 percent of the estimated 4,000 Cowlitz residing in western Washington are killed by diseases introduced by Europeans.

1847   Canadian artist Paul Kane travels along the Lewis River but is unsuccessful in persuading any Native American to escort him to Spirit Lake.

1853   Thomas Dryer leads the first recorded ascent of Mount St. Helens.

1860   Guided by a Native American, a group of prospectors ascends the volcano from the south.

1873   Members of a funeral party are jolted by earthquakes as they lower the body into a grave near the mountain. They look up to observe a steam eruption.

1883   A climbing party includes the first woman to reach the volcano's summit.

c. 1887   Robert Lange hikes for two days to begin prospecting at Spirit Lake. Logging is underway along the Lewis River and south of the Toutle River.

1892   The St. Helens Mining District is officially created, with Henry Waldo Coe of Portland a major participant.

1894   Sampson Mine is built by the Milwaukee Company. Low-grade ore is extracted, but transportation proves a problem, and the mine shuts down. The company later disbands.

1896   U.S. Army Lieutenant Charles Elliott explores and maps Mount St. Helens' foothills for the National Geographic Society.

1897   Mount St. Helens is included in a national forest reserve.

1899   Norway Mine at Spirit Lake is in operation.

1901   Cowlitz County Commissioner Studebaker approves the construction of a road into Spirit Lake after being pressed by prospectors. The Norway, Chicago, and Yellow Metals Mines are in full operation. Mining claims in the Spirit Lake vicinity include the Grizzly (on Grizzly Creek), Sweden, Bronze Monarch (Michigan copper mines), Cascades Calumet, Young America, Washington Chief, Washington Treadwell, Polar Star, Goat Mountain, Minnie Lee, and Ripper.

1903   The *Oregon Daily Journal* reports that two climbers witnessed the volcano erupt on September 12. "Glacial ice that had been there ever since I could remember was fast melting and the whole north side of the mountain was unlike anything I ever saw before. Had I not known it was St. Helens I was on I would never have recognized it," said one of the climbers, S. P. White of Vancouver. A second group of people at timberline also experienced an eruption "so severe" they were "thrown to their knees."

1905   The Lange Mine is in full operation.

1908   President Theodore Roosevelt designates the newly created U.S. Forest Service as the administering agency for what was known as Columbia National Forest, which includes Mount St. Helens and Spirit Lake.

1908	A fire started at Lange's Mine burns the south slopes of Mount Margaret.
1910	The Forest Service erects a small ranger station at Spirit Lake.
1912	Lange's gold mine ceases operation, along with most other mines in the area.
1913	The Forest Service's St. Helens Ranger District is head-quartered at Spirit Lake.
1917	A fire lookout is built on the volcano's summit, then torn down in 1928.
1920–1923	The Forest Service leases lakeshore plots to families who wish to build cabins on the south shore.
1925	The first motor boat is operated on Spirit Lake.
c. 1926	Harry Truman and Jack Nelson arrive at Spirit Lake. Truman operates a small store.
c. 1928	Jack Nelson operates Harmony Falls Lodge on the eastern shore of Spirit Lake until the 1950s.
1928	The Portland YMCA builds its Holmstedt Memorial Lodge on Spirit Lake's south shore.
1937	The Longview Ski Club builds a cabin at timberline.
1938	A two-lane road to Spirit Lake is opened, and bridges are built over the Toutle River.
1939	Harry Truman builds his Mount St. Helens Lodge, which remains standing until the eruption.
1946	The Portland YMCA acquires lakefront property at the northeastern tip of Spirit Lake and builds a lodge and camp there, that remain until the eruption. The old Holmstedt Lodge becomes an Episcopal Church camp until the 1970s, when it is torn down.
1949	The Columbia National Forest is renamed the Gifford Pinchot National Forest.

1962   Hurricane Frieda hits Mount St. Helens on October 12, with winds gusting at 75 miles per hour. Trees are blown down in the Spirit Lake basin, creating a meadow near the lake's outlet and destroying buildings at the Portland YMCA camp.

1965   The Duck Bay boat launch is built.

1973   The Cowlitz people are awarded $1,550,000 from the U.S. government for their territory but are not formally recognized as an American Indian tribe.

1975   In April, a 29-member climbing party camps near Forsyth Glacier, in the path of an avalanche that kills five persons.

1978   A coalition of 23 environmental groups proposes the Roadless Area Review and Evaluation (RARE II), a plan to increase national wilderness areas. Spirit Lake and its backcountry are included in the proposal but are not approved by the U.S. Department of Agriculture, leaving the areas vulnerable to logging and mining.

1980   March 20, an earthquake under the mountain measuring 4.2 (Richter scale) marks the first major reawakening in the volcano's 123-year dormancy. The volcano then erupts regularly with ash and steam from March 27 until May 18. On May 18, 1,300 feet of its 350-year-old summit collapse into a 14-mile-long debris avalanche, releasing a lateral blast that sweeps a 230-square-mile area at 650 miles per hour. Fifty-seven people are killed.

Glossary

Ablation: the loss of glacial snow and ice through melting and erosion. Geologist Carolyn Driedger discovered that glacial ablation at Mount St. Helens was slowed by heavy ashfall that blocked solar radiation.

Andesite: one of four major types of volcanic rock (originally underground magma) that contain silica. Andesitic magma contains 54 to 62 percent silica and forms diorite if it solidifies below ground.

Arthropod fallout: a rain of dead, windblown insects from the upper atmosphere. An important food source for glacial scavengers on high mountains, arthropod fallout was also a food source for carnivorous beetles on the Pumice Plain after the 1980 eruption.

Ash: As geologist Don Swanson and others have pointed out, volcanic ash is not really ash (as in burned organic material) but fine-grained particles originating from a volcanic action.

Ashfall: volcanic ash that falls from the sky. Geologists estimated that Mount St. Helens' May 18 ashfall was enough to bury a football field 150 miles deep. The May 18 ash cloud circled the Earth in 15 days.

Basalt: one of four major types of volcanic rock (originally underground magma) that contain silica. Basaltic magma contains 45 to 54 percent silica and forms gabbro if it solidifies underground.

Biological legacy: a concept developed at Mount St. Helens by ecologist Jerry Franklin that emphasizes the role of survivors after the 1980 eruption. The concept countered the popular notion that all living things in the blast zone were killed by the eruption.

Blast: the explosion that initiated the cataclysmic eruption on May 18, 1980. Estimates for blast winds run from 220 m.p.h. to 670 m.p.h. The heat of the blast was roughly 570 degrees Fahrenheit. It blew down an estimated 4 billion board feet of timber.

Blast zone: the fan-shaped area affected by the May 18, 1980 eruption. It is usually estimated to be 230 square miles wide and contains scorched, downed, and buried trees.

Blowdown: the area in the blast zone where whole forests were knocked over. These areas were found to have a high percentage of surviving plants and even some animals.

Cataclysmic eruption: the climax eruption on May 18 that marked the pinnacle of the mountain's eruptive events during the spring of 1980.

Cinder cone: a volcanic cone made of pyroclastic particles—particles ground fine by an explosion.

Climax community: a composition of plants and animals that remains more or less the same until a disturbance occurs. Ancient forests, such as the one at pre-eruption Spirit Lake, are usually considered climax forests.

Colonizer: a species of plant, animal, or bacteria that arrives in an area from somewhere else.

Composite cone: also called a stratovolcano because it is made up of many layers, or strata. Like most of the world's volcanoes, Mount St. Helens is a composite cone.

Crater: a depression on a volcano formed by an explosion or collapse. Mount St. Helens' crater is 2,100 feet deep and runs 1.2 miles across, from east to west.

Crevasse: a deep crack in a glacier.

Dacite: one of four major types of volcanic rock (originally underground magma) that contain silica. Dacitic magma contains 62 to 70 percent silica and forms granodiorite if it solidifies underground.

Debris avalanche: an avalanche of heterogeneous material, including rock, glacier ice, water, snow, and trees. Mount St. Helens' debris avalanche swept through a 25-square-mile area at 70 to 150 miles per hour. Its volume was estimated to be .6 cubic miles.

Dike: a layer of magmatic rock cutting across other layers of rock. Dikes can represent old magma conduits.

Dome: usually short for volcanic dome or lava dome. Domes are usually produced by pasty lava such as dacite or rhyolite. Mount St. Helens' crater dome is roughly 1,000 feet higher than the crater floor and represents 5 percent of the volume lost by the volcano in the 1980 eruption.

Ecological succession: change in the composition of an ecosystem as organisms compete over time. Primary succession takes place in an area previously devoid of life-forms; secondary succession takes place after disturbances such as fire.

Ecology: the study of how organisms interact with their environment.

Ecosystem: an area comprising both physical environment and living organisms that has controlled cycling of energy and nutrients.

Eon: a unit of time representing one billion years.

Era: one of five major divisions of geologic time.

Fault: a fracture in one of the Earth's plates.

Fumarole: a vent, usually on a volcano's slopes, that emits gases. Fumaroles on Mount St. Helens' north flank remained active for two years after the 1980 eruption.

Glacier: a mass of recrystallized snow of a certain density that moves under the pull of gravity.

Humus: the organic portion of soil resulting from decomposing plant or animal matter.

Igneous: rock formed by the cooling of magma.

Lahar: a type of mudflow containing high-temperature, water-saturated volcanic material traveling at high speeds. The lahar on the North Fork of the Toutle River originated at the debris avalanche and came to rest at the Columbia River, depositing enough sediment to fill the 40-foot channel to 15 feet for a two-mile stretch.

Lateral blast: a volcanic blast (see above) that is directed laterally across the land instead of vertically upward; also called a directed blast.

Lava: magma that has surfaced above ground.

Magma: molten rock that often contains gases that force it upward.

Montane: a biogeographic zone made up of cool, moist slopes below timberline that are usually covered with large conifers. Spirit Lake was considered a mid-elevation montane area before the eruption.

Mudflow: a flow of water-saturated, fine-grained particles usually moving at least 80 m.p.h. Also called a lahar (an Indonesian term). The 1980 Toutle River mudflow destroyed or damaged 27 bridges, 200 homes, and 185 miles' worth of roads. Thirty-one ships were stranded upstream on the Columbia River.

Neotene: an organism that has become sexually mature in the larval stage.

Phreatic explosion: an explosive eruption that does not involve magma but is produced when water flashes to steam after hitting superheated rocks.

Plate tectonics: the theory, first proposed by Alfred Wegener and refined later, that the Earth's crust is made up of a dozen or so oceanic and continental plates. The drifting plates were once part of a supercontinent dubbed Pangaea, which split apart 180 million years ago.

Plinian column: first described by Pliny the Younger in reference to the eruption of Vesuvius in A.D. 79, this is a vertical eruption plume of ash, gas, and steam forming a cauliflower-shaped cloud over the volcano.

Pumice: porous volcanic rock formed by gas expanding in cooling lava. Mount St. Helens' pumice has been found as far north as British Columbia.

Pyroclastic flow: an extremely hot and turbulent lateral flow of explosive gases, pumice, and other volcanic material. At Mount St. Helens, pyroclastic flows created the Pumice Plain.

Rhizome: a plant stem that runs sideways underground, usually used for self-propagation.

Rhyolite: one of four major types of volcanic rock (originally underground magma) that contain silica. Rhyolitic magma contains 70 to 78 percent silica and forms granite if it solidifies underground.

Scorch zone: also called the singe zone. That part of the blast zone where trees were scorched to death by the lateral blast but not blown over.

Scoria: a porous volcanic rock that does not float like pumice.

Seismic swarm: a series of shallow earthquakes under volcanoes.

Seral: opposite of climax (see above). Describes a community that is still changing over time or in an early stage of ecological succession.

Shield volcano: a volcano that is built by liquid lava to form gentle slopes that look like a warrior's shield lying on the Earth. Hawaiian volcanoes are shield volcanoes.

Stratigraphy: the study of the Earth's strata, or layers.

Subalpine: the elevation just below timberline. In the Cascades, it is marked by heavy winter snows.

Talus: rock debris piled at the base of cliffs.

Tephra: all kinds of dry rock ejected by a volcano.

Timberline: an elevation that marks the climatological limit of plant growth. Because of Mount St. Helens' many eruptions, its timberline was still advancing upward before the 1980 eruption.

Tuff: volcanic rock made up of fine-grained pyroclastic material.

Sources: U.S. Geological Survey, U.S. Forest Service, Washington Department of Natural Resources

Selected Bibliography

Beckey, Fred. *Cascade Alpine Guide*. Seattle: The Mountaineers, 1973.

Bilderback, David, ed. *Mount St. Helens 1980: Botanical Consequences of the Explosive Eruptions*. Berkeley: University of California Press, 1987.

Bunnell, Clarence Orvel. *Legends of the Klickitats*. Portland: Binfords & Mort, 1935.

Carson, Rob. *Mount St. Helens: The Eruption and Recovery of a Volcano*. Seattle: Sasquatch Books, 1990.

Cascade Mountains Study: State of Washington. Olympia: Washington State Planning Council, 1940.

Case, Robert and Victoria. *Last Mountains: The Story of the Cascades*. Portland: Binfords & Mort, 1945.

Clark, Ella E. *Indian Legends of the Pacific Northwest*. Berkeley: University of California Press, 1953.

Crandell, Dwight and Donal Mullineaux. *Potential Hazards from Future Eruptions of Mount St. Helens Volcano*. Geological Survey Bulletin 1383-C. Washington, D.C.: U.S. Geological Survey, 1978.

Decker, Robert and Barbara, "Mount St. Helens," in *Volcanoes*. New York: W. H. Freeman and Co., 1981.

Dryer, Thomas. "The 1853 Ascent of Mount St. Helens," reprinted in *Mazama*, vol. L, no. 13 (December 1968).

Dyrness, C. T. and Jerry Franklin. *Natural Vegetation of Oregon and Washington*. Portland, OR: U.S.D.A. Forest Service General Technical Report PNW-8, 1973.

Elliott, Charles P. "Mount St. Helens," *National Geographic*, July-August 1897.

Foxworthy, Bruce L. and Mary Hill. *Volcanic Eruptions of 1980 at Mount St. Helens: The First 100 Days* (U.S.G.S. Professional Paper 1249). Washington, D.C.: U.S. Geological Survey, 1982.

Frenzen, Peter et al. *Mount St. Helens, Biological Research Following the 1980 Eruptions: An Indexed Bibliography and Research Abstracts (1980-1993)*. General Technical Report PNW-GTR-342. Portland: U.S.D.A., Forest Service, 1994.

Guggenheim, Alan. *Spirit Lake People: Memories of Mount St. Helens*. Gresham: Salem Press, 1986.

Harris, Stephen. *Fire and Ice*. Seattle: The Mountaineers/Pacific Search Press, 1980.

Hilton, Alice, "Our Mount St. Helens," in *Cowlitz Historical Quarterly*, vol. 22, no. 4 (Winter 1980), pp. 7–34.

Holmes, Kenneth L. "Mount St. Helens' Recent Eruptions," *Oregon Historical Quarterly*, 56, no. 3 (September 1955), pp. 197-210.

Keller, S.A.C., editor. *Mount St. Helens: Five Years Later*. Cheney: Eastern Washington University Press, 1986.

——————————. *Mount St. Helens: One Year Later*. Cheney: Eastern Washington University Press, 1982.

Lawrence, Donald B. "Diagrammatic History of the Northeast Slope of Mount St. Helens, Washington," *Mazama*, 3, no. 13 (December 1954), pp. 41–44.

_____. "The 'Floating Island' Lava Flow of Mount St. Helens," *Mazama* 13, no. 12 (December 1941), pp. 56–60.

_____. "Continuing Research on the Flora of Mount St. Helens," *Mazama* XXI, no. 12 (December 1939), pp. 49–54.

_____. "Trees on the March," *Mazama* XX, no. 12 (December 1938), pp. 49–54.

Lipman, P.W. and Donal Mullineaux, editors. *The 1980 Eruptions of Mount St. Helens, Washington.* (U.S.G.S. Professional Paper 1250). Washington, D.C.: U.S. Geological Survey, 1981.

Loo-wit Lat-kla (pseudonym). "Gold Hunting in the Cascade Mountains," *Cowlitz County Historical Society Quarterly*, vol. 9, no. 4 (Feb. 1968), pp. 1–25.

Macaulay, Tom. "Mount St. Helens: Beautiful Mountain of Death," *Northwest Magazine*, January 23, 1977, p. 29.

Perry, Ronald W. and Michael K. Lindell. *Living with Mount St. Helens.* Pullman: Washington State University Press, 1990.

Phillips, Kenneth. "Fumaroles of Mount St. Helens and Mount Adams," *Mazama*, 13, no. 12 (December 1941), pp. 37–42.

Pringle, Patrick. *Roadside Geology of Mount St. Helens National Volcanic Monument and Vicinity.* Olympia: Washington Division of Geology and Earth Resources, 1993.

Pryde, Philip R. "Mount St. Helens: A Possible National Monument," *National Parks*, May 1968, pp. 7–10.

Rosenfeld, Charles, and Robert Cooke. *Earthfire: The Eruption of Mount St. Helens.* Cambridge, MA: MIT Press, 1982.

Shane, Scott. *Discovering Mount St. Helens: A Guide to the National Volcanic Monument.* Seattle: University of Washington Press, 1985.

Sterling, E. M. *The South Cascades: The Gifford Pinchot National Forest.* Seattle: The Mountaineers, 1975.

St. John, Harold. "The Flora of Mount St. Helens," *The Mountaineer*, 70, no. 7 (1976) : pp. 65–77.

Teale, Edwin Way. "A Day with the Fern Gatherers," in *Autumn Across America.* New York: Dodd, Mead, and Co., 1956.

Tilling, Robert, et al. *Eruptions of Mount St. Helens: Past, Present, and Future.* Washington, D.C.: U.S. Geological Survey, 1990.

Williams, Chuck. *Mount St. Helens National Volcanic Monument: A Pocket Guide.* Seattle: The Mountaineers, 1988.

_____. *Mount St. Helens: A Changing Landscape.* Portland: Graphic Arts Center, 1980.

Williams, John H. *The Guardians of the Columbia.* Tacoma: Williams, 1912.

Zimmerman, Jack. "Mount St. Helens: Saint or Devil?" in *The Sunday Oregonian*, July 5, 1953, pp. 8–9, 12.

Acknowledgments

The scientific information in this book derives mostly from the painstaking research of Mount St. Helens' research community. I owe a significant debt to each researcher's intellectual passion and determination. Published articles, books, and personal information given in interviews were all used extensively in building this book. My sincere thanks to every scientist who is quoted in the text, as well as many others whose research was a tremendous contribution.

Many people were especially kind and helpful. I must first of all thank Monument Scientist Peter Frenzen for his friendly and indefatigable assistance. Peter spent many hours answering questions, offering crucial information, and reading an initial draft. I must also thank Charlie Crisafulli for his wonderful enthusiasm, and for sharing his unique, hard-earned knowledge of the blast zone with me.

Don Swanson and Dan Miller were also generous and helpful, as were many others, including Carolyn Driedger of the U.S. Geological Survey, James Strassmaier and Sieglinde Smith of the Oregon Historical Society, staff members of the Castle Rock Exhibition Center and the Cowlitz County Historical Museum, Vincent Lee of the California Academy of Sciences, Robert Allerman of the Soil Conservation Service, Dave Bean of the Washington Department of Natural Resources, Lorna Goldsby of the Fern Barn, Roy Wilson of the Cowlitz Tribe, and naturalist Daniel Mathews. Many thanks as well to Wendell Berry and to the participants of the 1995 Institute of Environmental Writing, and to Marcy Houle and Melissa Scanlan, who reviewed the initial draft.

Chuck Tonn and Karen Jacobsen shared their vast knowledge of Spirit Lake with me, as did conservationist Susan Saul, cabin owners Sam and Dorothy White, and Harmony Falls co-owner Julia Bernard. I shall forever remember Jim and Pauline Lund, who died before the publication of this book. Thanks, Jim, for teaching me a sure-fire way to summon a pack of coyotes. All I can say is the world lost the Clown Prince of Spirit Lake too soon.

A thousand special thanks to my dear friends Louisa Jones and Laura Bernard, who have helped me in many ways. Thanks as well to Gloria Bowles, Meg and Dick Scanlan, José Olavarrieta, Colleen Wilson, and many others too numerous to name.

Finally, this book could not have been written without the constant help of my parents, Marie and Angelo John, who first taught me the value of wild places. My parents helped house me during my research trips, and both shared photos, news clippings, memories, and other precious things relevant to the lake and mountain. My brothers and sisters—Marita, Terese, John, Bernie, Michael, Jeanine, Celeste, and Elizabeth—provided wonderful friendship at Spirit Lake and elsewhere. Marita and Michael accompanied me on post-eruption excursions; Jeanine read an initial draft and offered crucial feedback and encouragement during the manuscript's production; and Celeste was an invaluable blast zone companion and reviewer of several drafts. Needless to say, my deepest gratitude goes to my husband, Tom Scanlan.

———•————————•———